THE LODGE AND THE CRAFT

ROLLIN C. BLACKMER

The LODGE _and the_ CRAFT

A PRACTICAL EXPLANATION
_of_
THE WORK OF FREEMASONRY

ROLLIN C. BLACKMER, _C.M., M.D., LLD._
Past Master, Past High Priest, Past Commander

Macoy Publishing & Masonic Supply Co., Inc.
Richmond, Virginia

TO THE CRAFT

In the hope that dark places shall be made
light and a clearer understanding had of our
glorious Institution this book is dedicated with
fraternal greeting.

ROLLIN C. BLACKMER

SOME books, like an artist's painting, receive only modest acclaim when they first see the light of day, then are almost forgotten for a time until rediscovered by some earnest seeker after Truth.

Such a book is *THE LODGE AND THE CRAFT* by Rollin C. Blackmer, C.M., M.D., LLD., Past Master, Past High Priest, Past Commander from the State of Missouri, written back in 1923.

We do not know if Dr. Blackmer wrote any other books, but we do know from his scholastic degrees and offices held in the various Masonic bodies, that he was well qualified to make this book available to the Craft "In the hope that dark places shall be made light and a clearer understanding had of our glorious Institution."

The book had only a modest sale and then became unobtain— able. But to those few who were fortunate to have a copy (and had good eye sight), the book became a treasured gem. Perhaps the small print discouraged many. In recent years there have been repeated requests for it — so many, in fact, we almost feel "obliged" to reprint the book.

We are indebted to the Cleveland Masonic Library for supplying a cherished copy in order that this very worth while book by Dr. Blackmer could be photo offset and once again made available to Freemasons everywhere. We have not changed the text, but we have enlarged the type to make it more readable. Because of the enlargement, you will find some rather faint letters and you may observe markings and underscoring where some brother added his own emphasis to passages which especially interested or bothered him. It tells something about the reader. The brother, or brothers, who borrowed this volume from the Library must have been serious students seeking to increase their Masonic learning for we found markings throughout the entire volume.

You, too, can enrich your Masonic education by the study of this excellent *practical explanation of the work of Freemasonry* written many years ago, but which is as worth while today as then.

1976   THE PUBLISHERS

INDEX TO CHAPTERS

LECTURE I

The Lodge and the Craft

THERE are at the present writing more than 100,000 men in the State of Missouri holding membership in Masonic lodges. If there are seventy-five of this number who have made sufficient study of the Institution to which they belong to have awakened in themselves any glow of interest in its symbolism, its philosophy, or even its history, the fact is certainly not shown in the articles published in the Masonic press of this state or in the speeches delivered before the general public or within the tiled lodges. It is a lamentable fact that the great mass of our membership are as densely ignorant of everything connected with Masonry, aside from the mere wording of the ritual, as the peasantry of Spain and Mexico of the true history, biography and political philosophy of the Church of Rome.

There are many reasons for this. The first and most prominent reason is, that they do not suspect the existence of the vast amount of literature extant, nor the relation which Freemasonry bears to the intellectual development of the world. To be sure, a very large number of our members do not suspect that the world has had any intellectual development. With all the advantages our free public schools are supposed to afford, very many men enter business life with scarcely more learning than might be described as a rudimentary acquaintance with the three R's. These men acquire property, occasionally wealth, and with the artistic aid of a good tailor and a good barber cannot be picked out from an assembly of college professors so long as they keep their mouths shut. Many of these men have good natural common sense, live respectable moral lives, speak with as good language as do most of those with whom they associate, and not a few possess kind and generous dispositions. In short, most are honorable and many are lovable. There is no reason why they should not, and every reason why they should be admitted to the rights and privileges of Freemasonry. However, Freemasonry pretends to be, and ought to be reckoned, a learned profession. The more need for their sakes. Many of these brothers would feel themselves highly insulted if they were mentioned as belonging to the ignorant classes. Yet it is cer-

[1]

tain they are not learned, and neither does Freemasonry as an organization make any attempt to relieve this condition, at least in this jurisdiction.

We profess valuable acquirements. Should these end with the material and financial benefits that may possibly come to a man through his association with the Order? We have demanded from him, in his petition, a disclaimer of all such hopes. We ought to give our candidate something that will remain with him, at least so long as mental integrity lasts and human emotion endures. We should not only restate, in a new and interesting manner, that faith which we require him to profess, but we should be able to present to him every evidence that learning and philosophy have discovered to confirm that faith and cause it to be within him a living thing. This learning does not stand for gold or lands, though it never made the capability of any man less to earn his daily bread, support himself and family and contribute to the relief of the worthy distressed. It ought to enable him to put such things in the place where they relatively belong.

The fair academic scholar, coming into Masonry, is, generally, deeply impressed with the dignity and solemnity of the ceremonies attending his initiation. He expected much on account of the great reputation of the Order, its hoary antiquity and the respectable character borne by its members, and he is not disappointed. He is instructed in his lectures, and is still further impressed with the extreme care apparently exerted, that all this work shall be acquired in its exact wording and also with the profound secrecy with which it seems to be surrounded and guarded. He is also struck with the archaic language used. Perhaps he is sufficiently learned to refer it to its approximate date, for the diction and rhetoric point unmistakably to the early eighteenth century. But, as he goes on, he finds an ever-growing inadequacy in the explanations given. This the uneducated candidate, of course, does not notice. Perhaps our scholar may inquire of his instructor why he is expected to conceal and never reveal and yet always to hail the mysteries which have been imparted to him? How can a man obey both parts of this injunction? How can he hail and conceal at the same time, or the same thing? His instructor, unless he be one of the seventy-five before mentioned, scratches his head and replies that he does not know and that he had never been asked that particular question before. Later, if persistent, the candi-

date discovers that neither the Wardens nor the Master are able
to answer his question. Some day he asks the District Deputy
and the Grand Master, and it is quite within the bounds of
possibility that neither of these dignitaries would be able, off-
hand, to give him the required information. But the Grand
Master always has within his telephone call, within the length of
his cable tow as the ancient manuscripts have it, one of the seventy-
five—"one poor wise man"—and he, by his wisdom, will deliver
the Grand Master from his predicament and enable him to
inform the persistent seeker after knowledge that two centuries
ago the word "heal" was pronounced as the Hibernians pronounce it today—"hail"—and that to "heal" meant to cover
over, or conceal, like healing a wound by covering it over with
new skin, and that when he promised to "hail" any of the
mysteries of Freemasonry he simply promised to cover them up
or hide them. It is very likely that the companion words "conceal" and "reveal" were at that time pronounced "concail" and
"revail", as most expressions of this sort rhetorically demand a
similarity of sound. He is further informed that the same root
syllable appears in the word "hell", and that the latter word
simply meant the grave, or the place where the dead were hidden
or covered up, and not a place of torment for lost souls, as it has
generally come to mean at the present day.

The fact that the rituals of Freemasonry have been transmitted, from generation to generation down through the ages, by
oral tradition, accounts for the change in pronunciation not
having been noticed. A similar thing occurred in relation to the
name of one "Peter Gower," a celebrated Mason held up for
veneration in the ancient manuscript, known as the Leland Manuscript. It seems that our English-speaking brethren acquired
the name from an account given them by certain French brethren
who had come over to work with them in the early eleventh
century on some of the great cathedrals. The French name for
Pythagoras was "Petigore", which word sounded to their English
ears like "Peter Gower", hence the difficulty in locating the
illustrious brother, when the English scholars of later years came
to study the contents and historical value of this same ancient
manuscript, concerning which I shall take opportunity to speak
further on in this book.

Soon our candidate passes his examination in the first and
second degrees and is raised to the Sublime Degree of Master
Mason. Here he witnesses a drama that is strange and unique,

yet representing what appears to be an historical event connected with the building of King Solomon's Temple. Again his
previous learning prompts him to ask questions. Whence is
derived the historic authority for these important and curious
events? Nothing in the Bible gives warrant for any such occurrences and he knows that up to the present time no other
record has been discovered of the existence of such a king as
Solomon, to say nothing of his adventures and contemporaneous
acquaintances. He asks and again receives no satisfactory information as to the truth or falsity of the singular narrative so
lately rehearsed in his presence.

Someone suggests that the required information might be
obtained in the higher degrees. So he joins the Scottish Rite or
the Chapter, Council and Commandery and finds that the
mystery, though here further elaborated, is rather obscured
than elucidated. Its real origin is hidden in the night of time.
In the Scottish Rite he is presented with a book entitled "Morals
and Dogma", written by the late General Albert Pike. He is
recommended to study this book. He reads a few chapters but
fails to perceive the connection between the literature here presented and the degrees he has taken. This is not so much the
fault of the book as of the lack of previous instruction along
these lines, and no one seems able or willing to prepare him.
Besides, he soon begins to find out that his Masonic brethren
around him are not at all interested in these fields of Masonic
study. Even the Lodge of Instruction frowns upon it. All seem
to be imbued, not with the desire for greater Light, but for more
brilliant shining under such titles as "Worshipful Brother,"
"Excellent Companion"—or "Eminent Sir"—"Thrice Illustrious",
or it may be to wear a "Red Cap" or a "White Cap" or a
"Diamond Cross". Some few become interested in the relief
work of the Order, or in the meandering and intricate adminis-
tration of Masonic politics. The Masonic literature within his
reach simply recounts the social events in Masonic circles, or
records the eulogistic speeches delivered by the Right Worshipfuls or the Most Worshipfuls who frequent these grand as-
semblages, and endeavor to climb to elevated stations by flatter-
ing their constituency. These addresses contain little information but overflow with panegyric, moral platitude and mutual
admiration.

Soon our Masonic student either imbibes the same ambition or
gradually declines from active lodge attendance. Thus he who

might have learned much to his own satisfaction and improvement, and who had the ability to have taught the same to his less-informed brethren, is lost to the work. In short, he gives it up. He abandons the search, the "Master's Word" still unfound. My brethren, things ought not so to be. Every year thousands of dollars are spent upon entertainment and parade, while there is no Masonic library accessible to the members of this jurisdiction. In order to partially correct and ameliorate this condition, for I am sorry to say that it has been almost universal, the Grand Lodge of Iowa established a Masonic library, *at an expense for buildings and books of approximately $200,000*, and prevailed upon Rev. Bro. Joseph Fort Newton to compile a book which should meet the demand for primary information, relative to the Order, and prepare the new Masonic student for a broader course of reading. This course, supported by the library and stimulated and encouraged by a large society organized for Masonic research, and a couple of the best Masonic periodicals which it has ever been our good fortune to read, is sufficiently liberal to promote a just appreciation of what Freemasonry is, what it has been in the past and what it may yet become.

The ordinary Masonic literature of the day ought to show any fair-minded man that the Order is not accomplishing the work it might well do, nor showing the great, broad, tolerant spirit which so well becomes it. A copy of Bro. Newton's book, "The Builders," is placed in the hands of every newly-raised Master Mason through the generosity of the Iowa Grand Lodge. We were previously acquainted with nearly all the facts recounted in this book and fully agree with the view here taken regarding our beloved Craft. Its beautiful language, its lofty conception of the mission of Freemasonry in the world and the considerable knowledge of symbolism and philosophy it exhibits have all excited our profound admiration, and while we could never hope to approach the grace of literature shown by this illustrious mind, the book has stimulated us to undertake, in our humble fashion, a work along similar lines, but more adapted to the needs of our own jurisdiction. We do not pretend that we have introduced very much original material into this book. The work is too small for such a purpose, nor is there need for it at this stage of the neophyte's education. We will, where possible, give due Masonic and literary credit where we have freely copied the words of others. Many beautiful passages have come down to us from great antiquity and we do not know who composed them first, nor in whose teeming brain they first originated. Others have copied them for many generations. It shall be our effort to arrange the information and emotion they bring in such a manner that our candidate may grasp their meaning and intention and share the Light that shines from them. We vaunt ourselves, whether wisely or not our readers shall be the judges, on possessing a good ear for beautiful Masonic oratory, and we trust no writer will have occasion to be ashamed of the setting which we may give to his Masonic eloquence.

The language of our ritual, as we have before suggested, is archaic, coming down from that rare age when men wrote for the ear and not for the eye. Two hundred years ago few knew how to read, but all might listen, and such literature as the plays of William Shakespeare, the King James Bible and much of the remaining literature of the times, and last, but not by any means least, the rituals of Freemasonry owe a great portion of their fame to this one fact. They represent the spoken word placed on the manuscript. Reading aloud is rapidly becoming a lost art, and in a very short time our spoken tongue will bear no closer relation to the written language than it does today in China. Only a few much despised story writers, who try to copy the dialect of the characters represented in their books, save our language from that condition now. We expect that most any of our modern scholars would be astonished and shocked if they could see their phonetically spelled conversation placed side by side with their best literary efforts.

We have always regarded the ancient forms of expression which prevail in Masonry as one of its most interesting attractions. Many of our brethren look upon these mannerisms of speech as being almost sacred, and it is true that the language of our ceremonies becomes weakened by every alteration in language that is attempted. This same idea was plainly illustrated some fifty years ago when a new translation of the Bible was placed before the public. The new version, doubtless far more accurate than the old, was written for the eye. It gave no satisfaction. *It was no longer the WORD OF GOD.* The publishers found that the public did not care whether the old translation was correct or not. It was the spoken word of God that they loved. The new book, just placed in their hands, seemed no more to them than a translation of Marcus Aurelius would have done. The strings of their hearts had come to vibrate in unison with the old Saxon cadences. The new book spoke only to the intellect, while the old one spoke to the emotions. This same thing may be noticed in the language of the Scottish Rite rituals, as well as in the language of the new rituals which have recently been prepared for the boys' Order of De Molay. No one could say that Albert Pike lacked learning, or that the writer of the De Molay rituals lacked in his knowledge of the English language, but both would have done better had they patterned their style of expression on the King James Bible and read every sentence aloud before they left it for the elocution of ordinary men.

So when we sit in Grand Lodge and listen to aspirants for future official honors trying to split hairs over some of these ancient expressions, arguing that it would be more correct, grammatically, to make the ritual say, "The Sun at its meridian height," than to say, as it did of old, "The Sun at high meridian," and offering other criticisms equally as important, we cannot help feeling a considerable degree of disgust. Let us not try to put new cloth onto old garments. When any addition or alteration becomes necessary let us invariably trust to the ear for the proper diction to use. The old Saxon derivatives have a strength and pungency, a beauty and charm, a grandeur and a feeling to which the more exact Latin scholastic words can never attain.

We wish to say a few words regarding Masonic study and research. We wonder how many scholars realize the unity of human knowledge? Take, for instance, the general subject of geometry or mathematics. There is nothing which can possibly become the object of contemplation by the human mind into which the idea of measurement and quantity does not enter; no human activity can be expressed without it. In short, it is one of the manifestations of the Infinite. One of our ancient charges declares that geometry and Masonry are synonymous terms, so every sort of knowledge is in a closer or more remote relation to that of Masonry. This must impress one that there can be no easy road to the attainment of any respectable knowledge of Freemasonry. The history of the Operative Art is as old as the human race, and the most ancient of its ruins are the remains of temples to the Living God, demonstrating that from the earliest days Speculative Masonry marched hand in hand with it. The very mounds describe circles, squares, triangles, octagons, all accurately drawn and preceding all history of any kind. The book that goes to the heart of Freemasonry will be a complete history of mankind upon the earth, with all that man has ever thought or said or done in all his life. It is interwoven with religion, with law, with government, with moral character, with family relations, with natural philosophy, with language and with every form of science known to the human mind or to human experience. The science and art of Freemasonry is in itself a liberal education.

We once read of a man who wrote a book entitled, "The Sources of Human Error." We feel that our subject is of much the same scope and requires a very similar preparation in the way of study and experience. To complete such a book would demand all our lives in all the worlds. But it is a subject whose center is here and now, and broadens out in ever-increasing circles until it compasses all space and time. Every man may start the foundation of such a temple as that of Solomon of old, and build at least a little way, even though he may realize that eternity will dawn e'er it be finished. There will be plenty of reward just in the work itself. In fact, no one's work is ever completed in Speculative Masonry. It will always be like the house of Aladdin, still one window unfinished, for which sufficient jewels cannot be found. Mr. Kipling's poem, entitled the "Palace," illustrates fully the idea which we have attempted to convey:

When I was a king and a Mason, a Master proven and skilled,
I cleared me ground for a palace, such as a king should build.
I decreed and cut down to my levels, but presently under the silt,
I came on the wreck of a palace such as a king had built.

There was no worth in the fashion, there was no wit in the plan.
Hither and thither aimless, the ruined footings ran.
Masonry, brute, mishandled, but carved on every stone
"After me cometh a Builder, tell him I, too, have known".

Swift to my use in the trenches, where my well-planned ground-
    works grew,
I tumbled his quoins and his ashlars, and cut and reset them
    anew.
Lime I made from his marbles; burned it, and slaked it, and
    spread,
Taking and leaving, at pleasure, the gift of the humble dead.

Yet I despised not, nor gloried; for as we wrenched them apart,
I read in the raised foundations the heart of that builder's heart.

As though he had risen and pleaded, so did I understand.
The form of the dream he had followed, in the face of the thing
    he had planned.

When I was a king and a Mason, in the open noon of my pride,
They sent me a word from the darkness, they whispered and
    called me aside,
They said—"The end is forbidden." They said—"Thy use is
    fulfilled.
Thy palace shall stand, as that other's, the spoil of a king, who
    shall build."

I called the men from my trenches, my quarries, my wharves
    and my shears,
All I had wrought I abandoned to the faith of the faithless
    years,
Only I cut on the timber—only I carved on the stone—
"After me cometh a Builder, tell him I, too, have known."

LECTURE II

ORGANIZATION

FREEMASONRY, according to the ancient definition, is "a beautiful system of morals, veiled in allegory and illustrated by symbols." In this definition the main ideas are system, allegory and symbolism. There has never been but one set of moral principles revealed to mankind, or developed in humanity. These principles were announced at a very early date in the Mosaic Law, as embodied in the Decalogue or Ten Words of the Hebrews, but they were just as clearly recognized in the Code of Hammurabi, published more than a thousand years previously, on the cylinders of Assyria. Brother Rudyard Kipling illustrates the germs of these same principles in a very beautiful manner in his poem, called 'The Law of the Jungle." It starts as follows:

> "This is the Law of the Jungle,
>   As old and as true as the sky,
>   And the wolf that keeps it shall prosper,
>   But the wolf that neglects it shall die.
>
> "As the creeper encircles the tree trunk
>   The law runneth forward and back,
>   For the strength of the pack is the wolf,
>   And the strength of the wolf is the pack.
>
> "The kill of the wolf is the meat of the wolf,
>   He may eat where he will,
>   And until he has given permission,
>   No other may eat of that kill.
>
> "But the kill of the pack is the meat of the pack,
>   One must eat where it lies,
>   And no wolf may carry away of that meat,
>   To his den, or he dies."

The poem may be read in its entirety in Kipling's Jungle Book. Every full-grown man recognizes at once, if of sound mind, the distinction between right and wrong, in any case, so far as the circumstances are all clear, no matter which path he may choose to follow. It is a part of the mathematical sense, the instinctive sense of equality. Masonic morals are the same as any other morals and the principles from which they derive their necessity and expediency are identical. It is a fact that the consequences of any act may be either immediate or remote, and so may be the consequences of neglect. So far as the consequences of action are immediate, men do not need to be taught what to do and what to refrain from doing, but where the consequences are remote, this is not the case. All men, at some period of their lives, must be taught either by their own experience, or by the experience of others, what consequences may be expected to follow certain lines of conduct. All agree that youth is the time when these instructions ought to be imparted. This instruction from parent to child, from elder to youth, from adept to neophyte constitutes the science of ethics. And those acts from which the young man should refrain, and those acts which he cannot neglect without ill consequences, either to himself or others, at some time in the more or less remote future are known as Moral Duties.

The manner in which any man performs his duty constitutes his moral character.

Freemasonry is a system of morals, a peculiar manner or process of instruction in morality. The method here employed for inculcating morals is allegory, a story or similitude, illustrated by symbols. Moral principles and moral philosophy are not tangible things. They relate to feelings and emotional states of mind, to appetites, desires and ambitions. They are not like a trade, occupation or art, to be taught by constant repetition of physical or mental actions until skill or ease in doing them is acquired. They are not like an abstract science, to be taught by demonstration, as one would teach the principles of arithmetic or chemistry. They must be taught by comparison, their likenesses illustrated by figures of speech or a story told which is calculated to arouse an emotion. In this way we liken the building of character to the erection of a temple, after the manner of an architect, applying the principles of morality even as the architect applies the principles of geometrical science. It is thus that we would apply the ancient definition to the work of the modern institution.

Once upon a time men used, to a very considerable extent, to apply the method of authority for the purpose of teaching morals. The parent orders the child to perform certain acts and forbids certain other acts. The sole and sufficient reason given is the mere fact that the parent orders it, and the sole penalty is the parent's displeasure and such punishment as the parent is able to inflict.

When the church wielded absolute moral authority the question of right or wrong conduct was determined only by her commands. During the greater part of the last two centuries the attempt has been made, with greater or less success, to transfer that absolute moral authority to the Holy Bible, the latter collection of sacred Scriptures being held to be the veritable word and commands of the Eternal God Himself. An act was right or wrong, according as it was commanded or forbidden in this Book. Such is the belief of many, we may call it the popular belief of today. While we do not believe any right-feeling and right-thinking man would ever be morally misled in following the principles of morality as taught in the Bible, yet this very notion which we have pointed out, of looking upon this Book as being an absolute literal sanction for action, has under erratic interpretation led to the shedding of more innocent blood than the love of gold or hope of glory. These great principles of righteousness and love and justice do not enjoy their existence, because God commands them through the mouths of His prophets. They are in themselves eternal and coexistent with God and appear in the record of human experience all over the world. They are the real foundation of our belief in God and for our belief in and respect for the Bible as well. In fact, the Bible derives its authority, as far as this generation is concerned, from them.

Freemasonry has always sustained the principles of private judgment as a private right, and must stand by that in opposition to all forms of moral authority. The authoritative method may be good for young children, but it is ruinous for grown-up men. Modern Freemasonry is arranged in degrees or gradations somewhat as ancient operative Masonry was arranged into Masters, Fellowcrafts and Entered Apprentices, over all of whom that might be engaged in performing any particular job of work of importance ruled a Grand Master. When the society had become fully organized under the Grand Lodge system (the ancient meetings being usually spoken of as General Assemblies of Masons), which event and regulation took place in the decade following a meeting held in the year 1717, Ancient Craft Masonry was said to consist of the degrees of Entered Apprentice, Fellowcraft, Master Mason, together with the Holy Royal Arch.

At the present time, in this State of Missouri, the Institution is found working under two distinct rites, the York or English Rite and the Scottish Rite, both systems enjoying the first three degrees in common. Of the history of the formation and development of these two rites we will speak later. The York Rite, so called, is composed of the Blue Lodge, consisting of the first three degrees before mentioned; also the Royal Arch Chapter, possessing authority over the four degrees of Mark Master, Past Master, Most Excellent Master and Royal Arch Mason. To the latter is appended a degree known as "The Order of Anointed High Priests," to which only those who have presided as High Priest of a Royal Arch Chapter are eligible to membership. Following this body is the Council, consisting of the degrees of Royal Master, Select Master and Super-excellent Master, and the Commandery, consisting of the Orders known as the Illustrious Order of the Red Cross, the Pass Degree of St. Paul or the Mediterranean Pass, the Order of Knight of St. John of Jerusalem, Palestine, Rhodes and Malta and the Order of Knight Templar. The entire system exhibits fourteen degrees.

The society known as the Order of the Eastern Star, composed of Master Masons and ladies who are the wives, widows, mothers, sisters or daughters of Master Masons, may be said to belong, in some manner, to this rite.

The Scottish* Rite in this state is composed of four closely associated bodies known as the Lodge of Perfection, consisting of fourteen degrees, the Chapter Rose Croix of four degrees, the Council of Knights Kadosh of eleven degrees and the Consistory of Masters of the Royal Secret of two degrees, all holding allegiance to the Supreme Council of Sovereign Inspectors General of the Thirty-third Degree of the Ancient and Accepted Scottish Rite of Freemasonry for the Southern Jurisdiction of the United States of America. The twenty-nine degrees conferred by this rite transact all their financial affairs in the Lodge of Perfection. To these two rites may be added the Institution known as the Ancient Arabic Order of Nobles of the Mystic Shrine, the Red Cross of Constantine, the White Shrine of

---

*NOTE:—This question has frequently been asked: Why should a rite of Freemasonry be named Scottish, which did not take its origin in Scotland, but was formed in the United States and from degrees which had previously been conferred only in France and England? Scotland had nothing to do with the Scottish Rite, neither did Scotchmen, so far as may be discovered. The following explanation has been offered: In the French lodges, when the question is asked, "Are you a Master Mason?" the reply is given, "I have seen the acacia." The Fraternity is often spoken of as the "Order of the Acacia." Now it happens, as in the case of "Peter Gower," which was mentioned in the previous lecture, that the French word for Scotch, "Ecossais," and the French word, "Acacia," are pronounced so nearly alike that English ears easily confound the one with the other. The degrees being conferred orally, the "Order of the Acacia" was understood and written down in English as the "Order of the Scotch (Ecossais)."

Jerusalem and the Grotto, the latter being a recently organized institution resembling the Shrine very closely and evidently having for its single purpose the entertainment of its members, all Master Masons being eligible to membership, while the Shrine makes eligible to membership only those who have attained to the Order of Knight Templar in the York Rite or to the thirty-second degree of the Scottish Rite, and who maintain membership in good standing in those bodies.

The supreme government of these Masonic bodies which I have mentioned is vested as follows: That of the Blue Lodges is vested in the Grand Lodge of Ancient Free and Accepted Masons of the State of Missouri, a body incorporated under the laws of the state. This Grand Lodge holds fraternal relations with nearly all regular Grand Lodges over the world, but its government is independent and sovereign over the three degrees of Ancient Craft Masonry within the boundaries of the state. The supreme government of the Chapters of Royal Arch Masons is, first, in the Grand Chapter of Royal Arch Masons of the State of Missouri, and secondly in the General Grand Chapter of Royal Arch Masons of the United States of America. The government of the Councils of Royal and Select Masters is vested, first, in the Grand Council of Royal and Select Masters of the State of Missouri, and secondly in the General Grand Council of Royal and Select Masters of the United States of America. The government of the Commanderies of Knights Templar is vested, first, in the Grand Commandery of Knights Templar of the State of Missouri, and secondly in the Grand Encampment of Knights Templar of the United States of America. The General Grand Chapter, the General Grand Council and the Grand Encampment all hold fraternal relations with similar bodies in other countries over the world.

The Scottish Rite, in the United States, is at the present time divided into two Supreme Jurisdictions, the Northern and Southern. The Northern Jurisdiction comprises fifteen states north of the old Mason and Dixon's line, while the Southern Jurisdiction claims authority over all the remaining states and territories. The headquarters of the Northern Jurisdiction is situated in the city of Boston and must meet there at least every three years. The headquarters of the Southern Jurisdiction is situated in the city of Washington, D. C., at the House of the Temple of Solomon. The latter is the elder and much the larger body and claims the title "Mother Council of the

World." Both bodies maintain fraternal relations with similar bodies over the world.

It may be mentioned that the government of the York Rite bodies is representative in character, the governing bodies being elected regularly by their constituent members, while the Scottish Rite Supreme Council is composed of thirty-three Sovereign Grand Inspectors General, holding office during life and absolutely controlling their own membership. The nearest system of government resembling it is the Roman Catholic Church, with its Pope and College of Cardinals, where the Pope appoints the Cardinals and when he dies the Cardinals elect a new Pope from among their own number. The constituent membership of the lower bodies have nothing to do with the government of the Scottish Rite and can only make their wishes known by way of recommendation and petition.

The primary qualifications for membership in a Blue Lodge, A. F. and A. M., in this state are that the petitioner shall be a white man, free born, over twenty-one years of age, a believer in a Supreme Being, having no disqualifying physical imperfection and engaged in no immoral or prohibited occupation. The question of physical disqualification is one regarding which somewhat more latitude is allowed than is known in many other jurisdictions. Here it is generally considered that the petitioner shall be physically able to comply with all the ceremonial requirements in the ritual of the several degrees. Saloon keeping and the manufacturing of intoxicating liquors are prohibited by statutes of the Grand Lodge. It is also held that a man whose mind is weakened by old age may not be admitted, though no particular age is mentioned. It is needless to say that the petitioner should be a man of sound mind and able to read and write and one who has been guilty of no crime which the laws forbid and punish. Membership and good standing in a lodge is essential to eligibility in any and all the other bodies. The Council of Royal and Select Masters and the Commandery of Knights Templar both require membership in good standing in a Chapter of Royal Arch Masons. The Commandery also requires that the candidate express a preference for the Christian religion, though no particular church or creed is mentioned. All the Masonic bodies in the state require the annual dues to be paid in advance for the current year, and delinquency for three months renders the member liable to suspension. In the lodge the candidates are required to learn the candidate's lecture in each degree and to pass an examination thereon in open lodge. This knowledge together with a receipt for dues for the current year is required of all visitors, unless vouched for by some member present as being a Mason in good standing of the particular degree to which admission is requested.

As our interest is to be particularly directed to the Ancient Craft, we will now speak of the organization of the Grand Lodge, the governing body of the Craft in this jurisdiction. As we have already said, this body is incorporated under the laws of the State of Missouri, with all the civil rights and privileges of any other business corporation. The membership of this body is composed of the present Grand officers, all Past Grand Masters, members of the several Grand Lodge committees, Masters, Senior Wardens and Junior Wardens of the various constituent lodges in the jurisdiction. Every Master Mason in the jurisdiction is entitled to a seat in the Grand Lodge, but except as before stated, without voice or vote. Those who are Past Masters of lodges are entitled to vote on all matters, including the election of Grand Lodge officers. According to the present rule, each member of the Grand Lodge present is entitled to one vote, unless a vote by lodges is called for. In such a case each lodge is entitled to five votes and the Master of the lodge, if present, shall cast such vote, but in his absence the Senior and Junior Wardens may cast it. Either of these officers may send a proxy in case he is unable to attend the meeting of the Grand Lodge, but this proxy must hold the same rank in the Order that is held by the officer he represents. From any decision of the Grand Lodge, assembled in regular session, there is no appeal. An appeal arising in any particular lodge lies first to the Grand Master and secondly to the Grand Lodge in regular session. It is the general practice to lay the matter before the Grand Master's District Deputy, though his powers, unless acting under express orders from his superior, are advisory only. In disagreements between Grand Lodges the final recourse is the severance of all friendly, fraternal relations. This is a remedy seldom resorted to.

The primitive body of Masonry is the particular lodge known in ordinary parlance as the Blue Lodge, blue being the color of its decorations. The peculiar color of the chapter is scarlet, that of the Council purple and that of the Commandery black and white. The ancient operative masons, in which society modern Freemasonry had its origin, while engaged in erecting those magnificent buildings which have made their names so justly celebrated in all ages, dwelt and worked in lodges. These lodges were small buildings of a temporary character, set up near the scene of their labors. These were called in Latin, "Logia." In the Teutonic languages they were called "Hutten" or "Hutts."

In speculative Masonry a lodge is defined to be a certain definite number of Masons, duly assembled, with the Holy Bible, Square and Compasses and a charter from a Grand Lodge authorizing them to meet and work. Seven Master Masons, one of whom must be the Master, or a Warden, all members of that particular lodge are necessary to form a working quorum for the transaction of business. All business, save that of conferring degrees, examination as to proficiency in the lectures of the degrees and trials for unMasonic conduct, is transacted in the third or Master's degree. Trials are always conducted in the highest degree to which the accused has attained; examinations are made in the degree to which they appertain.

The jurisdiction or territory of a particular lodge, unless limited by a statute of the Grand Lodge, extends half way, by air line, to the meeting place of the nearest lodge in all directions. In cities and towns, where two or more lodges are established, these lodges have what is termed "concurrent jurisdiction," within the corporate limits of said city or town and then half way to the nearest lodge, measured air line from said town limits. A man desiring to unite with the fraternity is expected to petition the nearest lodge and is reckoned as their material. Should any man desire to petition any other lodge than the one in whose jurisdiction he resides, the lodge receiving the petition must secure a waiver of jurisdiction from the lodge to which he should have applied. This waiver, if granted, may require that the fee for initiation be turned over to the lodge whose material the candidate is. Should he live in a concurrent jurisdiction of several lodges, a waiver must be secured from the nearest of these lodges to that to which he applies before the petition can be acted on.

It is almost a universal custom among Freemasons all over the world to require a unanimous vote of all the members present on all candidates for initiation. The rule is for the petition to remain before the lodge for the period of one calendar month, during which time a committee of investigation inquires into the character of the candidate and his standing in the community.

At the end of that time the committee makes a report, either favorable or unfavorable, and a ballot is held, at which all the members of the lodge present must vote, and the appearance of a single black ball is sufficient to reject. In case any member is unable to be present at the meeting at which the ballot is held he may make objection to the initiation of the candidate, either in writing or verbally to the Worshipful Master, and said objection has all the effect of a black ball. This objection, unless removed by the member making it, holds for one year; this or a rejection by ballot remains a bar to the further petition of the same candidate to this or any other lodge for one year, when he may apply again, if he so desires. In case he lives in a concurrent jurisdiction he is not obliged to apply to the same lodge in which he was rejected, though the fact of his previous rejection must be stated in any subsequent petition. Some Grand Jurisdictions claim perpetual jurisdiction over rejected candidates, but the Grand Lodge of Missouri claims jurisdiction for one year only. In case the petition is from a man who is already a Mason and is for membership in another lodge, a rejection does not prevent him from making another petition as soon as he desires. Such a petitioner must be vouched for or found by examination to be a Mason before his petition can be received, and he must present a dimit from the lodge of which he was last a member. In the jurisdiction of Missouri it is customary for a member desiring to join another lodge to secure from his lodge a certificate of good standing, which he presents with his petition. Such certificate entitles him to apply to any lodge. In case he is accepted his former lodge grants him a dimit, transferring his membership, while in case of his rejection he still remains a member in good standing in his original lodge. In this way he is able to make his transfer without any danger of forfeiting his Masonic standing.

LECTURE III

ANCIENT LANDMARKS

ALL regular Grand Lodges pretend to follow and observe what are known as the "Ancient Landmarks." There exists some difference of opinion as to what principles of conduct can properly claim the dignity of "Ancient Landmarks," but it is universally conceded that when it is agreed as to what they are, it is not within the power of any man or any body of men to infringe upon them or neglect them.

Regarding the definition as to what constitutes a Landmark, it may be said that a Landmark is a distinctive characteristic of the Fraternity that became established at a very early date in its history and, in a measure, sets the Order apart and separates it from all other societies. The sum of these characteristics constitutes what is known as the "Body of Masonry."

The list or code which follows consists of twenty-five of these characteristics compiled by Dr. Albert G. Mackey, a very illustrious authority in all matters Masonic. Any brother may have the same right, as he did, to arrange a list of principles which, in his opinion, constitute the "Body of Masonry," or any Grand Lodge may adopt a list, but such adoption does not create landmarks. Whatever they are they have existed from time immemorial, and can neither be created nor annihilated. They are like "natural laws," things to be discovered and not legislated into existence.

I.   The modes of recognition, for instance, the signs, grips and words.

II.   The division of Symbolic Masonry into three degrees.

III.   The legend of the third degree.

IV.   The government of the fraternity by a presiding officer, called a Grand Master, elected from the body of the Craft.

V.   The prerogative of the Grand Master to preside over every assembly of the Craft wheresoever and whensoever held.

VI.   The prerogative of the Grand Master to grant dispensations for conferring degrees at irregular times.

VII.   The prerogative of the Grand Master to grant dispensations for opening and holding lodges.

VIII.   The prerogative of the Grand Master to make Masons at sight.

IX.   The necessity for Masons to congregate in lodges.

X.   The government of every lodge by a Master and two Wardens.

XI.   The necessity for every lodge, when congregated, to be duly tiled.

XII.   The right of every Mason to be represented in all general meetings of the Craft and to instruct his representative.

XIII.   The right of every Mason to appeal from the decision of his brethren in lodge convened to the Grand Lodge or general assembly of Masons.

XIV.   The right of every Mason to visit and sit in any regular lodge.

XV.   That no Mason, not known to some brother present as such, can enter a lodge without undergoing an examination.

XVI.   That no lodge can interfere with the business or labors of any other lodge.

XVII.   That every Freemason is amenable to the laws and regulations of the Masonic jurisdiction in which he resides.

XVIII.   That every candidate for initiation must be a man, free born, and of lawful age.

XIX.   That every Mason must believe in the existence of God, or the Supreme Architect of the Universe.

XX.   That every Mason must believe in a resurrection to a future life.

XXI.   That a Book of the Law of God must form an indispensable part of the furniture of every lodge.

XXII.   That all men in the sight of God are equal and meet in lodge on one common level.

XXIII.   That Freemasonry is a secret society, in possession of secrets that cannot be divulged.

XXIV.   That Freemasonry consists of a speculative society founded upon an operative art.

XXV.   That these Landmarks can never be changed.

Much comment and discussion might be had upon each and all of these propositions, but in a general way they may be considered as sound and they are pretty closely adhered to by the Judiciary and Appeals Committees of the Grand Lodge of the State of Missouri.

Regarding No. XIV, it may be said that visiting any particular lodge under the jurisdiction of the Grand Lodge of Missouri, other than the lodge to which the brother belongs, is considered rather as a privilege than as a right, for if any member of the lodge objects to the visitor's admission or presence in the lodge, he must retire. This objection holds good for that particular meeting only and only when the objecting brother himself is present.

Regarding No. VIII, while the prerogative of the Grand Master to make Masons at sight is not actually denied, it is very generally disapproved. The prerogative and right of the Grand Master to grant dispensations to form and open new lodges is undoubted, and that lodges so formed and opened may make Masons is also undoubted. This would seem to include the right to make Masons at sight, on the principle that the greater includes the less. Still it is only on rare occasions that such a prerogative ought to be exercised, and when it is exercised it does not include the power of making the Mason, so created, a member of any regular lodge against the will and pleasure of that lodge. This is a prerogative that has come down to us from a time when Masons were more frequently made in lodges congregated and opened especially for the purpose of conferring degrees and which were dispersed immediately after that work had been accomplished than at the present day. At that time the mere making a Mason of a man was not supposed to make him a member of any particular lodge. He was generally advised to attach himself to a lodge as soon as he could find it convenient to do so. Today all lodges are regular and attached to some Grand Lodge, and permanent in their establishment and possessing a territorial jurisdiction, and the Masons that are made in them become, ipso facto, members of that lodge, unless the degrees are merely conferred at the request of some other lodge upon candidates elected by it. Unattached Masons are not considered to be in good Masonic standing, unless it can be shown that the fault is not their own, but is due to their having been rejected in a regular lodge.

In other jurisdictions several other propositions not here mentioned are regarded with great veneration, and come so near the rank of Landmarks that any Grand Lodge disregarding them would run great danger of forfeiting friendly and fraternal relations. This would seem especially true of any jurisdiction permitting the admission of a person of the black race. The governing bodies of France, Italy and Mexico long ago lost the fraternal recognition of all English and American Grand Lodges by disregarding Numbers XIX, XX and XXI. Still it must be remembered that circumstances in these countries are vastly different from those which prevail in England and America. When the Grand Orient of France was organized the rule which prevailed among Masons might be exhibited in the article on religion, to be found in the "Ancient Charges," to be quoted in the succeeding lecture of this book. The French claim that the change was made by the English and American lodges and not by them, that the latter Grand Lodges have created an entirely new requirement, which they are under no possible obligation to follow.

It is a fact that the Roman Catholic dominance in matters of religion prevailed to a much later date in the Latin countries and still exercises great influence. The Church discouraged in every way possible the possession and use of the Bible by the laity, so that the Bible never became a household book as in England and America, neither was it regarded with anywhere near the same degree of reverence, even by the most religious people. Neither was there ever, in the Latin mind, any middle ground between the creeds and government of the Roman Catholic Church and absolute free thought. When that Church ceased to be counted as absolute religious authority, no such authority existed. If rebellion against that authority had been delayed in England and America for another two hundred years such might have been the case in those countries.

At the time of the reformation the English set up a national church to take the place of the Roman Catholic Church, and which differed from it only in matters of government and in one or two points of belief and in America Protestantism has vested an authority in the Bible that was never pretended elsewhere. The former the Latin countries had no reason to accept, and the latter is a thing of slow growth, which the French Revolution was not calculated to encourage, and which would never have taken place in the presence of modern scientific knowledge. Even with us the Volume of the Sacred Law is regarded more as a symbol of Divine Light than as a rule and guide for faith and practice, and while its presence on the altar as a symbol is considered as indispensable, it is almost never read in the lodge. In thirty years of almost constant attendance at lodge in many jurisdictions, the writer has never heard the Bible read in the lodge, though portions of Scripture are occasionally quoted in the ritualistic work.

Many things led up to the break which are now matters of history too lengthy to deal with in this connection. The controversy has developed much prejudice and uncharitable opinion not very creditable to either side. During recent years there have been organized in these countries new bodies of Masons which our Grand Lodges have recognized as holding to the "Ancient Landmarks." These bodies are, at present, very weak and do not obtain much encouragement from the older Masonic bodies in these countries, as may be well supposed. These bodies have not seemed to be inimical to the Scottish Rite, and it is not an infrequent sight to meet a brother of French, Italian or South American origin in a Consistory of the thirty-second degree, whom, acting as a member of an examining committee in a Blue Lodge, we would have been obliged to have refused admission.

The Ancient Charges and Regulations, prepared and presented to the Grand Lodge of England in 1721 by Dr. Anderson and Dr. Desaguliers and adopted by that body on the 25th of March, 1722, are also held in great veneration by all regular Masons and state as nearly as possible what it was thought at that time the conduct of a Mason ought to be. They seem to be copied very closely from the laws and regulations of the Ancient Operative Masons that had been handed down from unknown antiquity. Many old copies of these laws have been unearthed since the day when Anderson presented them by students of Masonic history, which confirm their authority. They may be said to constitute the standard of Masonic ethics throughout the world. We will repeat them here:

CONCERNING GOD AND RELIGION—A Mason is obliged by his tenure to obey the Moral Law, and if he rightly understands the art he will never be a stupid *atheist* or *an irreligious libertine*. But though in ancient times Masons were charged in every country to be of the religion of that country or nation, whatever it was, it is now thought more expedient only to oblige them to that religion in which all men agree, leaving their particular opinions to themselves. That is, *to be good men and true,* or men of honor and honesty, by whatever denominations or persuasions they may be distinguished, whereby Masonry becomes the center of union and the *means of conciliating true friendship among persons who would otherwise have remained at a perpetual distance.*

OF THE CIVIL MAGISTRATES SUPREME AND SUBORDINATE—A Mason is a peaceable subject to the civil powers wherever he resides or works, and is never to be concerned in plots or conspiracies against the peace and welfare of the nation, nor behave himself undutifully to the inferior magistrates. For as Masonry has always been injured by wars and bloodshed and confusion, so most kings and princes have been much disposed to encourage the Craftsmen because of their peaceableness and loyalty where-

by they practically answered the cavils of their adversaries
and promoted the honor of the Fraternity which has ever
flourished in times of peace. So that if a brother should be a
rebel against the state he is not to be countenanced in his rebellion, however he may be pitied as an unhappy man, and if
convicted of no other crime, though the brotherhood must not
and should not own to his rebellion and thus give umbrage or
ground for political jealousy to the government for the time being,
they cannot expel him from the lodge and his relations to it
remain indefeasible.

OF LODGES—A lodge is a place where Masons assemble and
work, hence that assembly and duly organized society of Masons
is called a lodge, and every brother ought to belong to one and
be subject to its by-laws and general regulations. A lodge is
either Particular or General and will be best understood by
attending it and by the regulations of the General or Grand
Lodge hereunto annexed. In ancient times Masters and Fellows
could not be absent from it, especially when warned to appear
at it, without incurring severe censure, until it appeared to the
Master and Wardens that pure necessity hindered him. The
persons admitted members of a lodge must be *good men and
true, free born and of mature and discrete age, no bondsmen, no
woman, no immoral or scandalous men but of good report.*

OF MASTERS, WARDENS, FELLOWS AND APPRENTICES—All
preferment among Masons is grounded upon real worth and
personal merit only, that so the lords may be well served and
the brethren not put to shame, nor the Royal Craft despised.
Therefore, no Master or Warden is chosen by seniority, but for
his merit. It is impossible to describe these things in writing
and every brother must attend in his place and learn them in
a way peculiar to this Fraternity. Only, candidates may know
that no Master should take an apprentice unless he has sufficient
work for him and unless *he be a perfect youth, having no maim
or defect in his body, that may render him incapable of learning
the art* of serving his Master's Lord and of being a Brother and
then a Fellow in due time, even after he has served such a
term of years as the custom of the country directs, and that he
should be descended from honest parents, that so, when otherwise qualified, he may arrive at the honor of being a Warden,
and then the Master of the lodge, the Grand Warden and at
length the Grand Master of all the lodges, according to his

merit. No brother can be a Warden until he has passed the part of a Fellowcraft, *nor a Master until he has acted the part of a Warden, nor a Grand Warden until he has been a Master of a lodge,* nor a Grand Master unless he has been a Fellowcraft before his election, who is also nobly born, or a gentleman of the best fashion, or some eminent scholar, or curious architect, or other artist, descended of honest parents, and who is of singular great merit, in the opinion of the lodges. And for the better, easier and more honorable discharge of his office, the Grand Master has the power to choose his own Deputy Grand Master, who must be then or have been formerly the Master of a Particular lodge, and has the privilege of acting whenever his principal, the Grand Master, should act, unless the said principal be present or interposes his authority by a letter. These rulers, supreme and subordinate of the Ancient Lodge, are to be obeyed in their several stations by all the brethren, according to the old charges and regulations, with all humility, reverence, love and alacrity.

OF THE MANAGEMENT OF THE CRAFT IN WORKING—All Masons shall work honestly on working days, so that they may live creditably on Holy Days and the times appointed by the laws of the land or confirmed by custom shall be observed. The most expert of the Fellows or Craftsmen shall be chosen or appointed Master or Overseer of the Lord's work, who is to be called Master by those who work under him. The Craftsmen are to avoid all ill language and to call each other by no disobliging name but Brother or Fellow, and to behave themselves cautiously both within and without the lodge. The Master, knowing himself to be able of cunning, shall undertake the Lord's work as reasonably as possible and truly dispense his goods as if they were his own, nor to give more wages to any Brother or Fellow or Apprentice than he really deserves. Both the Master and the Masons receiving their wages justly shall be faithful to their Lord and honestly finish their work, whether task or journey, nor put the work to task that hath been accustomed to journey. None shall discover envy at the prosperity of a brother nor supplant him, nor put him out of his work, if he be capable to finish the same, for no man can finish another's work so much to the Lord's profit unless he be thoroughly acquainted with the designs and drafts of him that began it. When a Fellow Craftsman has been chosen Warden of the work, under the Master, he shall be true both to the Master and the

Fellows, shall carefully oversee the work in the Master's absence to the Lord's profit and the brethren shall obey him. All Masons employed shall meekly receive their wages without murmuring or mutiny and not desert the Master until the work be finished. A younger brother shall be instructed in the working to prevent spoiling the materials for want of judgment and for the increasing and continuing of brotherly love. All tools used in working shall be approved by the Grand Lodge. No laborer shall be employed in the proper work of Masonry, nor shall Freemasons work with them, that are not free, without an urgent necessity, nor shall they teach laborers or unaccepted Masons as they would teach a Brother or Fellow.

OF BEHAVIOR WHEN THE LODGE IS CONSTITUTED—You are not to hold private committees or separate conversations without leave from the Master, nor to talk of anything impertinent or unseemly, or interrupt the Master or Wardens, or any brother speaking to the Master, nor behave yourselves hilariously or jestingly while the lodge is engaged in what is serious and solemn, nor use any unbecoming language upon any pretence whatever, but to pay due reverence to your Master, Wardens and Fellows and put them to worship. If any complaint is brought the brother found guilty shall stand to the award and determination of the lodge, who are the proper and competent judges of all such controversies (unless you carry it by appeal to the Grand Lodge) and to whom they ought to be referred, lest the Lord's work be hindered meanwhile, in which case a particular reference may be made. But you must never go to law about what concerneth Masonry without absolute necessity apparent to the lodge.

AFTER THE LODGE IS OVER AND THE BRETHREN NOT GONE— You may enjoy yourselves with innocent mirth, treating one another according to ability, but avoiding all excess or forcing any brother to eat or drink beyond his inclination, or hindering him from going when his occasions call him, or doing or saying anything offensive, or that may forbid any easy and free conversation, for that would blast our harmony and defeat our laudable purposes. Therefore, no private piques or quarrels must be brought within the door of the lodge, far less any quarrels about religion, or nations, or state policy. We being only Masons of the catholic (universal) religion, above mentioned, we must not forget that we are also of all nations, tongues, kindreds and languages, and are resolved against all politics as what never yet conduced to the welfare of lodges and never will. This Charge has been strictly enjoined and observed, but especially since the Reformation in Britain, or the descent or secession of these nations from the Communion of Rome.

WHEN BRETHREN MEET, WITHOUT STRANGERS, BUT NOT IN LODGE FORMED—You are to salute one another in a courteous manner, as you will be instructed, calling each other Brother, freely giving mutual instruction as shall be thought expedient, without being overseen or overheard and without encroaching upon each other or derogating from that respect which is due to any brother, were he not a Mason. For although all Masons are brethren upon the same level, yet Masonry takes no honor from any man that he had before, nay, rather it adds to his honor, especially if he has deserved well of the brotherhood, who must give honor to whom it is due and avoid ill manners.

IN PRESENCE OF STRANGERS NOT MASONS—You shall be cautious in your words and carriage, that the most penetrating stranger shall not be able to discover or find out what is not proper to be intimated, and sometimes you shall divert a discourse and manage it prudently for the honor of the Worshipful Fraternity.

AT HOME AND IN YOUR NEIGHBORHOOD—You are here to act as becomes a moral and wise man, particularly not to let your family, friends and neighbors know the concerns of the lodge, but wisely to consult your own honor and that of the Ancient Brotherhood for reasons not to be mentioned here. You must also consult your own health by not continuing together too late or too long from home after the lodge hours are past and by avoiding all gluttony and drunkenness, that your family be not neglected or injured, nor you disabled from working.

TOWARDS A STRANGE BROTHER—You are cautiously to examine him in such a manner as prudence shall direct you, that you may not be imposed upon by an ignorant, false pretender, whom you are to reject with contempt and derision, and beware of giving him any hints of knowledge. If you discover him to be a true and genuine brother you are to respect him accordingly, and if he be in want you must relieve him, if you can, or else direct him how he can be relieved. You must employ him for some days or recommend him to be employed. But you are not charged to do beyond your ability, only to prefer a poor brother, that is a good man and true, before any other poor people in the same circumstances. Finally, all these charges you are to observe and also those that shall be communicated to you in another way, cultivating brotherly love, the foundation and capstone, the cement and glory of the Ancient Fraternity, avoiding all wrangling and quarreling, all slander and backbiting, not permitting others to slander any honest brother, but defending his character and doing all good offices as far as is consistent with your honor and safety and no farther. And if any of them do you an injury you must apply to your own, or to his lodge, and from thence you may appeal to the Grand Lodge, at the quarterly communication, and from thence to the annual Grand Lodge, as has been the ancient, laudable conduct of our forefathers in every nation and age, never taking a legal course, but when the case cannot be otherwise decided, and patiently listening to the honest, friendly advice of the Master and Fellows when they would prevent you going to law with strangers or would excite you to put a speedy period to all law-suits, that so you may mind the affairs of Masonry with the more alacrity and success. But with respect to Brothers and Fellows at law, the Master and brethren should kindly offer their mediation, and if that submission is impracticable they must, however, carry on their process or law-suit without wrath or rancor, nor, as in the common way, saying and doing things which may hinder brotherly love and good offices to be renewed and continued, that all may see the benign influence of Masonry, as all true Masons have done from the beginning of the world and will do to 'the end of time.—"So mote it be!" Amen!

Every Mason should read and reread these Ancient Charges, as they, together with the Particular Charge that goes with each degree, practically demonstrate what the general conduct of a Mason ought to be under all circumstances, in the lodge, to his brethren and to the world at large. The standard so set up is dignified and kindly, but does not place any puritanical damper on rational enjoyment. It is normal and reasonable and requires nothing that the ordinary honest, upright, decent citizen could not comfortably and easily comply with. Every man would admit that he ought to live by such a standard, whether he was a Mason or not. Yet if Masons invariably lived up to this standard the lodge and the world would be a much pleasanter place to live in than it is today.

LECTURE IV

RITUAL AND CEREMONIES

A PAST GRAND MASTER once remarked in our presence—
"The ritual is the vehicle on which the principles of Freemasonry ride into the hearts and minds of men." In
discussing such a subject it is somewhat difficult for the writer
to know where to begin and where to stop. There are many
things which can be only partially explained in writing; some
that cannot be explained at all. A portion of our work is
esoteric and secret, and a portion is exoteric and may be known
to anyone who cares to interest himself in the subject. The
workings of the spirit of Masonry, like the "Kingdom of Heaven,"
spoken of by a Great Teacher, is partially internal and secret,
like the leaven or yeast that works in the measure of meal until
the whole is leavened and partially outward and visible, like the
growth of the mustard-seed into a tree capable of supporting
the fowls of the air. It is of the latter only that we are permitted to speak in full. Of the former we may only hint and
draw comparisons.

One might say—"If the Mysteries of Masonry are replete with
such advantages to mankind, why are they not divulged for the
general good of society?" To that a Mason might make answer
—"Masonry is an art. Could Raphael divulge the art of painting Madonnas? Can a mathematician divulge the science of
geometry? Can any of the great arts be divulged? They are
acquired only after a lifetime of labor, and many of them require genius and love and devotion besides, which can never be
taught save by example." Were the privileges of Masonry indiscriminately bestowed the entire design of the Institution
would be subverted, and, being familiar, like many other important matters would soon lose their value and sink into disregard.
In fact, they would become mere statements in words, mere
pictures of something that had no existence or countertype in
the emotions of men. As mysteries they have dynamic power
which may goad men to action, but as mere ceremonies they
would become worthless and without effect. It may be a weakness in human nature that men are generally more charmed with
novelty than with real merit and intrinsic value in things.
Novelty influences many of our acts and determinations. What

is new or difficult of acquisition, be it ever so trivial or insignificant, readily captivates the imagination and insures a temporary admiration, while what is familiar or easily obtained, however noble or eminent for its utility, is certain to be disregarded by the giddy and unthinking.

Did the particular secrets or peculiar forms prevalent among Masons constitute the essence of our Art, it might be alleged that our amusements were trifling and our ceremonies superficial, but this is not the case. Having their uses they are preserved and from the recollection of the lessons they inculcate the well-informed Mason derives instruction. Drawing them to a near inspection he views them through a proper medium, adverts to the circumstances that gave them rise, dwells upon the tenets they convey, and, finding them replete with useful information, adopts them as keys to the privileges of his Art and prizes them as sacred. These mysteries and these ceremonies are useful, only as they serve to create emotions in the hearts of men and firm resolutions to live noble and worthy lives. For this reason our officers that find it their duty to instruct candidates during their introduction into these ceremonies, should look well to their ability, not only to convey the necessary information, but also to awaken the much more necessary emotion. Remember that the letter killeth while the spirit maketh alive. Let these officers learn to read and speak understandingly and feelingly, and what is more important, display in their own deportment an example and similitude of the results of Masonic study and discipline.

Some time early in the year 1717 the members of the Society of Operative Masons, in and about that portion of the city of London known as Westminster, determined to change the character of their institution to that of a purely speculative science and to place it under a more comprehensive and better organized government. This they certainly accomplished, and our Grand Lodge system with its theory of territorial jurisdictions and chartered constituent bodies resulted. They also adopted at that time a ritual. No person can say with a certainty that there ever was a time when the wise and accomplished Architect was not aware that a fine similitude existed between the qualities of a great and sublime architecture and those of a noble character and greatness of soul. The analogy is so striking that it is almost impossible to suppose that a good man should fail to see it and to point out these likenesses to those who looked to him for

Masonic instruction along purely operative lines. How much of the present work of the degrees already existed in the teachings of the Fraternity, previous to the reorganization of the society in 1717, and how much was introduced at that time or subsequently we can never know. Many ancient manuscripts were destroyed about that time, possibly through fear that they would be made public, and that through the records of meetings, etc., political capital might be made against some men then living. Many manuscripts have been lost since and not a few manufactured out of whole cloth in modern times. It is certain that there was sufficient knowledge and learning among the Fraternity to attract to the organization at once many eminent scholars and many men of high social standing in the community, including some names of royal greatness.

The renewed Order flourished beyond all precedent. It seems likely from what we can discover at this date that the main portion of the ceremony was conferred in a single degree and that the information that distinguished the different grades between Apprentices, Fellowcrafts and Masters consisted purely of certain signs and words that might enable those of the higher ranks to recognize each other. If Dr. Anderson and Dr. Desaguliers and other prominent Masons of that time were sufficiently acquainted with the import of the Ancient Mysteries of Egypt, India, Assyria, Greece and Rome to have copied the many resemblances that since their time have appeared in the ritual, they must have been head and shoulders above many other scholars of that period. It must be remembered that most of the information that we now possess relating to such matters appeared in English literature at a much later date. Not one word of Egyptian hieroglyphic or Babylonian cuneiform writing had been translated and the knowledge of Hebrew and Sanscrit was exceedingly limited, the former to Biblical translation and the latter to a simple acquaintance with the fact that it was the mother tongue to Hindustani. The great science of comparative philology was not yet born, nor would it be for a century yet to come. Yet it was a fact that the drama of the Third Degree was promulgated by Dr. Desaguliers as early as 1723 and introduced by him into the working Masonry of Scotland and Ireland. How was it possible for the learned doctor at that date to pick out the only name mentioned in the Bible that in its etymology meant "The Daylight of the Month of the Ram"? and at the same time was historically connected with the only profession or occupation that Masons acknowledged to be superior to their own. I refer to the craft of the metal worker. The tool sharpener must always be king among stone cutters. Again the learned doctor must pick out another tool sharpener, to accompany the legend, one Tubalcain, which name we also find in the ancient manuscripts before the days of the reorganization. Bel-Can or Baal-Can was the Vulcan of the Syrian mythology. We think it quite possible that Dr. Desaguliers simply arranged the old secret tradition of the builder of the temple into a drama, as we now find it, but the idea is so primitive and so interwoven with similar dramas of the Men's House, found among all kindreds and tribes of savage humanity scattered over the broad earth, that it seems utterly out of the question that any man living in the year 1720 could have invented and made it up out of whole cloth, so to speak. As for the lectures and monitorial work, the matter is quite different. Here we have historical data from which to reconstruct the story which we shall proceed to relate at this time.

There lately appeared in "The Builder," the journal of the National Masonic Research Society, published in Anamosa, Iowa, a reprinted article on the history of the ritual, which is said to have first appeared in the Masonic Monthly of Boston in 1863. Concerning this article, Brother Joseph Fort Newton, the editor, says: "It is of unusual value, not only from its completeness, but for its revelation of the growth of the ritual, as much by subtraction as addition, and especially as showing the introduction of Christian symbolism, imagery and interpretation, first by Martin Clare in 1732 and by Dunkerly and Hutchinson later. One need only to turn to the 'Spirit of Masonry' by Hutchinson, deservedly one of the most popular Masonic books ever written, to see how far this tendency has gone, when it was checked in 1813 at the great Masonic Union, which took place in that year between the Ancients and the Moderns, so called. At this time a committee made a careful examination and comparative study of all the rituals then in use among Masons, and the result was the Preston Webb lectures now generally in use in this country." * * *

"Of the thousands upon thousands of candidates who annually pass through the ceremonies of the three degrees conferred in Masonic lodges, but very few ever know anything of the history of the ritual of the Order. This is especially to be regretted, for the reason that there is among the Craft generally a strong aversion to any change, however slight, in anything connected with the ritual, for fear that some of the Ancient Way Marks may be infringed upon or obliterated. This veneration for the ancient usages and customs is highly commendable, and care should ever be taken that it be not weakened, as the stability, universality and usefulness of the Order are to a very considerable extent dependent upon it. Rude hands should not be allowed to tamper with our ceremonies, our language or our usages. But it is of the greatest importance that there should be an intelligent appreciation of what really are ancient usages and what actually constitute 'Landmarks' of the Order, as it is these alone that should be carefully preserved and from which we should never suffer the slightest deviation.

"In the minds of men every word of the ritual, as it has now come down to their individual ears, is invested with all the sanctity of a Landmark, to deviate from which,' even in the slightest degree, would be a stab at the heart of the venerable Institution and shake the very foundations of the Temple itself. In order that this fidelity to obligations and convictions may be intelligently directed, as far at least as what are technically called the 'lectures' of the lodge are concerned, the following brief history has been prepared. The uninformed brother may safely rely upon the truthfulness of this narrative.

"Previous to the revival of Masonry in 1717 and the organization of our present system of Grand Lodges and chartered lodges, the secrets of the Order were undoubtedly communicated, and the instructions and explanations given to candidates in such form of language as the presiding Master and Wardens could command at the time. If he were a person gifted in language, and his mind well stored with facts and lessons of scriptural Masonic history, his explanations would be full and interesting and his instructions clear and explicit. If, on the other hand, the presiding officers were less fortunate in these respects, the traditions and moral instructions would be set forth in style and language corresponding even to a meager and barren explanation of the most vital points. It is very probable, but not certain, that these explanations and instructions, 'Lectures,' as they were technically called, by long usage and frequent repetition, gradually assumed very nearly a set form of words, which form was transmitted orally from one generation to another.

"Soon after the reorganization of the Order in 1717 the Grand

Lodge of England ordered the Ancient Charges and Constitutions of the Order to be compiled and printed, which was done by Dr. James Anderson, a distinguished scholar and Freemason. This volume, known as the Anderson Constitutions, was published in 1723 and was one of the first printed books on Freemasonry ever issued. Simultaneously with the publication of this book of Constitutions, Dr. Anderson, assisted by Dr. Theophilus Desaguliers, arranged the lectures, for the first time, in the form of questions and answers. Dr. Oliver informs us that the first lecture extended to the greatest length, but the replies were circumscribed to a very narrow compass. The second lecture was shorter and the third, called the Master's part, contained only seven questions and answers. So favorably were these lectures received that the Grand Lodge of England, then the only Grand Lodge in existence, save the old Grand Lodge or Assembly at York (which soon after expired), adopted the form and ordered them to be given in all the lodges. Thus was compiled and disseminated the first regular form or system of Masonic lectures.

"The progress of the Order, subsequent to the date above mentioned, was unprecedented in all its previous history, and in a few years the imperfections of Dr. Anderson's lectures loudly called for revision. This was finally accomplished in 1732 by Martin Clare, an eminent Mason and who was afterwards Deputy Grand Master. Clare's amendments consisted of but little more than the addition of a few moral and scriptural admonitions and a simple allusion to the five human senses and to the theological ladder. A few years later Thomas Dunkerly, an accomplished scholar and who was considered the most intelligent Mason of his day, considerably extended and improved the lectures. Among other things he first gave the theological ladder in its three most important rounds. According to Dr. Oliver, Dunkerly added many 'Types of Christ.' This, be it remembered, was only one hundred and sixty years ago, 1763, and is an explicit statement of the addition of the first Christian allusions to be found in the ritual of Freemasonry.

"The lectures of Dunkerly continued to be a standard in England until 1763, when the Reverend William Hutchinson revised and improved them. Hutchinson boldly claimed the third degree to be exclusively Christian. He considered the three degrees to refer to the three great dispensations, viz., the Patriarchial, the Mosaic and the Christian. He even argued that the name 'Mason' signifies or implies 'member of a religious sect' and a professed devotee of the Deity. He regarded the degrees as progressive steps or schools in religion. He believed that a knowledge of the God of Nature was the first step or estate of our profession; that the worship of the Deity after the Jewish Law is described in the second stage of Freemasonry, and that the Christian Dispensation is distinguished in the last and highest Order. In the lectures of Hutchinson are first introduced the three great pillars, Wisdom, Strength and Beauty, as the supports of a lodge. He also appears to have introduced for the first time the four cardinal virtues, Temperance, Fortitude, Prudence and Justice. He also gave to the Star its Christian signification. In fine, he appears to have exerted his utmost ingenuity to render the degrees emphatically Christian in their allusions and teachings.

"Hutchinson's system continued in force only a few years. His lectures gave place in 1772 to the revision of William Preston. The latter not only revised but greatly extended the lectures, and his system continued to be the standard in England until the union of the two Grand Lodges of England, which took place in 1813, when a committee, of which Dr. Hemming was the chairman and the leading mind, compiled the form now generally in use in the English lodges and known as the Hemming lectures. During the unhappy division of the Craft in England, between 1739 and 1813, differences had crept into the work of the lectures, and at the union above mentioned the committee endeavored to compile a system which, while it should be in conformity with the spirit of Freemasonry and in harmony with the 'Ancient Landmarks,' should be a sort of a compromise between the forms in previous use by the two rival organizations.

"The Hemming lectures differ widely from those of Preston, or from any others previously introduced. A few of these differences may properly be mentioned. English lodges are now dedicated to Moses and Solomon, instead of the two Saints John, as before, and their Masonic festival falls on the Wednesday following St. George's Day, April 23, that saint being the patron saint of England. The symbolic *working tools* of an Entered Apprentice are a 24-inch gauge, a gavel and a chisel. Those of a Master Mason are a pair of compasses, a skirett and a pencil. Instead of following the precedent and example of his predecessors in introducing new Christian allusions, Dr. Hemming expunged several in use previously. The *ornaments* of a Master

Masons' lodge were a porch, a dormer and a stone pavement. The system, however, never met with cordial approval, even of the English brethren, and though 'beautifully elaborate' contains so many incongruities and departures from the more simple lectures of Preston that it can never be recognized as a universal system.

"The verbal ritual of Preston was introduced into this country by two English brethren, who had been members of the principal Lodge of Instruction in London and was by them communicated to Thomas Smith Webb, an accomplished and distinguished Mason of New England. According to the testimony of Webb himself he made but little change in the system of Preston. In his first edition of 'The Freemason's Monitor,' published in 1797, he says: 'The observations on the first three degrees are principally taken from Preston's "Illustrations of Masonry" with some necessary alterations. Mr. Preston's division of the first lecture into six, the second into four and the third into twelve sections, not being agreeable to the present mode of working, they are arranged in this work according to the general practice.' It is plain that Webb followed Preston quite closely and one who will take the trouble to compare will find that Cross, and after him all the rest have copied nearly verbatim from Webb, so that the exoteric portion of the ritual as contained in our monitors, charts, manuals and trestle boards are but little more than reprints of Preston's 'Illustrations of Masonry.' In 1801 and 1802 Benjamin Gleason, an intelligent and zealous brother, then a student in Brown's University at Providence, Rhode Island, received the lectures of Preston as modified by Webb directly from Webb himself. Gleason, by his zeal and other excellent qualities, became a great favorite with Webb, through whose influence he was induced to become a Masonic lecturer.

"July 2, 1804, Isaiah Thomas, then Grand Master of the Grand Lodge of Massachusetts, commissioned Brother Gleason as Grand Lecturer to the lodges in his jurisdiction, the Grand Lodge having left the subject of the uniformity of the work to his discretion as Grand Master. Early in the year 1806 the Grand Master of New Hampshire, Thomas Thompson, wrote to the Grand Master of Massachusetts, requesting that a committee might be chosen by the two Grand Lodges to meet and confer upon Masonic subjects, and especially upon the subject of the uniformity of the work and lectures. The proposition was favorably received and such a committee was appointed. Rev. George Richards, editor of Richards' 'Preston's Illustrations of Masonry,' Lyman Spawlding, Grand Secretary, and John Harris represented New Hampshire and John Fowle, Benjamin Gleason and Stephan Bean represented Massachusetts. The committee met at Newburyport in that state and before rising adopted a report, signed by each member of the committee, from which we make the following extract—'The respective committees of New Hampshire and Massachusetts are also fully agreed and are positively unanimous in their opinion that the mode of work, as exemplified by Brothers Gleason, Fowle and Bean, as practiced in Massachusetts and adopted in New Hampshire, according to the acknowledgment of Brothers Harris, Richards and Spawlding, is as correct as can possibly be expected under existing circumstances, and they deem it expedient that in the three degrees every Master of a lodge should be indulged with the liberty of adapting historical details and the personification of the passing scene as most agreeable to himself, his supporting officers and assisting lodge.' The report was approved by the respective Grand Lodges and the Preston-Webb Ritual continued to be taught by Brother Gleason. This is the committee from which Brother Jeremy L. Cross, long and well known as a Masonic lecturer and as the author of the Masonic Chart and other works, claimed to have received the work and lectures and to have been formally commissioned as a lecturer. He also affirms that he never afterwards changed a word or letter of the ritual as it was communicated to him by them.

"There are, however, some differences between the lectures as taught by Cross and as taught by Gleason, though they are practically such as may be called non-essential. In 1810 the Grand Lodge of Massachusetts formally adopted the Preston-Webb Ritual and voted to employ Brother Gleason to communicate it to the lodges under its jurisdiction. In the performance of this duty he was employed most of the time for several years, and he continued to impart his instruction at intervals until his death in 1847, visiting for that purpose various sections of the country."

Thus closes the historical article which appeared in the Masonic Monthly of Boston. The lodges that originally constituted the Grand Lodge of Missouri were chartered some by the Grand Lodge of Pennsylvania and some by the Grand Lodge of Tennessee, so that the ritualistic work in use here was most likely brought from the latter jurisdiction. It has undergone changes since the organization of our Grand Lodge in 1821, but these alterations have not been many or material. For more than a quarter of a century Brother Alan McDowell was custodian of the work and most of the District Grand Lecturers received their instruction from him in person. Brother McDowell was a fine English scholar and his desire was to render the language of the ritual as brief and concise as possible, without altering the sense or the archaic form of the rhetoric. Until within the last ten years no particular monitor had ever been adopted by the Grand Lodge. The printed portion of the ritual most in use was what was known as the Parson's monitor, and wherever this work differed from the old monitors of Webb, Cross and Mackey the change was most likely made either by Brother McDowell or Past Grand Master Thomas Garrett. The funeral ceremony most in use was compiled by Brother Garrett. Most Worshipful Brother Garrett was a journalist of considerable reputation and his knowledge of English was at least respectable. About ten years ago Most Worshipful Brother W. F. Kuhn, at that time a member of the Committee on Ritual, induced the Grand Lodge to publish a monitor of its own. It was proposed to copy the Parson's monitor as closely as possible without infringing on the copyright of that book, the ownership of that copyright having passed out of the hands of the original publishers and the book, for the time at least, out of print. He also proposed that wherever in the ritual the word "Mason" was used, either in the esoteric or exoteric portion of the work, it be changed to the word "Freemason." Whether wisely or otherwise, the resolution was adopted. In the opinion of many this change weakened the language for the sake of a doubtful move in favor of historical truth.

This question naturally opens up the discussion of the name of the Fraternity to which we belong. Whence the origin of the term "Freemason" in contradistinction to any other Mason? Certainly in this country and at this time all Masons are free, one as much as another. Some have claimed that the name referred to workers in "free-stone." This definition would shut out all workers in granite, marble and caen stone, which certainly could not be made to apply to the Ancient Craft. Others think that the word was intended to mean "Free of the Guild," a member of a society properly initiated into its mysteries in contradistinction to a "rough Mason," or mere "stone layer," who had never been admitted to the Ancient Fraternity. Others hold, and we believe with sufficient evidence, that the word was originally intended to signify "free of feudal tenure." In the Middle Ages all ordinary people were bound to the soil, as serfs, on the estate of some nobleman. But the Freemasons, on account of the very nature of their profession, were a traveling guild. All other occupations were local. A member of the shoemakers' guild was expected to obtain his business patronage in the place where he was born, while the Mason, and especially the skillful architect or cunning sculptor of stone, was obliged to go where the temporary need for his services called him. For this reason it was not at all desirable that he should be bound to the soil by feudal tenure. This was the reason why the society required that every Entered Apprentice should be free born and no serf or slave whose lord or owner could claim his services. For at least one year subsequent to having completed his time as Apprentice he was required to travel to complete his education.

Therefore, we believe that a member of our ancient brotherhood was called a "Freemason" in contradistinction to a "Local Mason," who simply did stone work at the command of his lord and who was never allowed to leave the place of his birth but was bound to the soil and to the service of the lord of the domain. Our ancient brother was free to travel in foreign countries, to work and receive Masonic wages, and was subject only to the rules and regulations that governed the Craft, and he took a solemn oath to preserve inviolate the secrets which belonged to the society, instructing no cowan or "Local Mason" or exhibiting to such person any pattern-stone, and to yield cheerful obedience to the Master and Wardens over the work on which he was engaged. When one job of work was completed the lodge in that place dissolved and the Mason betook himself at once where he might be needed. The Craft was charged to give him employment wherever he went or to furnish him with sufficient money to pay his expenses to the next lodge. In all the ancient manuscripts the term used is "Mason," while the local stoneworker is called a "layer" or "cowan." So while we have no fault to find with the word "Freemason," where such a designation is required or proper, the term "Mason" answers all purposes when employed inside a lodge or in connection with the Ancient Craft where there is no necessity to indicate a distinction between a member of the Fraternity and a mere stone layer by occupation, who has never joined the society.

LECTURE V

OPENING AND CLOSING LODGE

IN any association the necessity for some preparatory ceremonies before proceeding to the dispatch of ordinary business has always been recognized. The decorum and dignity
of the meeting alike suggest, even in popular assemblies called
only for a temporary purpose, that a presiding officer shall with
some formality be inducted into the chair, and he then, to use
the common phraseology, opens the meeting with the appointment of his necessary assistants and his announcement, in an
address to the audience, explanatory of the object that has
called them together.

If secular associations have found it expedient to adopt some
preparatory form, to avoid the appearance of unseemly abrupt-
ness, it may well be supposed that religious societies have been
still more observant of the custom, and that as their pursuits
are more elevated their ceremonies of preparation should be
still more impressive. As the Herald in the Ancient Mysteries
announced the commencement of the ceremonies by the proclamation, "Depart, ye profane," so the first attention of a Masonic
lodge is to secure privacy. The officers assume their stations
and the Master announces his intention to open the lodge. The
officers clothe themselves in a manner appropriate to their rank
and quietly seat themselves. The next duty is to see that all
present are entitled to remain. No stranger should be permitted
to remain in the room, unless known to some member present
to be a Mason. The fact of having previously sat in lodge with
the person under question enables one to vouch for his character,
either in the lodge or to any brother outside the lodge, all three
being present.

In the absence of such voucher the stranger must retire and
a committee be appointed to examine him as to his Masonic
qualifications. This committee first examines the stranger's
receipt for dues for the current year and compares his signature
with that upon the certificate. The signature on the certificate
is supposed to have been written in the presence of the officers
who issued and signed it and affixed the regular seal of the lodge.
This certificate also bears the facsimile signature of the Grand
Master and Grand Secretary and seal of the Grand Lodge,

which in a sense vouches for the regularity of the lodge to whom it was delivered. If the signatures are identical the evidence of the stranger's membership in good standing is very strong. The committee then satisfies itself that the lodge mentioned in the certificate is in good and regular standing, and working under a charter from some Grand Lodge having fraternal relations with our Grand Lodge. The book of Grand Lodge proceedings for the last session will answer this question for our own jurisdiction, in case of any doubt. Most lodges keep a book in which are printed the names of all recognized lodges listed under their separate jurisdictions. The only fault with this is that the book in question is seldom up-to-date. It is more useful where the name of the lodge in question appears than where it is absent, as new lodges are being organized all the time. Then the committee administers the oath customary with our Grand Lodge on these occasions, after which they proceed to satisfy themselves that the stranger has been regularly initiated and is in possession of the degree in which the lodge is open and in which he desires to visit. Being so satisfied the visiting brother is introduced into the lodge, is properly welcomed by the Master and invited to a seat, according to his rank.

All present being entitled to remain in the lodge, the lodge is then *"tiled."* The avenues of entrance to the lodge are properly guarded. A portion of a lecture is then rehearsed by the Master and Senior Warden, and th. Master proceeds to ascertain from each officer his familiarity with the duties of his station. The ceremony of *"opening"* follows, in which all the brethren assist. An *"ode"* is sung and the following *"prayer"* is repeated by the Chaplain or the Master:

"Most Holy and Glorious Lord God, the Great Architect of the Universe, Giver of all good gifts and graces, in Thy name we have assembled and in Thy name we desire to proceed in all our doings. Grant that the sublime principles of Freemasonry may so subdue every discordant passion within us, and so harmonize and enrich our hearts with Thine own love and goodness that the lodge at this time may humbly reflect the order and beauty that reign forever before Thy throne. Amen!" Response by the brethren: *"So mote it be!"*

This prayer is printed in the Missouri Monitor. The following prayer appears in the Webb Monitor of one hundred years ago, from which the above was doubtless derived:

"Most Holy and Glorious Lord God, the Great Architect of the Universe, the Giver of all good gifts and graces, Thou hast promised that where two or three are gathered together in Thy name that Thou wouldst be in the midst of them and bless them. In Thy name we have assembled, most humbly beseeching Thee to bless us in all our undertakings so that we may know and serve Thee aright and that all our actions may tend to Thy Glory and to our advancement in knowledge and virtue. And we humbly beseech Thee, O Lord, to bless our present assembling, to illuminate our minds so that we may walk in the Light of Thy Countenance, and when the trials of our probationary state are over be admitted to that Temple not made with hands, Eternal in the Heavens. Amen!" Response by brethren: *"So mote it be!"*

The Master then declares the lodge open in the name of God and the Holy Saints John, gives the brethren an admonition against improper debate and un-Masonic conduct, which closes with the 133rd Psalm: *"Behold how good and how pleasant it is for brethren to dwell together in unity. It is like the precious ointment on the head that ran down upon the beard, even Aaron's beard that went down to the skirts of his garments, like the dew of Hermon, the dew that descended upon the mountains of Zion, for there the Lord commanded a blessing, even life forever more."*

The opening in each degree is very similar, though the devotional exercises are omitted. At all stated or regular meetings the lodge must be opened on the first degree. If no business appears it is opened on the second degree. If no business appears in the second degree the lodge is opened on the third degree. All the business that can be transacted in the first and second degrees is to confer the same or to hold an examination of a candidate, as to his proficiency in the work of that degree, or conducting a trial for un-Masonic conduct on one who has never received the third degree. When the lodge is regularly opened on the third degree the regular business of the lodge is transacted. This custom does not hold in all foreign jurisdictions, as many of them dispatch the regular business of the lodge in the first degree. The trial of a brother for un-Masonic conduct must take place in the highest degree to which the accused brother has attained in the lodge. When the entire work of the lodge is completed the lodge closes in due form in the degree on which it is then at work. The first opening and the final closing must be in due form. During the meeting the temporary transfer from one degree to another may be in short form, which consists merely in giving the Tiler at the door proper orders and the Master and Wardens making the usual proclamation. The closing ceremonies are to a great extent a repetition of the opening ceremonies. The following prayer is used:

"Supreme Architect of the Universe, accept our humble thanks for the many mercies and blessings which Thy bounty has conferred upon us, and especially for this friendly and social intercourse. Pardon, we beseech Thee, whatever Thou hast seen amiss in us since we have been together, and continue to us Thy presence, protection and blessing. Make us sensible of the renewed obligations we are under to love Thee, and as we are about to separate and return to our respective places of abode, wilt Thou be pleased so to influence our hearts and minds that we may, each one of us, practice out of the lodge the great moral duties that are inculcated in it, and with reverence study and obey the laws, which Thou hast given us, in Thy Holy Word. Amen!" Response by the brethren: *"So mote it be!"*

The following appears to be the prayer from which the above was taken: "Supreme Architect of the Universe, accept our humble thanks for the many mercies and blessings which Thou hast conferred upon us, and especially for this friendly and social intercourse. Pardon, we beseech Thee, whatever Thou hast seen amiss in us since we have been together, and continue to us Thy presence, protection and blessing. Make us sensible of the renewed obligations we are under to love Thee supremely and to be friendly to each other. May all our irregular passions be subdued and may we daily increase in faith, hope and charity, but more especially in that charity which is the bond of peace and the foundation of every virtue. May we so practice Thy precepts that we may finally obtain Thy promises and find an entrance through the gates into the Temple and City of our God. Amen!" Response of the brethren: "So mote it be!"

The following has been thought by many to be a very beautiful closing prayer:

"And now, Great Master of the Universe, that the cares and labors of another day are ended and the silence of the night has fallen upon the world, permit us to retire to our homes and to our rest and resign ourselves to Thy protection. In Thine everlasting arms support us, by Thy mighty power defend us and let Thy goodness and Thy mercy follow us all our days, and finally, when we shall have finished our labors on earth, receive us into that land where the storms of life come not and the shades of evening do not gather, where we shall see Thee without obscurity, know Thee without imperfection and love Thee without end. Amen!" Response by the brethren: "So mote it be."

The following Charge is rehearsed:

"Brethren, we are about to quit this sacred retreat of friendship and virtue to mix again with the world. Amidst its concerns and employments forget not the duties you have heard so frequently inculcated and so forcibly recommended in this lodge. Be diligent, prudent, temperate and discreet. Remember that around this altar you have promised to befriend and relieve every worthy brother who shall need your assistance. Remember that you have promised to remind him in the most tender manner of his failings and aid his reformation. These generous principles are to extend further. The whole world has a claim upon your kind offices. Do good to all. We recommend it more especially to the household of the faithful. Finally, my brethren, be ye all of one mind and live in peace and may the God of Love and Peace delight to dwell among you and bless you."

The foregoing Charge is very ancient, dating back, at the shortest, to the reorganization of Masonry in 1717. The same may be said of the beautiful benediction which closes the lodge.

"So may we ever meet, act and part. May the blessing of Heaven rest upon us and all regular Masons. May brotherly love prevail and every moral and social virtue cement us. Amen!" Response by the brethren: *"So mote it be."*

As a short reminder to the Masonic student of the opening and closing ceremonies, the lodge is first congregated, then purged, then tiled, then lectured and finally opened.

LECTURE VI

SYMBOLISM OF THE LODGE

THE expression occurs, *"The lodge is symbolically a representation of King Solomon's Temple."* Why this particular edifice was selected as typical of human character or the morally enlightened human soul is a historical question not so easy to determine at this period of time. This Temple was the dwelling place of the Living God, the God worshiped by all nations who knew Masonry. Physically, if it ever so existed, it was the only prominent public building erected by the Jews, whose religion was so intimately connected with the Christian religion as to be spoken of as a preparation for it. The city of Jerusalem, where this building stood, was not only the Holy City of the Jewish people, but was the type of the New Jerusalem, that celestial city revealed in the Apocalypse of Saint John, which was four square, a perfect cube, with walls of jasper, streets of pure gold, gates of pearl, its foundations garnished with all manner of precious stones and illuminated by the Glory of God. So this Temple of Solomon, whatever it was, appears as a microcosm, or smaller pattern or model of the magrocosm or Great Temple on High. In short, the smaller Temple represents the world. The larger represents the Universe. In the same way the smaller Temple represents the human soul, the larger Temple, God, the Soul Universal, in which everything else has its existence. So in the Biblical description of the Temple of Solomon we read of immense cost, the vast number of workmen engaged in building it, the wisdom, more than half miraculous and magical, of the great king, himself, his fabulous wealth and prominence. All served to strike the mind of the religious Mason of the Middle Ages with wonder and admiration and made a profound impression upon him. This is a part of the explanation why this building was selected.

The Great Teacher said to Nicodemus: "Before you can enter the Kingdom of Heaven you must be born again." The initiation into the Ancient Mysteries was spoken of as regeneration, and the man who had received these Mysteries was said to be "twice born." In this sense the lodge is a type of the Temple, for here light is sought and here a new life is begun, which deals with the higher realities. Again the lodge is the symbol of the world.

[45]

The ancient Sanscrit word for world was "loga" and the Greek word for that emanation of the Deity, through which the world was created, was "logos." This is a very curious fact, though most Masonic scholars do not believe that such was the origin of the word "lodge," as we use it. Still the assembly of Masons duly opened certainly exhibits the symbolism just indicated. Its *covering is the clouded canopy or starry-decked heaven*, to reach which, as the abode of those who do the will of the Supreme Architect of the Universe, it is furnished with a *theological ladder which extends from earth to heaven*. It is illuminated, as is the world, with the refulgent rays of the sun, symbolically represented as rising in the East, attaining its meridian in the South, and finally setting in the West, and lastly, its very form, an oblong quadrangle or square, may refer to the early tradition, previous to the days of Columbus, that such was the shape of the earth. At the west end are the two pillars of Hercules, Gibraltar and Ceuta, which mark the entrance to the Mediterranean sea.

The word to which most of the students look for the origin of the word "lodge," is from the Latin, "logia," meaning a small temporary dwelling place. The Roman Colleges of Architects employed the word "logia" to represent the small temporary buildings which the Masons erected near the great edifice on which they were working. In these "logia" they dwelt and worked. It served as a shop, bunk-house and eating house combined. While engaged upon the edifice they were building, it may be for months or years, the number of Masons dwelling together, as we have stated, acquired a solidarity so that the group of men would be given the name of the building in which they dwelt and would be spoken of as a lodge of Masons. It cannot be doubted that previous to the reorganization of the Order in 1717 lodges could be convened at any time or place where the requisite number of Masons happened to be, and these were authorized, under the customs then prevalent, to make Masons. When the work was finished the lodge dissolved, perhaps never to meet again. The mere fact that a man is a Mason today carries with it the fact that he is a member of some lodge. Such was not the case in the old days, for then a Mason could not join a lodge until he had been made or initiated. The Ancient Charges admonish him to do so and take part in meeting its expenses and living in obedience to its rules. There were no Grand Lodges or chartered lodges, in the sense in which we speak of them. There was a general assembly of Masons once a year, which adjudicated all questions of interest to the Craft and elected a Grand Master.

When the Grand Lodge of England was formed, some of the lodges then in existence which formed it insisted on remaining exempt from the effects of the constitution which that Grand Lodge then and there promulgated. These four original lodges permitted the Grand Lodge to govern the lodges which had been organized under its auspices. There were no such things as charters until subsequent to 1739, as they came into being as an invention of the Dermott system, or, as they called themselves, the Grand Lodge of Ancients, which was organized in that year. This condition endured for a good many years. Many of the most honored Masons in history received their degrees in such a temporary lodge as we have mentioned, simply constituted for that particular purpose. The Marquis de Lafayette was made a Mason, in a military lodge opened for that purpose, in the army of which George Washington was commander, and it is said that Washington himself received his degrees in the same manner, though he afterwards became a member and Master of Alexandria Lodge, a regular lodge and where at the present date many of his Masonic relics are kept. Among them is the chair in which he sat as Master.

This condition has now ceased in all jurisdictions of the United States, so that the mere fact of receiving his degrees in a lodge constitutes a Mason, so made, a member of said lodge, save where a degree may be occasionally conferred at the request of another lodge to which the candidate is already elected, the ballot electing the candidate always taking place before the initiation.

The nomadic customs and career of the Ancient Operative Craft made the right to make Masons in a private lodge both a convenience and a necessity, but the attachment of speculative Masonry to definite, permanent localities led to its discontinuance, but we still speak of a lodge of Entered Apprentices being composed of three Masters and four Entered Apprentices, a Fellowcrafts Lodge of three Masters and two Fellowcrafts and three Master Masons as constituting a lodge of Master Masons, and this is what we mean when we speak of a lodge being duly and legally constituted. The situation of a lodge being due east and west is what is known as its orientation. Of course, in speculative Masonry this is not a question relating to the particular room or hall where the lodge meets, but of the symbolic lodge itself. *A lodge is a certain number of Masons duly assembled with the Holy Bible, square and compasses, and a charter from a Grand Lodge authorizing them to meet and work.* Nevertheless it is a great convenience to have the lodge hall situated due east and west and in erecting a Masonic Temple some considerable sacrifice should be made to have it so situated. All the famous cathedrals erected by our ancient brethren were strictly orientated, as also were the great and celebrated buildings of antiquity. The great Pyramids of Egypt face exactly the cardinal points of the compass and so did most of the noted Greek buildings. The Temple of Solomon, according to the Bible, was situated with its most sacred place at the west end and the main entrance at the east end, for some unexplainable reason. It may be that some key to an explanation may be had from the passage in Ezekiel, where it says: "He brought me back by way of the outward gate of the sanctuary that looketh towards the east, and it was shut. And the Lord said unto me, 'This gate shall be shut. Let no man enter in by it for the Lord of Hosts, He hath entered in by it, therefore it shall be shut'." This indicates that although this gate was at the east end it was not employed by the priests nor by the people.

For speculative Masons the great fact that religious and philosophical light ever seems to come from the east is a sufficient reason for our lodge orientation, and the expression, "Ex oriente lux," falls upon the ear of the student of Masonry with a double meaning. As the sun rising in the east floods the world with its life-generating rays, so the Worshipful Master of the lodge from his station in the East regularly distributes Masonic light to all within the circle of his obedience.

It is a curious fact regarding symbolism that the sign and the thing signified may have existed side by side since the beginning of the world, without any man perceiving their analogous relation, when suddenly it blazes out, almost like a revelation of God. A great many students do not seem to realize this. They seem to think that about all the old philosophers had to do was to invent cryptograms under cover of which they might conceal their wisdom and the facts in nature which they had discovered. We do not believe this to have been the case at all. We believe that where they used symbols to conceal thought once, they employed them a thousand times to illustrate and teach thought. We are living in a different age, where learning is free and of

making books there is no end. No one is striving to hide the
great facts of astronomy or geometry, or political economy or
religion, but the number of men who really know a single thing
about the basic facts of these great sciences are, to our minds,
considerably fewer, in an equal population, than were the
priestly caste of Egypt or India. Those who taught science
by oral tradition, even with the use of every form of symbolic
illustration, could teach but few, even the little that the professors themselves knew.

What of religious truth today? Is the result better? Are
the common, ordinary people walking in any closer communion
with the Living God than when Rameses II of Egypt made
war upon the inhabitants of Syria? We are sorry to say that
we see very little improvement in this respect evidenced, though
perhaps there is less superstition. When we find some great
truth buried, not concealed, but buried by the decaying influence
of time and change, we may never know with what endless care
some ancient brother had striven to leave some memorial, some
key to future generations so that they might be led to think
his thoughts over again and know that he, too, had known.
Speculative Freemasonry evolved quietly and gradually from its
operative progenitor and religious philosophy came down to us
from the Ancient Mysteries, and they dwelt side by side for
many generations, until all of a sudden a real philosopher happened to become a Freemason and the wonderful adaptation of
the structure was perceived and recognized. The original stone
squarer we do not believe ever developed any remarkable religious truth. The advent of philosophy in Freemasonry was
late in the history of the Art, and this is the reason so many
historians have arrived at hasty conclusions regarding the
history of the Order. The ancient philosopher did not invent
speculative Freemasonry to conceal, but to reveal the truths of
morality and religion. He found it with this phase imperfectly
developed, first as an amusement, but under his influence it
became the serious worship of the sculptor. As the circumstances
of the operative art changed and the necessity of the Craft declined, the speculative element in the society alone remained.

No one can tell the exact day when Masonic symbolism was
first born, but the advent of the society of the philosopher accounts for the many curious allusions, theories and allegories
that have been discovered or revealed, at what would seem to
be a comparatively recent date. The man who is willing to

assert that the lodge was intended to symbolize any certain doctrine or thing and nothing else, is very apt to find himself, at no distant date, alone in his opinion. The lodge was, at first, a simple assembly of a number of Masons engaged in the erection of a stone building, and did not symbolize anything save friendship, hospitality and common business relations. The philosopher had not yet appeared.

It is evident that either history or nature or fate intended the lodge to symbolize many things and it doth not yet appear what it shall be. The alchemists, the Rosicrucians and the philosophers of the early seventeenth century found themselves under the persecution of the church and found in Masonry, on account of its peculiar legal privileges, a safe and welcome asylum, and they exerted the influence on the activity of the Craft that learned men invariably exert among the less informed. To illustrate some of the lines of thought which pass among the present philosophers of the Craft, we will describe a late theory that a certain brother, than whom there is none brighter among our acquaintance. Said he, "The lodge is a representation of King Solomon's Temple and the Temple was calculated to symbolize the maternal human body, wherein the candidate must enter to be born again. The uterus and vagina represent the porch of the Temple, the pillars of the porch represent the fallopian tubes, the network, the broad ligament with its accompanying blood vessels, the lily-work, the ampulla or fimbriated extremity of the tube, and the pomegranate, the ovary and its exuberant seeds, the ova cells. The winding stairway is represented by the three divisions of the intestine. The three steps, are represented by the ascending, transverse and descending colon, the five steps by the coils of the ilium and the seven steps by the coils of the jejunum. The veil of the Temple represents the diaphragm, the shechinah and the altar represent the heart, which is the source of life, the first to live and the last to die. This is overshadowed by the wings of the cherubim, in the shape of the lungs. The seven-branched candlestick is represented by the arch of the aorta, the great artery of the chest, which is itself the sanctum sanctorum, while the abdomen was the holy place or Middle Chamber. The brain represents the Deity, which governs all things, and is the analogue of the Holy Royal Arch, whose ark contains the Ineffable Name of God." There are many other analogues which might be mentioned, which suggest themselves to the trained anatomist.

Should our good brother some day be able to demonstrate that this figure or type was in the mind of our ancient brethren, or even in the mind of King Solomon himself, he will indeed have wrought a great work for symbolic Masonry. There is no need to do this. The figure or type is of just as much utility and importance as it is, as it would be if he possessed a perfectly authenticated manuscript direct from the hands of our Grand Master, Hiram Abiff, in which his plan was specifically set forth. The Great Teacher did not have to introduce His disciples to the Good Samaritan, so that they might hear His story in person, or to the Prodigal Son or the Sower that went forth to sow, in order to inform them of the doctrine of pity and mercy or tenacity of religious conviction. So far as the mysteries are concerned we have no doubt that the lodge is the representative of the Men's House. We have never heard of any nation, tribe or people that did not have among the men some sort of secret society where the mysteries of their religion were taught and the boy of the tribe initiated into the estate of manhood.

We expect to refer further to this primitive initiation when we come to the description of the third degree. What we desire to convey here is, that at some time in the seventeenth century, or very early in the eighteenth, the remnant of what among our race and nation was once the Men's House became merged with the Masonic Lodge, probably through its members joining the lodge as accepted Masons and without any ostensible junction of the two institutions. It is quite possible that a partial union had previously taken place early in the fourteenth century, subsequent to the suppression of the Order of Knights Templar, which took place in 1312. There exists considerable legendary evidence of the persecuted knights having found refuge among the Masons at that period, especially in Scotland. The ancient halls of the Order of Mythra have been discovered in several places, as they were generally situated under ground rather than in the higher stories of buildings, and these subterranean halls resemble very closely our modern lodge rooms. A very elaborate set of apartments have recently been unearthed in the island of Malta, which date back at least three thousand years.

The ancient Roman Basilicon or judgment halls also indicate the same manner of construction. These, after the time of Constantine, were occupied as Christian churches. The aspe, which was the former seat of the judge, was in the east and the altar was in the middle of the room in front of him, while

the assembled litigants arranged themselves on either side.
These buildings became a sort of prototype of the great mediæval
cathedrals, in the erection of which our ancient brethren attained such fame, though the latter were a thousand time more
beautiful and symbolic. Again, the ancient Gothic dwellings
of the wealthy classes usually possessed a great central banquet-
ing hall, very closely resembling our lodge halls. The seat of
the proprietor was upon a diaz in the east, where he and his
family presided as the dividers of the bread, and with them were
placed all the guests of equal rank, while the remainder of the
household ate from the long table in front, also arranged according to rank. At the west was the entrance and the watch
fire, where the sentinels stood. An entrance at the south led
to the kitchen and cooking department, the place of refreshment.
In the north were the private apartments of the women of the
household. The main ranking was into earls, churls and thralls.

It may be added that the arrangement of the Arabian tent
dwelling is very similar. The main apartment, or seraglio, was
where all the business of the household was transacted, visitors
received and orders given. The patriarch or proprietor had his
seat on a diaz in the east. At the west was the entrance and
the fire around which the sentinels gathered. At the south was
the kahn, where all the work of the household was carried on,
while in the north was the zenana or harem, the private apartment of the ladies of the family. In permanent dwellings this
apartment was separated from the seraglio by a lattice-work, so
that the ladies might listen to the entertainment which took
place there. So the lodge room is simply a convenient arrangement.. for carrying on the work of the Fraternity, as well as
symbolic of its teachings. The symbolism of the furniture and
decorations will be described in their appropriate place. In the
study of Masonic philosophy the symbolism that must be closely
borne in mind is that of the universe, as it appeared to our
ancient brethren, with all its sun, zodiac, planetary bodies and
fixed stars, with their revolutionary periods and other phenomena. The word "temple" is derived from the word "tempus," or
time, and was constructed for the purpose of teaching the calendar, as it is calculated from the various movements of the
heavenly bodies. This interpretation will appear more clearly
as we proceed.

LECTURE VII

DEGREE OF ENTERED APPRENTICE

IT has been said that the *"youth as an Entered Apprentice should industriously occupy his mind in the accumulation of useful knowledge."* That the Fellowcraft, in his manhood, should engage in active work, applying the knowledge so acquired in the duties of his profession, while the elderly Master Mason should find his employment in teaching and reflection, and by his learning and experience develop the designs from which others may work. The candidate for this degree is expected to give acceptable answers to the following questions:

1st. *"Do you seriously declare upon your honor that unbiased by improper solicitations of friends and uninfluenced by mercenary motives you freely and voluntarily offer yourself a candidate for Freemasonry?*

2nd. *"Do you seriously declare upon your honor that you are prompted to solicit the privileges of Masonry by a favorable opinion conceived of the institution, a desire for knowledge and a sincere wish of being serviceable to your fellow creatures?*

3rd. *"Do you seriously declare upon your honor that you will cheerfully conform to all the ancient usages and established customs of the Fraternity?"*

Having signified his assent to these questions, the candidate is prepared for the ceremonies that await him. Primitive man was about the most defenseless of the entire animal creation. He was without natural weapons, but half protected against the elements, blind in ignorance, yet urged to action by powerful passions and appetites, some good and necessary to his life and happiness, some pernicious and deadly. In this condition he groped his way over rough and rugged paths, beset with difficulties and dangers, struggling towards the Light. In his heart the germ of love for his fellows glowed with a feeble flame. It is here in this trembling spark of altruism that he is first prepared for the great mystery of existence. At this stage the following text of Scripture is suggested: *"ASK and it shall be given you. SEEK and ye shall find. KNOCK and it shall be opened unto you."*

In the three words indicated the student of Masonic philosophy may behold the three, four and five of the celebrated Pytha-

[53]

gorean 'Triangle. The door opens and as he enters, the old world with its cares and distinctions, its dissensions and its vices, its pride and its ignorance is left behind.

This step ought not to be allowed to pass, without some attempt to impress upon the candidate in a manner which would ever remind him of the pains of death, from the outward life he is leaving, and the pangs of his new birth to better thoughts and aspirations, purer motives and brighter hopes. As he starts out upon his journey in search for the Light, he should at this point be reminded of that universal dependence upon that Great Source and Giver of all Light and Life, whereby the world exists.

The following prayer is very old:

"Vouchsafe Thine aid, Almighty Father of the Universe, to this our present convention and grant that this candidate for Masonry may dedicate and devote his life to Thy service and become a true and faithful brother among us. Endue him with a competency of Thy Divine Wisdom, so that by the influence of our art he may be better enabled to display the beauty of holiness, to the honor of Thy Holy Name. Amen!" Response by the brethren: *"So mote it be."*

The next lesson to be inculcated and the first real lesson to be impressed upon the candidate after his admission to the lodge is "Faith in God." The man, if such there be, who acknowledges no higher power than himself, will never consider a purely moral obligation binding. To such a man there is no such word as "ought," no such word as "duty." The words "expediency" and "inclination" will take their place. Freemasonry, among English-speaking people, has always required a declaration of belief and trust.

There are three different kinds of belief in God. The first sort is in no way religious, though it ought to be. It is simply a confidence in the persistency and uniformity of natural laws, a belief that suns will rise and set, that seed time and harvest will come and go, that cold and heat, rain and dry weather will follow each other as they have always done since the beginning of history. Sir Bulwer Lytton illustrates this sort of belief in his poem, entitled, "There Is No Unbelief":

> There is no unbelief—
> Who ever plants a seed beneath the sod
> And waits to see it push away the clod,
> Believes in God.

Who ever says, when clouds are in the sky,
Be patient heart. Light cometh by and by,
Trusts the Most High.

Who ever sees 'neath winter's shroud of snow
The golden harvests of the summer grow,
God's power doth know.

Who ever lies down on his bed to sleep,
Content to shut each sense in slumber deep,
Knows God will keep.

Who ever looks on, when the eyelids close,
And dares to live, when life has naught but woes,
God's comfort knows.

Who ever says—"tomorrow"—"the unknown",
The "future"—trusts that power alone,
He dares disown.

And so from day to day, and night to night, unconsciously,
The soul lives by that same faith the lips deny,
God knoweth why.
There is no unbelief.

But to the reverent and serious man Nature is the Great Confirmation. He does not need to reason or to study, he feels the Infinite and calmly waits the revelation of God's majesty. To him justice is instinctive, and doing justly he pities those who suffer from injustice and oppression and relieves them as he has the power and opportunity. As he marvels at the vastness of the universe around him he perceives his own relative insignificance and dependence on that Power that holds the worlds in their courses. With this man the more he learns the more humble he becomes. Freemasonry cares but little for the pride of successful dialectic.

The second kind of belief is purely intellectual. It is the acceptance of theological dogma. The best that this sort of belief can do for a man is to help him form a picture, or at most an inward mental conception of the Deity. There are but two sources of evidence of the existence of God, the universe and the experience of the human soul. In proportion as these truly and correctly reveal the nature of God and His attributes, so the will of God becomes manifest, and at the same time His justice is revealed in the accuracy of His laws. Where no particle of matter and no feather-weight of energy is lost but all accounted for by sure arithmetic, just so certainly is that justice demanded in the lives and experiences of men. As His love and benevolence is shown in His care over every swallow that falleth to the ground, so is that love demanded of men to Him and to each other.

The third class or variety of belief is the "conscious presence", what some would call the "witness of the spirit". This is a vision vouchsafed to those only who do His will and live His life. This is the "ultima thule" of Masonic science. This is the substance of things hoped for and the evidence of things not seen of which the apostle speaks. Many deny its experience. Many claim to have it who in their daily lives show no evidence of it. Even with the purest in heart the vision is not constant nor the visitations frequent, but those who do justly, love mercy, walk humbly, keeping themselves unspotted from the world, will at some time behold the Light, the Light which, as they say, was never on sea or land, sufficiently at least so that they will be assured of its existence, its comfort and help in time of trial, its support in time of danger and its power to banish the fear of those things which can only kill the body.

CIRCUMAMBULATION—This term is employed in ceremonial language to indicate walking around something. If you study the plans of the mediæval cathedrals you will at once perceive that they were not built for audience chambers, where a congregation assembled twice on Sunday and once in the middle of the week to listen to preaching. The mass of the Middle Ages was a private ceremony, performed and attended by the officiating priests alone. These cathedrals exhibited a series of long aisles around and around the large central altar, up and down which the penitents journeyed, halting at the different shrines, chapels and stations of the cross to say their prayers. The cathedral was indeed the house of God, who in the shape of the Incarnate Eucharist rested continuously on the altar. It was a house of prayer and temple of remembrance, but it was not a meeting house or synagogue.

Their ceremonies were copied from the Ancient Mysteries, and it is likely that our own Masonic brethren had these ceremonies from the ancient world in their minds and had frequently beheld these parades before they adopted the Masonic ceremonies of circumambulation. In Greece the priests and the people, when engaged in offering sacrificial rites, walked three times around the altar, at the same time chanting a sacred hymn. Necrobias tells us that the ceremony had reference to the movement of the heavenly bodies, which according to the ancient poets and philosophers produced a harmonious sound, inaudible to mortal ears, which was known as the "music of the spheres." Hence in making their procession around the altar great care was taken to move in the same direction as the apparent course of the sun. For that reason they commenced at the East and proceeded to the West by way of the South, and thence by way of the North they arrived at the East again, keeping the right side always nearest to the altar.

This ceremony was, among the Romans, so intimately connected with every religious rite of expiation and purification that the word "lustrare" came to signify both to purify and to walk around anything. Thus for Masonic moral symbolism it signifies purification. The ancient peoples thought to purify themselves by imitating the motions of the gods and doing and acting as the heavenly bodies did. The Hindus used this rite and the Druids used it also. It certainly originated among peoples who adored the heavenly bodies as representatives of the Deity, the lodge representing the world. The three principal officers represent the sun in three different parts of the day, morning, noon and evening. The intellectual symbolism is to illustrate the journey from intellectual darkness towards intellectual light. The 133rd Psalm here recited was one of the Psalms of Degrees, so called by the Hebrews. It used to be sung as the people marched up the steps to the door of the temple, and commemorated to the Jews the return journey from their captivity in Babylon back to their home in Jerusalem:

"Behold how good and how pleasant it is for brethren to dwell together in unity. It is like the precious ointment upon the head, that ran down upon the beard, even Aaron's beard, that went down to the skirts of his garments. Like the dews of Herman and the dew that descended upon the mountains of Zion, for there the Lord commanded a blessing, even Life forever more."

This was a great hymn of rejoicing; so the candidate for Masonry should rejoice, coming out of the blindness and darkness of the profane world to seek for Light and Truth within the sacred precincts of the lodge. The allusion to the three gates of the temple is purely symbolic, for there is no mention in the Bible of more than one entrance to the Temple of Solomon, and that was through the porch at the east end of the building. Symbols are not to be taken for historical facts, either in the ritual of Freemasonry or elsewhere. The temple

of Character, of Virtue and Honor and Purity and Justice, while
it has an existence just as surely and just as certainly as did
the Temple of Solomon of old, is not subject to the limitations
of the material world. Allegory must needs be somewhat flexible
because the lesson to be taught is of far more importance than
the consistency of the similitude.

Next the candidate receives a short address regarding the
nature of the institution. This varies in different jurisdictions,
but in Missouri it has been cut as short as possible. When Webb
published his monitor, about one hundred years ago, he introduced the following brief lecture:

"From the commencement of the world we may trace the
foundations of Masonry. Ever since symmetry began and
harmony displayed her charms our Order has had a being. During many ages and in many different countries it has flourished.
In the dark periods of antiquity, when literature was in a low
state and the rude manners of our forefathers withheld from
them that knowledge we now so amply share, Masonry diffused
its influence. This science unveiled, arts arose, civilization took
place and the progress of knowledge and philosophy gradually
dispelled the gloom of ignorance and barbarism. Government
being settled, authority was given to laws and the assemblies
of the Fraternity acquired the patronage of the great and the
good, while the tenets of the profession were attended with
unbounded utility.

"Masonry is a science confined to no particular country but
diffused over the whole terrestrial globe. Wherever arts flourish,
there it flourishes, too. Add to this that by secret and inviolable
signs, carefully preserved among the Fraternity throughout the
world, Masonry becomes a universal language. Hence many
advantages are gained. The distant Chinese, the wild Arab
and the American savage will embrace a brother Briton, Frank
or German, and will know that beside the common ties of
humanity there is still a stronger obligation to induce him to
kind and friendly offices. The spirit of the fulminating priest
will be tamed and a moral brother, though of a different persuasion, engage his esteem. Thus through the influence of
Masonry, which is reconcilable to the best policy, all these dis-
putes which embitter life and sour the tempers of men are
avoided, while the common good, the general design of the Craft
is zealously pursued. From this view of the system its utility
is sufficiently obvious. The universal principle of the art unites

men of the most opposite tenets, of the most distant countries and the most contradictory opinions in one indissoluble bond of affection, so that in every nation a Mason finds a friend and in every climate a home." *

"Freemasonry is a beautiful system of morals veiled in allegory and illustrated by symbols. Its tenets are brotherly love, relief and truth. Its cardinal virtues are temperance, fortitude, prudence and justice. Its religion, if religion it may be called, is an unfeigned belief in the One Living and True God."

In some jurisdictions the tenets of a Mason's profession are "friendship, morality and brotherly love." In most of the Latin countries the tenets are "liberty, equality and fraternity." This opens up the fact that there are minor differences in the traditions that have come down to this generation, owing to want of care in oral teaching. This should prompt the student to a sense of responsibility in transmitting the mysteries exactly as he receives them.

Regarding the point of religion it would seem to be much more important that it should be genuine and unfeigned, and constitute an actual guide and restraint over the conduct of the individual than that it should be a mere creed to which he mentally consents, perhaps because it is the prevailing profession of his neighborhood, or perchance assumed for the purpose of leading his acquaintances to put confidence in his honesty because of his outward piety. A great teacher once remarked: "If the Light that is within you be darkness, how great is that darkness." Here again the lesson to be taught is of far more importance than the consistency of the similitude. It is of far more importance that the brethren know that the candidate is serious minded and sincerely seeks the Light, than that he is the communicant of any well-known persuasion.

OBLIGATION OF SECRECY—Secrecy is in itself a virtue. If it were possible for some wise man to collate the sources of human error and sin, the loose tongue would be found to rank next to selfish desire in its evil influence. Masonry has always been a secret profession, whether speculative or operative. The true explanation of all the ancient religious dogmas was known only

---

* This was undoubtedly the original design of the brethren who sought to organize and build up speculative Masonry, but it is an ideal state and not likely to be soon realized in a land where there is such an intolerant spirit prevalent that a Christian dares not believe it possible for Masonry to exist among a people of any other faith, or Masonic honor among those whose religious opinions differ from their own.

to the inner circle of the initiated. Sometimes we fear, a selfish priesthood, while keeping secret the true explanation, gave the ignorant and unenlightened public one entirely false and misleading. Even Jesus Christ, in talking with His disciples regarding the meaning of some of His parables, said: "Unto you it is given to know the mysteries of the Kingdom of Heaven, but unto them it is not given." "Cast not your pearls before swine lest they trample them under foot and turn again and rend you." "Give not that which is holy unto dogs." "He that hath ears to hear, let him hear." The secrets of mediæval Freemasonry included everything appertaining to the operative art. The application of the science of geometry and trigonometry to the art of building, the patterns for sculpture, the proportions of weight in piers and walls necessary to sustain vaults and roofs, the different methods of working out the symbol of the cross in a cathedral ground-plan and all usual and customary decorations. When the Reformation occurred in Europe and the separation occurred between the Protestants and Roman Catholics, belief in the actual presence of the living God in the Eucharist, so called transsubstantiation, ceased over a considerable part of the continent and Great Britain. This was the death-blow to operative Masonry. The moment that belief lost its foothold a cathedral or a church became, instead of the dwelling place of the living God, a mere meeting house. There was no incentive for such wonders in stone. Henceforth, such displays became mere extravagant waste, pride of skill or just vain ministry to the desire of the eyes. Again with the advance in popular education the science of geometry became public knowledge and was no longer confined to the craft. Masonic knowledge having thus become common to the laity and the profane at the same time, political freedom rendered their peculiar legal privileges useless. When any man could travel in foreign countries and work for master's wages, what availed it that the Freemason had enjoyed these privileges for untold ages?

At the present time the Mysteries of Freemasonry are reduced to the *means of recognition among Masons*, and the ceremonies of admission into the society and the meaning of our symbols. These can never be divulged. The great secret of all is a living faith in God, and this can only be attained by obedience, even by Masons. There have been times and occasions in the past when the true and faithful servant of God and the Truth was in danger from the wrath of the forces of idolatry. It was necessary that the very fact of their connection with the Fraternity should be hidden. Meetings were indeed held on the *tops of high hills and in low valleys* and well guarded from the approach of cowans and eavesdroppers, who sought not only their secrets but their destruction.

A visit to the catacombs of Rome will show some of their ancient meeting places today, hidden even in tombs and graves. Even as late as 1820 the lives of men have been forfeited under great torture for being Masons. Not only was it necessary for societies of primitive Christians to flee to the catacombs to escape the violence of pagan Rome, but Freemasons of comparatively modern times, and in this land of the free and home of the brave, have been in danger from the fanaticism of their Protestant neighbors. In the old days, in ancient Rome, a ceremony closely analogous to that of our lodges might have veiled in allegory the passion of Him whom a few believed to have been the Redeemer of the world. It has only been a few years since a man could be a Mason, without danger of capital punishment, in such countries as Spain, Italy, Portugal or even France and Austria.

The secret doctrines of all the ancient peoples were never committed to writing, but were handed down from adept to neophyte by oral tradition. The Holy Books of India were handed down in this manner for many centuries with the utmost precaution to secure accuracy. They were not content by learning to recite them word for word, but many committed them backwards and in many other complicated methods, so that by no possible chance could the ancient text be altered. The secret mysteries of the Hebrew Cabalah (Kabbalah) (Queballah) were transmitted by this method down through all the celebrated characters of Jewish history, and formed the basis of the famous "Wisdom of Solomon." The Christian Church of the age immediately succeeding the apostolic observed the same custom of orally instructing postulants. St. Basil says: "Lest the vulgar, too familiar with our dogmas, should lose due respect for them." Secrecy was necessary in the days of operative Masonry, as the dignity, influence and the continued prosperity of the Craft, even their freedom depended upon it. This custom descended to speculative Masonry, as a wise precaution to prevent improper disclosure of our valuable teachings and to prevent impostors robbing the Order through fraudulent claims on its charity. Poverty and distress ought to be able to secure relief without the necessity for those who are charitably inclined to be imposed upon.

ENLIGHTENMENT—*"In the beginning God created the Heavens and the Earth and the Earth was without form and void and darkness was upon the face of the deep, and the Spirit of God moved upon the face of the waters, and God said, 'Let there be Light,' and there was Light."*

To the poet, speaking in those far distant ages, God commanded and Light immediately burst forth. We know now that such was not the case. The battle between Chaos and Natural Light occupied countless centuries, but at last Light was victorious. So in the human soul the struggle of the passions and desires of the animal nature rages on, but the Word may go forth in that soul and Light be kindled, to burn ever brighter and brighter to the perfect day. This is the chief end of speculative Masonry, to illuminate the dark places with intellectual and moral Light, to build character.

THE HOLY BIBLE, SQUARE AND COMPASSES—*"The Holy Bible, Square and Compasses are thus used. The Holy Bible is given us as a rule and guide to our faith and practice, the Square to square our actions and the Compasses to circumscribe our desires and keep our passions in due bounds with all mankind, especially with a brother Freemason.*

Let us examine this ancient paragraph a little. First comes the moral interpretation. There are three sources of moral improvement which are indicated in these articles of furniture found in every well governed lodge, first, the material universe in continuous action, second, what we may learn from our intercourse with our fellowmen, as well as the insight obtained regarding human character from their daily conduct, and lastly the moral experience of the race in the past. The points of the Compass are widely extended, and would seem to enjoin upon a man to keep his eyes open and interpret correctly the movements of the multitudes of worlds circulating in boundless space around him, the affairs of the infinitely large, and also the affairs of the infinitely small, the atoms of matter, the electrons of energy, the no less minute germs wherein life manifests itself.

The Square teaches the duties we incur in our relations with our fellowmen. It is the great measuring principle of Justice and Truth that sees things as they are. How close it is to that narrow, golden line of Truth, which the very virtues and attributes that lean upon it bend, which policy and prudence strive to conceal, which kindness and courtesy modify, which courage covers with his shield, imagination overshadows with her wings and even Charity dims with her tears. The footprints of the ancient of days both in the material world and in the souls of men are hidden only from the hard of heart. The Divine was ever revealed in the great love of man for his kind. "If a man love not his brother whom he hath seen, how shall he love God, whom he hath not seen?" speaks a great teacher. Love itself is a kind of light, the following of which leads to blessedness, if not invariably to happiness, because if the love is strong enough it is able to make a man forget self and thus losing his life in altruism he finds it. One has said, "He who seeks for heaven to save his soul, may keep the path, yet never reach the goal, while he who walks in love may wander far, yet God will bring him where the angels are." I cannot here do justice to my theme, for down beneath both Square and Compass lies the great record of the spiritual experience of our race. Here another pen will speak to you with an authority I cannot claim. Let me repeat the words of Rev. Bro. Joseph Fort Newton, the editor of the "Builder":

"Time is a river and books are boats. Many volumes start down that stream only to be wrecked and lost beyond recall in the sands. Only a few, a very few, endure the testings of time and live to bless the ages following. Tonight we are met to pay homage to the greatest of all books, the one enduring Book that has traveled down to us from the far past, freighted with the richest treasure that ever any book has brought to humanity. What a sight it is to see so many men gathered about an open Bible, how typical of the genius and spirit of Masonry, its great and simple faith and its benign ministry to mankind. No Mason needs to be told what a place of honor the Bible has in Masonry. One of the Great Lights of the Order, it lies upon the altar at the center of the lodge. Upon it every Mason takes the solemn vow of love, of loyalty, of chastity, of charity, pledging himself to our tenets of brotherly love, relief and truth. Think what it means to a young man to make such a covenant of consecration in the morning of life, taking that wise old Book for his guide, teacher and friend. Then as he moves forward from one degree to another the imagery of the Bible becomes familiar and eloquent and its mellow haunting music sings its way into his heart. And yet, like everything else in Masonry, the Bible so rich in symbolism becomes itself a symbol, that is, a part taken for the whole. It is a sovereign symbol of the Book of Truth, the Will of God, as man has learned it in the midst of years, that perpetual revelation of Himself which God is making to mankind in every land and in every age. Thus by the very honor that Masonry pays to the Bible it teaches us to revere every book of faith in which man finds help for today and hope for tomorrow, joining hands with the man of Islam as he takes oath on the Koran, and with the Hindu as he makes covenant on the Book he loves the best. For Masonry knows what so many forget, that religions are many, but religion is one. Perhaps we may say that one thing includes everything. The life of God in the soul of man and the duty and hope of man which proceeds from his essential character. Therefore, Masonry invites to its altar men of all faiths, knowing that if they use different names for the Nameless One of a Hundred Names, they are yet praying to the one God and Father of all, knowing also that while they read different volumes they are in fact reading the same Book, the same vast Book of Faith of man, as revealed in the struggle and sorrow of the race in its quest for God. So that great and noble as the Bible is, Masonry sees it as the symbol of that Eternal Book of the Will of God, which Lowell describes in these immortal lines:

" 'Slowly the Bible of the race is writ,
    And not on paper leaves or leaves of stone,
    Each age, each kindred adds a verse to it,
    Texts of despair, of hope, of joy or moan,
    While swings the sea, while mists the mountains shroud,
    While thunder surges burst on cliffs of cloud,
    Still at the Prophet's feet the nations sit.'

"None the less, much as we honor every Book of Faith in which man has found courage to lift his hand above the night that covers him and lay hold on the mighty hand of God, with us the Bible is supreme. What Homer was to the Greeks, what the Koran is to the Arab, that and much more, that grand old Book is to us. It is the mother of our literary family, and if some of its children have grown up and become wise in their own conceit, they yet rejoice to gather round its knees and pay tribute. Not only was the Bible the loom on which our language was woven, but it is a pervasive, refining, redeeming force bequeathed to us with whatever else is good and true in the very fiber of our being.

"Not for a day do we regard the Bible simply as a literary classic, apart from what it means to the faiths and hopes and prayers of men, and its inweaving into the intellectual and spiritual life of our race. There was a time when the Bible formed almost the only literature of England, and today, if it were taken away, that literature would be torn to tatters and shreds. Truly did Macaulay say that if everything else in our language should perish, the Bible would alone suffice to show the whole range and power and beauty of our speech. From it Milton learned his majesty of song and Ruskin his magic of prose. Carlisle had in his very blood, almost without knowing it, the rhapsody and passion of the prophets, their sense of the Infinite, of the littleness of men and the sarcasm of Providence. As Burns before him had learned from the same fireside Book of the indestructibleness of honor and the human pity of God, which thrilled in his lyrics of love and liberty. Thus from Shakespeare to Tennyson the Bible sings in our poetry, chants in our music, echoes in our eloquence and in our tragedy flashes forever its truth of the terribleness of sin and the tenderness of God and the inextinguishable hope of man.

"My brethren, here is a Book whose scene is in the sky and the dirt and all that lies between, a Book that has in it the arch of the heavens, the curve of the earth, the ebb and flow of the sea, sunrise and sunset, the peaks of the mountains and the glint of the sunlight on the flowing waters, the shadow of the forests on the hills, the song of the birds and the color of the flowers. Its two great characters are God and the soul of man; and the story of their Eternal Life together is its one everlasting romance. It is the most human of Books, telling the old forgotten stories and secrets of the heart, its bitter pessimism and its death-defying hope, its pain, its passion, its sin, its sob of grief and its shout of joy, telling all without malice, in its grand style, which can do no wrong, while echoing its sweet-toned pathos of pity and mercy of God. No other book is so honest with us, so mercilessly merciful, so austere yet so tender, piercing the heart yet healing the deep wounds of sin and sorrow. Take this great and simple Book white with age, yet new with the dews of each new morning, tested with the experience of centuries, rife in memories and wet with tears of the multitude who have walked this way before us. Lay it to heart. Love it. Read it and learn what life is and what it means to be a man. Aye, learn that God hath made us for Himself and unquiet are our hearts until we rest in Him. Make it your friend and teacher and you will know what Sir Walter Scott meant when, as he lay dying, he asked Lockhart to read to him. 'From what book?' asked Lockhart, and Scott replied, 'There is but one Book.'"

"*As the sun rules the day and the moon governs the night, so should the Worshipful Master rule and govern the lodge with equal regularity and justice.*"

These lesser lights are intended to remind us of that symbolism which makes the lodge the type of the world, and hence the Master presiding and dispensing light may be compared to these luminaries, which were created, "The Greater Light to rule the day and the Lesser Light to rule the night." Following this scriptural indication, Freemasonry does not set the day against the night, nor the night against the day. The Greater and the Lesser Lights are both beneficent, each having honor in its place. In the Ancient Mysteries, the Master or Presiding Priest was known as Hermes or Chr-mes, translated "Son of Light." Hermes was the ancient name for the planet Mercury, which always sets a little before the sun or rises a short time before it.

Thus, astronomically speaking, the reference is to the Sun, Moon and the Planet Mercury. In astrology, the house of the Sun is in the Zodiacal sign of the Lion, which is the fifth house; the house of the Moon is in Cancer or the Crab, which is the fourth house, and the Day house of the Planet Mercury is in the Twins, which is the third house. These numbers three, four and five are the dimensions of the Pythagorean Triangle in which the square of the five is equivalent to the sum of the squares of three and four—25=9+16.

An ancient system of philosophy taught by the Persian Magi held that the powers of Light were all beneficent, bringing every good and perfect gift, haunted by good angels, who guided the affairs of men, alike right and fortunate and presided ever by Ahura Mazda, the God of Light. At night the powers of evil held sway. All the malevolent demons were let loose under the leadership of Ahrymanus, the God of Darkness. In Masonry, evil is lack of Light, not a negative power but the absence of positive force. "God maketh the works of the wicked to praise Him." And the Greater and the Lesser Lights are all regulated by Him with mathematical harmony.

THE LAMBSKIN—The meaning of the word "candidate" is he

of the white robe. All the aspirants for the Ancient Mysteries were clothed in white garments. Even men who were running for office in the gift of the people assumed them. All religious societies have some distinguishing badge. The priests of Israel wore a curious girdle. The Brahman caste among the Hindus were distinguished by the Zennaar or Holy Cord of three strands. The Essenes clothed their novices in a white robe. In the Persian Mysteries of Mythra the candidate was invested, as in Masonry, with a white apron. The Egyptian priests wore symbolic aprons. Many of the secret societies among the American Indians wear an embroidered apron on which is painted the totem of the tribe or clan. Even the sculptured statues of Yucatan represent gods and men clothed in emblematical aprons. The shape, the color of the material and the material itself may all be symbolic. The color of the Masonic apron should be white, its material lambskin, its shape square with a triangular flap. This constitutes an emblem of purity and innocence.

Mackey, a great authority in things Masonic, says: "The material of a Mason's apron must be lambskin. No other substance, such as linen, silk or satin, can be substituted without entirely destroying its symbolic character, because it is the lamb which is the emblem of innocence. The Mason's apron should be fifteen inches square, and the flap about five inches deep to the point, and entirely without ornament. The silk and satin aprons, bespangled and embroidered, which have been gradually creeping into our lodges, are of French origin and have nothing to do with Ancient Craft Masonry." Of course, this is only the opinion of Brother Mackey and governs no one. Further, the symbolism, while it originally applied to the lamb, did not attach to the lamb's innocence, but to the fact that the lamb or ram was the first or leading constellation of the Zodiac, and to the shape of the apron, as being very important in certain geometrical calculations connected with the squaring of the circle, and certain zodiacal and solar phenomena. The Grand Lodge of Missouri specifies that in funerals and processions the apron shall be worn outside of the coat.

"The lambskin is an emblem of innocence and the badge of a Freemason, more ancient than the Golden Fleece or the Roman Eagle, more honorable than the Star and Garter or any other Order that could be conferred upon you at this or any future period by king, prince, potentate or any other person except he

be a Freemason. I hope you will wear it with pleasure to your-self and honor to the Fraternity."

In the little ceremony of presenting the apron many beautiful and sentimental addresses have been added to this. It has been the tendency of late for the custodians of the ritual to attempt with all their influence to crystallize the work into a set form, not only in this but in most other jurisdictions, to boil it down and contract it into the least possible space and endeavor to bring its rendition within the capacity of the most illiterate rural Master that could by any accident be elected to preside over the lodge. It would seem to the writer that when time permitted and the candidate appeared to be sufficiently intelligent to absorb and appreciate a sentimental impression, this is a place where such an impression might be offered to advantage. The benefits of absolute uniformity of work do not seem to us to be commensurate with the loss of such an impression, where such is possible. The following has been taken from the official monitor of the state of Alabama. It also appears in nearly the same language in the monitor published by the late General Daniel Sickles:

"It may be that in coming years upon your head will rest the laurel wreaths of victory, or from your breast hang jewels fit to grace the diadem of an Eastern potentate, nay, more than this, with Light added to coming Light your ambitious feet may tread round after round the ladder that leads to fame in our Mystic Circle, and even the purple of the Fraternity rest upon your honored shoulders. But never again from human hands, never again until your enfranchised spirit shall have passed upward and inward through the pearly gates shall an honor so distinguished, so emblematical of purity and all perfection be bestowed upon you as this I now confer tonight. It is yours to wear through an honorable life, and at your death, should you so will, be placed upon the coffin that contains your earthly remains and with them be laid beneath the turf and flowers. Let its fair and spotless surface be to you an ever-present reminder of a purity of life and rectitude of conduct, a never-ending argument for nobler deeds, for higher thoughts and better actions. And when at last your weary feet shall have come to the end of life's toilsome journey, and from your nerveless grasp shall drop forever the working tools of life, may the record of your actions be as pure and spotless as this fair emblem which I place in your hands tonight, and when your trembling soul shall stand before the Great White Throne, may it be your portion, my brother, to receive from the Supreme Grand Master the welcome words, 'Well done, good and faithful servant, enter thou into the joy of thy Lord.'"

The following is attributed to Brother F. S. Elliott: "My brother, I have the pleasure of presenting to you a lambskin or white leather apron. It is the emblem of innocence and the badge of a Mason, more ancient than the Golden Fleece or Roman Eagle, more honorable than the Star and Garter, when worthily worn and from a time to which the memory of man runneth not to the contrary this emblem plain and unadorned has been the peculiar clothing of all Free and Accepted Masons. The prince commanding the resources of empires and the citizen toiling in humble poverty have alike worn it with the consciousness that it has lightened the labor of the one and added dignity to the power of the other. It may be that you are, or yet will be, so firmly entrenched in the hearts of your fellowmen and so deserving of their gratitude and esteem that they will elevate you to the highest positions of trust and emolument and cause your name to be inscribed on the pillars of worldly fame, but never before have you and never again, my brother, will you have a higher mark of favor and confidence bestowed upon you than this which I, as the representative of these brethren and the Craft throughout the world, am about to confer.

"This emblem which King Solomon wore when arrayed in all his glory, and which invested with additional dignity the immortal Washington, and which has been eagerly sought and worthily worn by the best men of your generation, I now present to you. If you disgrace it the disgrace will be augmented by the consciousness that in this lodge you have been taught the correct principles of morality and virtue. Its spotless white is emblematical of the purity of life and uprightness of personal manhood which we hope and expect will hereafter distinguish you in all your social and personal affairs. It is yours to wear as a Mason so long as the vital spark shall animate your mortal frame, and when at last, whether in youth, manhood or age, your spirit shall wing its flight to that house not made with hands, and amid the tears and sorrows of your surviving relatives and friends the hands of sympathizing brother Masons shall lower your body into that still and narrow house prepared for all the living, it will still be yours, yours to be placed with the evergreen upon the coffin that contains your lifeless remains and be buried with you beneath the turf and flowers.

"And may you so wear this emblem that no act of yours may stain its purity nor cast reflections upon that institution which has outlived the fortunes of kings and the mutations of empires. May you so wear it and so live that when your summons comes to join the innumerable caravan that moves towards that mysterious realm, where each must take his chamber in the silent halls of death, that thou go not like the quarry slave at night, scourged to a dungeon, but sustained and soothed by an unfaltering trust approach thy tomb like one who, wrapping the drapery of his couch about him, lies down to pleasant dreams."

The following compilation, arranged by the writer, has been thought beautiful and appropriate:

"My brother, it now becomes my duty to present to you a lambskin or white leather apron. It is the emblem of innocence and the badge of a Mason, more ancient than the Golden Fleece or Roman Eagle, more honorable than the Star and Garter or any other Order that could be conferred upon you at this or any future period by king, prince, potentate or any other person except he be a Mason. I hope you will wear it with pleasure to yourself and honor to the Fraternity.

"My brother, heroes, prophets, priests and emperors have worn this emblem and have worn it worthily. It lies on coffins draped with costly velvets and with jewels rare that only the powerful of the earth could buy, and richly carved mausoleums note the spot. Yet once it lay within a grave marked only by a slender evergreen upon the body of a humble artizan, a widow's son, who bore his life with such a dignity and grace that even kings acknowledged that he surpassed them all. Poets whose tuneful lyres are now hushed forever tell how brave warriors in days of old have worn this little apron with more pride and glory than all their trophies of victorious battle, and the wise and good of every age have deemed it nobler far to be innocent than to be great, and he that buildeth, even though it be but a humble cot for some poor peasant's home, is much more honorable than he who devastates and lays waste a city, and that the humblest Mason hewing to the line is just as worthy as a great designer if he but do his best.

"This task of life will soon be o'er and from your nerveless grasp the working tools will fall, but when the Grand Inspector views what you have wrought, be it cope or arch or base or cornerstone, he will not reject it, if he but find it level, square and plumb. The race is not to the swift always nor the battle to the strong, and this little apron's fair and spotless surface may give you courage to resist temptations that degrade the soul, so that with heart and hands like it, unblemished, pure and clean, you may receive your wages at the Great White Throne, and having been a good and faithful servant enter and share the Glory of thy Lord."

LECTURE VIII

MEMORIAL TESSERA AND METALLIC SUBSTANCE

IN ancient times, before writing became general, people were accustomed to give pledges to memory in the shape of some small metallic substance like, for instance, half a broken coin, a peculiar seal ring or one of a pair of matched dice, or as in Egypt, scarabeii, on which part of some sacred proverb had been engraved on the one and a part on the other, somewhat after the manner of a Chinese laundry ticket. If a certain man showed particular hospitality, saved another's life, or performed for another some great service, the recipient would break a coin with his benefactor and if in after years the benefactor should be in need of assistance he had only to show his half of the coin to the man who had presented it to him, or to any of his family, and the debt would be repaid. Sometimes the party who had received the favor would give a seal ring or some other talisman, which would have the same effect.

These memorial tessera were very common among the Romans and are occasionally used among primitive people even to this day. In associations like the Masonic the newly initiated member received some sort of a token, which was almost equivalent to a certificate of membership. At the present time the custom is employed to teach a lesson in charity, though in this particular instance the gift is asked of the newly-initiated brother. In the degree of Mark Master the brother is supposed to adopt some sort of a device which, when properly recorded, furnishes a kind of identification mark for this particular brother, which device, engraved on some piece of metal of a certain shape, may be employed for the same purpose as the memorial tessera. These marks were originally placed on the stones, cut or engraved by this particular brother, to identify the work by him wrought.

The most primitive form of signature was the cattle mark, which the owner burned into the hide of his cattle so that they might be distinguished when they accidentally got mixed with another herd. The brand was recorded in the office of the headman of the villa or wick in which the herdsman dwelt. This brand could not be defaced even by tanning the hide, and thus served as evidence in case of theft. This fact, among others,

[72]

led to the employment of leather as a writing material, especially in all legal business. Many legal documents such as charters and diplomas are printed on parchment to this day. In connection with the metallic substance a short address is given to impress the lesson of charity. Among these we would like to introduce the following, which was delivered before the Grand Lodge of Missouri by Bro. Walter Williams. It is calculated to remind the candidate that his duty is not to himself and to his own immediate family alone, but that he has a certain responsibility for the good of the community in general in proportion to his ability:

"My brother, once upon a time, far away in the fabled Orient, there stood, so runs an ancient legend of the Craft, the master city of the world. Its lofty towers and gold-tipped spires and polished domes greeted the gaze of the approaching traveler while yet far out in the desert. Its frowning battlements looked down on large meadows of ripening grain and orchards and vineyards, thick laden with mellow fruit, and in happiness and security a vast population dwelt within the shadow of its walls. At the entrance to that city, at its very gateway, there stood a great golden vase, and every day, as at the dusk hour the weary toilers returned into that city from their toil and goings afield, each man took from out that which his labor and effort had won for him that day a goodly portion, no mean and stinted part, but a goodly portion, and placed it in that great golden vase. And when the dawn appeared and ran its roseate streaks along the eastern sky, the High Priest of that city came and read aloud the inscription carved on that great golden vase, and this is what he read: 'From each according to his ability, unto each according to his need.' And the High Priest took from out that great golden vase the offerings which the people had made and distributed them throughout the city, to that city's health and beauty and the common good of all. And the blessing of God was upon that city from the high altar down to its cold and granite walls, and yet beyond to the fair and fertile fields whereon that city stood and yet beyond to the cattle on a thousand hills.

"And the blessings came and never went until the time that custom failed. Then each man toiled as formerly but, as if with one common consent, that which he had made he hugged it to himself. And it came to pass that as he hugged it to himself his soul shrivelled within him, and as the days went on sloth

crept into the mart and scism into the temple. Envious brawls
festered to rebellion and that city's just and equable laws rotted
away to dust on their antique parchments. And if you should
go today to view that master city of the world you would find
the bats roosting in its market places, its lights gone out, the
ashes on its altar cold and black, its walls all crumbling down,
its magnificence and grandeur all departed and naught to
awaken the echoes of its empty courts and ruined palaces save
the cry of the jackal and hyena. Portrait statues of its once
mighty kings still stand mournful and desolate in their di-
lapidated judgment halls, but no knee is there in all that master
city of the world to do them reverence. My brother, we have
no great golden vase and each man under God is his own High
Priest, but the lesson is the same as it was then and it is to you,
my friend and brother, the same as it was then: 'From each
according to his ability, unto each according to his need.' "

There are many who seem to think that Masonic charity must
be confined to financial assistance, when a brother has been
reduced to such abject poverty that he and his family will starve
without it. In our opinion, financial assistance should be an
emergency resort only: "If a brother be naked and destitute
of daily food and one of you shall say unto him, depart in peace
and be ye warmed and filled, notwithstanding ye give him not
those things which are needful to the body, what doth it profit?"
True Masonic charity should never allow a worthy brother to be
brought down to such a situation.

In the days of our ancient brother, Benjamin Franklin, one
might well say, "Take care of the cents and the dollars will
take care of themselves." This proposition is no longer true.
It takes a much wiser man in these days to keep money than it
does to save it. In this relation keeping and saving are quite
different things. Never since the beginning of the world was
there such a vast proportion of the population leading predatory
lives. Of course, improvidence, indolence and vice play an important part in the causation of poverty and misfortune, even
among Masons, we are sorry to say, but where there is a single
case of delinquency there are a hundred cases of mental inadequacy. Masonic charity should extend to such advice, such
support, such friendship in business as may enable a brother
to keep what he earns. It should extend to giving brother
Masons the preference over any other persons in the matter
of employment and trade, providing the worthy brother is

capable of filling the position and is willing to deal fairly with his Masonic employer.

The present condition will continue just as long as the employer thinks that because his employe is a Mason he ought to do twice as much work for another Mason for the same pay as he would for anybody else, a Roman Catholic for instance. And the employe thinks, just because his employer happens to be a Mason, he ought patiently to allow said employe to loaf on the job and accomplish about half what the employer might expect from a profane. Each is under solemn obligation to deal with the other upon the square. It is the shepherd's duty to feed the sheep and not to shear them only.

Moreover, charity should extend to other things. It ought to be synonymous with toleration, even social toleration, if necessary. Caste distinctions do exist and we could not destroy them in a moment, even should we so desire, yet they are purely subjective, mere states of mind. No man or woman that was ever of the slightest use to his fellowmen, or that was ever able to impart any real strength to society was ever deprived of any of that worth or value by associating with his inferiors of either the moral, intellectual, financial or social variety. The man who is so easily injured by such associations is too susceptible and soft for any utility, and belongs among the dependent classes somewhere. The strong man or woman, the true man or woman, the courageous man or woman is not afraid to go out into the world and set an example for those who are below them in education, even in moral and social standing. Masonic acquaintance and association and friendship should lead to such a degree of brotherly love as will bring the strong to support the weak, the rich to help the poor, the young to reverence the old, the educated to instruct the ignorant, the well to nurse the sick and all good men to imitate the changeless goodness of the Father of all men.

Mohammed once said that the world rested upon three pillars, the Learning of the Wise, the Charity of the Good and the Valor of the Brave. This does not differ greatly from the three pillars which support Masonry, under the names of Wisdom, Strength and Beauty. Where a worthy brother lacks wisdom, Masonry should supply it. Where a brother lacks strength or valor, Masonry should encourage and stimulate him. Where a brother lacks the ornamental embellishments and amenities that education and refinement yield, Masonry should by its gentle, simple, unostentatious example surround him with such an environment as can never fail to influence him in this direction.

The words of St. Paul regarding charity should be borne in the mind of every Mason and sink deep into his heart: "Though I speak with the tongues of men and of angels and have not charity, I am become as a sounding brass or a tinkling cymbal. Though I have the gift of prophecy and understand all mysteries and all knowledge, and though I have all faith so that I can remove mountains and have not charity, I am nothing. Though I bestow all my goods to feed the poor and though I give my body to be burned and have not charity, it profiteth me nothing. Charity suffereth long and is kind. Charity envieth not. Charity vaunteth not itself, is not puffed up, doth not behave itself unseemly, seeketh not her own, is not easily provoked, thinketh no evil, rejoiceth not in iniquity, but rejoiceth in the truth, beareth all things, believeth all things, hopeth all things, endureth all things. Charity never faileth. Whether there be prophecies they shall fail. Whether there be tongues they shall cease. Whether there be knowledge, it shall vanish away. Faith, hope and charity alone abide, these three, but the greatest of these is charity."

We believe that all Masons ought to read this 13th Chapter of Corinthians occasionally, so that they may have some idea what true charity means and correct their own charity by it. It does not take a very profound thinker to perceive that financial donation forms but a very small part of its attributes. If every Mason's individual charity was patterned after this system there would be very small and infrequent necessity for the lodge to interfere. Alas! such is not the case, and the lodge whose treasury should be held for emergency only becomes the main, cold dependence in all cases of destitution. We intend later in this work to discuss more freely the methods most useful for lodges in their dealings with destitution in general.

LECTURE IX

WORKING TOOLS AND NORTHEAST CORNER

*T**HE** working tools of an Entered Apprentice are the twenty-four-inch gauge and the common gavel. They are thus used: The twenty-four-inch gauge is an instrument used by operative Masons to measure and lay off their work, but we as Free and Accepted Masons are taught to use ours for the more noble and glorious purpose of dividing our time. It being divided into twenty-four equal parts is emblematical of the twenty-four hours in the day, which we are taught to divide into three equal parts, whereby are found eight hours for the service of God and a distressed worthy brother, eight for our usual vocations and eight hours for refreshment and sleep.*

"The common gavel is an instrument used by operative Masons to break the corners off from rough stones the better to fit them for the builder's use, but we as Free and Accepted Masons are taught to use ours for the more noble and glorious purpose of divesting our hearts and consciences from all the vices and superfluities of life, the better fitting our minds as living stones for that spiritual building, the house not made with hands, eternal in the Heavens."

The emblematical allusion here is to a good use of time and purity of heart. It demonstrates that the tools and implements of the operative Mason's Art are to be sanctified and dedicated to the veneration of God and the erection of a spiritual temple in the heart, pure and spotless and fit for the dwelling place of Him who is the Author of Purity, where God is to be worshipped in spirit and in truth and right intent, not only where evil thoughts and unruly passions are banished and subdued, but where positive good deeds are designed and carried on through the entire day. Negative purity is simply a preparation and fitting for the reality of life, but it is not life itself, any more than transparency in the tissues of the eye is sight. It bears no fruit, erects no buildings, feels no happiness by itself, and unless applied energy accompanies it, it is a failure and no better than a glass eye is for sight. In the symbolism of the Scottish Rite the gavel stands for force and power, while the rule stands for measure and control of that power that grades the strength of the blow of the hammer according to the nature of the work to be accomplished.

THE NORTHEAST CORNER—Standing in the northeast corner of the lodge, immediately after his initiation, the candidate is pronounced to be *a just and perfect Mason*. In the ancient Brahmanical philosophy of India it was written: "If any man have an incurable disease, let him travel directly northeast, feeding on water and air until his natural body shall be entirely dissolved away and his soul will be united with the Supreme Soul of the World." The allusion is that the candidate starts a new life at this point. Here he lays his foundation stone, his corner stone, his perfect ashlar, the cubic stone of the old Masons. The only absolutely perfect ashlar is the Deity. The foundation of the Mason's spiritual and moral building is God alone. Here the last vestige of darkness ends and the Perfect Light appears, in the dawn of a new day. The work says that the first stone of a building is or ought to be laid in the northeast corner. It generally is so laid, but purely for speculative reasons, for as far as its stability and solidarity, as far as its ornamentation or usefulness is concerned, it might just as well have been started in the southwest corner.

It has been said that in all things Masonic a great solar myth has lurked from the very beginning. We are not inclined to deny this. The ancient philosophers were accustomed to draw a design of the zodiac in the following manner: A perfect square was divided into sixteen smaller squares. This causes the perimeter of the figure to be bounded by exactly twelve of the smaller squares, leaving four of the smaller squares in the center. In the four corner squares were placed the signs, first of the vernal equinox, second the summer solstice, third the autumnal equinox and fourth the winter solstice, while the remainder of the twelve signs were placed so as to occupy their correct positions in the other squares, while the sun occupied the four squares in the center. The vernal equinox was considered the beginning of the year, with the sun showing in Aries or the Lamb. This was the sign of the northeast corner. Here was the place where all the years began. Therefore, in all the ancient solar mysteries the neophyte begins his journey in the northeast corner. So far as speculative Masonry is the direct descendant of the ancient mysteries, either by legitimacy or by adoption, to that extent the candidate ought to begin his building in the northeast corner.

SECTION TWO—*"The Degree of Entered Apprentice is divided into three sections."* The first is initiatory, the second explanatory of the first and the third treats of a lodge and its appurtenances. We have already treated of the first section, as far as we may in a work of this sort, and the second section is nearly all esoteric and not to be made public. The best place to learn it is by attending lodge, where one may hear it frequently repeated. For the sake of aiding the memory, the official monitor contains the following:

At the building of King Solomon's Temple there was not heard the sound of axe, hammer or any tool of iron. The question might arise, how so stupendous an edifice could have been erected without the aid of metal tools, but are informed that the stones were squared and numbered in the quarries, whence they were raised; that the timbers were fitted and prepared in the forests of Lebanon, conveyed on floats, by sea, to Joppa and thence overland to Jerusalem, where they were put together by the aid of wooden instruments prepared for that purpose. And when the building was completed, its several parts fitted together with such exact nicety that it resembled more the handiwork of the Supreme Architect of the Universe than of human hands."

Whether this truly explains the reason for which this paragraph was written we very much doubt. Our ancient brethren would have considered it a lasting disgrace if any cutting had to be done on a stone, in order to make it fit, after it had left the work-shop to be delivered at the building. Every stone in the ancient cathedrals was wrought to an exact design. They not only feared that the metal tools might mar the beautiful work, but it implied that the Mason who wrought it was only half-learned and could not work to the design before him.

"Freemasonry regards no man for his worldly wealth or honors—it is the internal and not the external qualifications of a man that recommend him to Freemasons."

"We read in the book of Ruth, concerning their manner of redeeming and changing, that to confirm all things a man plucked off his shoe and gave it to his neighbor, and this was testimony in Israel."

"Ask and it shall be given you. Seek and ye shall find. Knock and it shall be opened unto you."

"No man, especially a Freemason, should ever engage in any great and important undertaking without first invoking the aid and blessing of Deity."

"The right hand has in all ages been deemed the seat of fidelity. The ancients worshipped a Deity under the name of 'Fides,' sometimes represented by two right hands joined, at others by an uplifted right hand."

"The Lamb has in all ages been deemed the emblem of innocence. He therefore who wears the lambskin as the badge of a Freemason is constantly reminded of that purity of life and conduct which is so essentially necessary to gaining admission to that Celestial Lodge above, where the Supreme Architect of the Universe presides."

According to that part of the Hebrew Talmud, called Beracoth, the ancient Israelites prepared themselves for entering the Temple as follows: "No man shall enter the House of the Lord with his staff or any offensive weapon, nor with his outer garment, nor with shoes on his feet, nor with money in his purse."

The primitive Roman King, Numa, was the first to erect a temple and altar to the god Fides, under which name the patron of oaths, vows and honesty was worshipped. The medals to Fides had on them two right hands joined. The right hand, for physical reasons, is held in great honor. It is supposed to carry good fortune with it. Even the word for the left hand, "Sinister," has come to be synonymous with ill-luck and unhappiness. The illegitimate child is said to have been born under the "bar sinister." In this subordinate situation a man often kept such children in his own house and educated them during the Middle Ages. Joan of Arc was supported in her victorious career by the most noble bastard of Orleans, who bore the bar sinister on his shield. The word "bastard" is but a contraction of "bar sinister-ed." The word dexter is frequently given as a Christian name, meaning skilful or capable with the right hand.

The following passage of Scripture is alluded to in this section and furnishes the authority for some of its teachings:

II Chronicles—XI—16th. "And we will cut wood out of Lebanon, as much as thou shalt need, and we will bring it to thee on floats, by sea to Joppa, and thou shalt carry it up to Jerusalem."

I Kings—VI—7th. "And the house when it was building, was built of stone, made ready before it was brought thither, so that there was neither axe, hammer or any tool of iron heard in the house while it was building."

Josephus says: "The whole structure of the temple was made with great skill of polished stone, and this was laid together so very harmoniously and skilfully and smoothly that there appeared to the spectator no sign of hammer or any other instrument of architecture, but as if without use of them the entire materials had naturally united themselves together, so that the agreement of one part with another seemed natural or organic, rather than to have arisen from the force of tools exerted upon them."

Ruth IV—7th. "Now this was the manner in former times in Isreal, concerning redeeming and changing, for to conform all things a man plucked off his shoe and gave it to his neighbor and this was a testimony in Israel."

Every Mason ought just for the sake of this passage to read the entire book of Ruth through at a sitting. It is short and he can easily do it any morning before breakfast. The circumstances that explain the meaning of the terms redeeming and changing were as follows:

Famine arose in the land of Israel, so that a man named Elimelech took his wife Naomi and his two sons Mahlon and Chilion and went into the land of Moab, quitting their family estate, property, pasture, water rights, etc., in the land of Israel, the intended sojourn in the land of Moab being temporary. The famine continued longer than was expected and the family was absent from the land of Israel for a period of ten years. The two sons married there, taking wives from the daughters of the land of Moab. Before any children had been born to either of the two sons an epidemic of sickness killed Elimelech and the two sons, leaving the three women widows. The three men were buried in the land of Moab. Shortly, Naomi and one of her daughters-in-law, the widow of Mahlon, decided to return to the land of Israel. This young widow's name was Ruth. Now Mahlon, leaving no issue, according to the law of Moses, it devolved upon his nearest male relative to provide for Naomi and to marry Ruth and raise up seed to inherit the family real estate, which formerly belonged to Elimelech, Mahlon and Chilion. Ruth fell in love with Boaz, a near relative of Mahlon, but not the next of kin. The man who was next of kin, being a poor man, declined to undertake his duty in the case, but Boaz, being a man of good property, called the elders of the family together as witnesses and bought him out, taking over the land, marrying Ruth and assuming the support of Naomi, and to confirm the bargain he took off his shoe and gave it to the next of kin. The name of the latter is not mentioned. Boaz and Ruth became the direct ancestors of David and Solomon and, incidentally, of Jesus Christ. The determination of Ruth to accompany Naomi back to the land of Israel was expressed in the following terms: "Entreat me not to leave thee or to cease from following after thee, for whither thou goest, I will go, and where thou lodgest, I will lodge; thy people shall be my people and thy God my God. Where thou diest, I will die, and there will I be buried. The Lord do so to me and more also if aught but death part thee and me."

LECTURE X

SECTION THREE

A VERY large portion of this third section of the degree of Entered Apprentice has always been considered as exoteric and is printed almost verbatim in all the monitors and illustrated by certain symbolic pictures. It runs as follows:

"The third section of this degree treats of a lodge, its form, supports, covering, furniture, lights, ornaments, jewels, how situated and to whom dedicated.

"A lodge is a certain number of Masons, duly assembled, with the Holy Bible, Square and Compasses, and a charter from a Grand Lodge, authorizing them to meet and work." Any lodge is said to be duly and legally constituted when a legal quorum of its members have assembled, one of whom is qualified to preside, if the Holy Bible, Square and Compasses be there and the charter or warrant under whose authority they exist and work. The charter or warrant should be signed by the Grand officers and it should have the seal of the Grand Lodge attached. The writing authorizes the persons named therein to meet as Masons and perform Masonic labor. Any visitor has a right to inspect this document before submitting to examination.

"Our ancient brethren held their meetings on the tops of high hills and in low valleys, the better to observe the approach of cowans and eavesdroppers and to guard against surprise." A cowan is a self-made Mason, a common stone layer, who has never been made a Mason in a regular lodge; equivalent to the modern term "scab." Regular Masons were forbidden under the severest penalties to work with them or to give them any information regarding the Craft. The reason given for holding meetings on the tops of high hills and in low valleys is not the true reason. It was simply due to the fact that high mountains and low valleys were deemed holy places respectively. In the Hebrew Scriptures nearly all the direct revelations of Jehovah were received on the tops of lofty mountains. Horeb, Sinai and Herman are instances. The Spirit was supposed to be very diffuse in those localities, most likely on account of the fact that the lightning and storms were attracted to them. Low valleys were also supposed to be haunted by spirits, usually of a malevolent character and disposition towards humanity. The

belief is in a great measure derived from the association of the Hebrews with the Persian Babylonians, whose religious system, as we have previously stated, was dual in character. These nations worshipped the personified powers of Light and Darkness as being almost of equal strength.

"The form of a lodge is an oblong square, from east to west, between the north and south, from center to circumference and from earth to Heaven. It is said to be of such vast dimensions to indicate the universality of Masonry and that a Freemason's charity should know no bounds." This symbol makes the lodge an analogue of the world. During the Middle Ages and, in fact, down to a much later period, illiterate people believed the world to be an oblong square. This figure from the surface to the center and from earth to highest heaven would constitute a double cube, expressive of the powers of Light and Darkness in creation. In the so-called miracle plays of the Middle Ages the stage was always so arranged as to show the world as a three-story contrivance. The middle floor was inhabited by men, the upper floor by the Trinity, the Virgin, the four Archangels, the Prophets, the Apostles, the Saints and Martyrs, while the lower floor was occupied by Satan and his attendant demons and tortured lost souls. The main hero was "Everyman," with his family, his friends and his enemies, representing his desires, appetites, passions, virtues and faults, performing around him, occasionally influenced by messengers from the other two worlds, in the one case prompting him to good deeds, and tempting him and leading him astray on the other—God and the Devil both, seeking to people their own dominions with human souls, as soon as they should depart from this life, with varying degrees of success. Such was the miracle play and such was the notion of the people of those ages regarding cosmos. This was by no means true of those nations inhabiting those countries where philosophy originated during the thousand years preceding the advent of Christ, especially among the learned castes.

"The supports of a lodge are three, denominated Wisdom, Strength and Beauty, because there should be wisdom to contrive, strength to support and beauty to adorn all great and important undertakings." To the ancients the covering of the world seemed to rest upon the summits of the high mountains. To the Israelites these mountains by tradition and legend were believed to be Mount Moriah, Mount Tabor and Mount Sinai. These were the mythical places where God had met and talked

name 'Mason' signifies or implies 'member of a religious sect' and a professed devotee of the Deity. He regarded the degrees as progressive steps or schools in religion. He believed that a knowledge of the God of Nature was the first step or estate of our profession; that the worship of the Deity after the Jewish Law is described in the second stage of Freemasonry, and that the Christian Dispensation is distinguished in the last and highest Order. In the lectures of Hutchinson are first introduced the three great pillars, Wisdom, Strength and Beauty, as the supports of a lodge. He also appears to have introduced for the first time the four cardinal virtues, Temperance, Fortitude, Prudence and Justice. He also gave to the Star its Christian signification. In fine, he appears to have exerted his utmost ingenuity to render the degrees emphatically Christian in their allusions and teachings.

"Hutchinson's system continued in force only a few years. His lectures gave place in 1772 to the revision of William Preston. The latter not only revised but greatly extended the lectures, and his system continued to be the standard in England until the union of the two Grand Lodges of England, which took place in 1813, when a committee, of which Dr. Hemming was the chairman and the leading mind, compiled the form now generally in use in the English lodges and known as the Hemming lectures. During the unhappy division of the Craft in England, between 1739 and 1813, differences had crept into the work of the lectures, and at the union above mentioned the committee endeavored to compile a system which, while it should be in conformity with the spirit of Freemasonry and in harmony with the 'Ancient Landmarks,' should be a sort of a compromise between the forms in previous use by the two rival organizations.

"The Hemming lectures differ widely from those of Preston, or from any others previously introduced. A few of these differences may properly be mentioned. English lodges are now dedicated to Moses and Solomon, instead of the two Saints John, as before, and their Masonic festival falls on the Wednesday following St. George's Day, April 23, that saint being the patron saint of England. The symbolic *working tools* of an Entered Apprentice are a 24-inch gauge, a gavel and a chisel. Those of a Master Mason are a pair of compasses, a skirett and a pencil. Instead of following the precedent and example of his predecessors in introducing new Christian allusions, Dr. Hemming expunged several in use previously. The *ornaments* of a Master

*vision saw extending from earth to Heaven, the three principal
rounds of which are Faith, Hope and Charity, which admonish
us to have Faith in God, Hope in Immortality and Charity for
all mankind. But the greatest of these is Charity, for Faith may
be lost in sight, Hope ends in fruition, but Charity extends beyond the grave into the boundless realms of eternity."*

According to the history of the ritual lately quoted, the presence of this theological ladder in the system of Masonry is due
to Hutchinson and back of him to Martin Clare. The original
conception was a ladder of seven rounds, consisting of the four
cardinal virtues which are known as the perfect points of
entrance, the same being Temperance, Fortitude, Prudence and
Justice, and the three theological virtues or Christian Graces, as
they are sometimes called, Faith, Hope and Charity. In the
Ptolemaic system of astronomy the ascent from earth to Heaven
passed through seven crystal spheres, occupied respectively by
the seven movable Heavenly bodies visible to the naked eye,
Saturn, Jupiter, Mars, Sun, Venus, Mercury and the Moon.
These in that pseudo science, known as astronomy's foolish little
sister Astrology, became taught as the "celestial ladder": "Divine Philosophy, thou art the Patriarch's Ladder, reaching from
earth to Heaven and bright with beckoning angels, but alas!
we see thee, only as did the patriarch of old, in visions and
dreams, dull slumbering on the earth."

Each planet had assigned to it a certain metal. To Saturn
was assigned lead, to Jupiter tin, to Mars iron, to the Sun gold,
to Venus copper, to Mercury the element known by that name,
to the Moon silver. Of all the Heavenly bodies the Sun occupies
the highest and noblest place and gold was the most beautiful
and costly metal, and resembling in color the rays of the Sun and
being found invariably in a pure state, was believed to be the
actual rays of the Sun which had become imprisoned in the rocks
and sands of the earth. This led to its peculiar use in the
ornamentation of all temples dedicated to the worship of the
Sun. The Mason hopes to be eventually elevated to this sublime
place by the means of Divine Love, which is synonymous with
charity. By the round named Charity the Mason hopes to
finally attain this sublime eminence of Truth which is Divine
Light. This is to the Mason the symbol of Heaven itself.

*"The furniture of a lodge consists of the Holy Bible, Square
and Compasses. The Holy Bible is dedicated to God, the Square
to the Master and the Compasses to the Craft. The Holy Bible*

is dedicated to God, because it is His inestimable gift to man. The Square to the Master, because it is the proper Masonic emblem of his office. The Compasses to the Craft, because by a due attention to their use they are taught to circumscribe their desires and keep their passions in due bounds."

"The ornaments of a lodge are the Mosaic pavement, the indented tessel and the blazing star. The Mosaic pavement is a representation of the ground floor of King Solomon's Temple; the indented tessel of that beautiful tessellated skirting or border which surrounded it, with the blazing star in the center. The Mosaic pavement is emblematical of human life, chequered with good and evil; the indented tessel or border of the manifold blessings and comforts which surround us and which we hope to enjoy by a faithful reliance upon Divine Providence, hieroglyphically represented by the blazing star."

Thomas Hutchinson says: "The blazing star or glory in the center of the lodge is the emblem of Divine Providence, and reminds us of that awful period when the Almighty delivered the two tables of stone which contained the commandments to His faithful servant Moses on Mount Sinai, when the days of Divine Glory shown so bright that none might behold it without fear and trembling. It also reminds us of the omnipotence of Divine Love overshadowing us and dispensing His blessings among us, and, being placed in the center, reminds us of that passage of Scripture which says: "Wherever two or three are gathered together in My Name, I will be in the midst of them and bless them." Thus wherever we may be assembled God is in the midst of us, seeing our actions and observing the secret intents and movements of our hearts. This star is not a star of five points, nor a star of six points, but a star of ten points, five of gold and five of silver. In Dunkerly's system it was said to represent the star that led the Wise Men of the East to the place of the Saviour's nativity, the star of guidance. This interpretation was not thought suitable for a universal system and was omitted at a meeting of Grand Lecturers held in Baltimore in this country.

The true star of the Ancient Mysteries was an eight-pointed star and was alluded to in Isaiah's description of a certain angel furnished with three pairs of wings: "With twain he covered his face, with twain he covered his feet and with twain he did fly." It represents a saltire cross, so called, the upright cross and the inclined cross combined. It is also indicated in the so-

called Maltese cross or star of eight points. It is also indicated
by the figure of the Babylonian God, "ILU"—"ALLA"—"AL"—
"EL," of which the Hebrew "Elohim" is the plural form. This
figure was a venerable man with arms outstretched; at his back
two pairs of wings arranged in the form of an inclined cross.
This is the name of Deity, used in the first verse of the Bible,
as having created the Heavens and the earth.

Of all forms of ornamentation which our ancient brethren
invented to illuminate and adorn their marvelous architecture,
none is more attractive than their mosaic work. With minute
particles of colored glass the old Masons accomplished something in the pictorial line that fully equaled, if it did not exceed
in beauty, the famous Gobelin tapestries, with which the needle-
work of the women covered the cold gray walls of many a
cathedral. A mosaic pavement was an ornament on which any
amount of time and money and genius could be expended. Sometimes they were of plain tiles set in small squares or diamonds
of marble, wrought of small pieces of waste of different colors.
Sometimes they were of gilded metal mixed with coral, agate and
chalcedony until it could well be said that it was paved like the
New Jerusalem in gold and precious stones. The tessellated
borders were, of course, in patterns by themselves and beautifully elaborate. Historical and Scriptural events and Christian
symbolism are often made the center-pieces, while the borders
would be wrought in some conventional design or some continuous procession of figures, something after the manner of the
frieze of the Parthenon at Athens, the subject of which was
the dedicatory procession of the building. Sometimes the pattern would be in wreaths and festoons of trees, fruits and
flowers. The olive tree, the rose of Sharon, the lily of the
valley, the lotus all figure frequently in these designs.

The symbolism of the lodge supposes the pavement to be in
large square checks, alternately white and black, and should be
in the proportion of three by four, thus making the diagonal
five. This represents the Pythagorean oblong, which is composed
of twelve squares arranged 3x4. The star should be gold and
silver and the border in flowers. The latter would not have
satisfied the Hebraic notion, because they considered themselves
to be forbidden in the law to draw any picture or likeness of anything in the Heaven above or the earth beneath, or in the waters
under the sea, so in the Hebrew temple the ornamentation would
have been what is known as arabesque. According to the Bible

Solomon was not so particular, as he believed himself commanded to ornament the Holy of Holies with cherubim and wreaths of lilies and pomegranates.

In the beautiful Congressional Library at Washington the pavement in the foyer or hall is exactly what we believe the original Masonic mosaic pavement was intended to illustrate. The pavement is in sixteen squares, each about five feet square. The four center squares are occupied by the star or Sun, which is a most brilliant Sun, inlaid with different colored metals in white marble. The remaining twelve squares form a row around these center squares, each containing a representation of one of the signs of the Zodiac in its center of some metal inlaid in a pictorial design. This pavement forms a very striking ornament to the most beautiful, perfect and complete building in the United States at the present time.

In the book of Exodus XXIV—10th—we find the following: "And they saw the God of Israel and there was under his feet, as it were, a paved work of a sapphire stone, and as it were the body of Heaven in his clearness." And in the XXVth chapter and 40th verse: "And look that thou make them after the pattern which was showed thee in the Mount." At the trial of Jesus, as represented in John XIX—13th: "When Pilate therefore heard this saying he brought Jesus forth and sat him down in the Judgment Seat, in a place that is called the 'pavement'." The Greek word here used is "lithostratum," but in the Hebrew it is "gabbotha." This word was used by Pliny, the Roman historian, to denote a "mosaic pavement." The word has nothing to do with Moses, but comes from the Latin "musicum opus." The word comes down in Italian, "musaico," and in French, "mosaque," which is pronounced the same as the English "mosaic." The Jewish Talmud also says that the apartment of the Temple where the Sanhedrim sat had a mosaic pavement.

"The Lights of a lodge are three, situated in the South, West and East. There is none in the North, because King Solomon's Temple was built so far north of the ecliptic that the Sun and Moon at their meridian height shown upon these three points only, the North remaining in darkness. The North is therefore Masonically termed 'the place of darkness'."

These Lights, like the Supports of a lodge, are represented by the Master, Senior and Junior Wardens. These are the sources of Light and Instruction in the work, as well as of superintendence and authority. If we can believe what we read of the history of operative Masonry, the Light of instruction was always freely given by the better informed to the unlearned, and whenever great and unexpected difficulties arose in the erection of some very important edifice, Grand Masters from cities far distant would often be summoned, on account of their great reputation, to assist the local architect in solving the problem. This was not so frequently necessary in the building of a new temple as in the repairing of a building that had been injured by fire, or in the devastation of a war or a storm. These came and rendered their services and advice as freely as did King Hiram of Tyre when he came to the assistance of King Solomon of old. The Lights alluded to in the work of Masonry are intellectual, moral and spiritual. The oldest worship known to the world is that which has come down to us from our Aryan ancestors in the quaint old hymns of the Rig Veda, and they were composed in worship of Indra or the Light. This worship was inherited by another branch of the same linguistic family, the ancient Persians, who through their instructor and law giver, Zarathrustra, were taught that Light was impersonated in Ahura Mazda, or God of the Day Light. This worship came down through the Order of Mythra, whose mysteries were celebrated by the Romans, though it originated in Persia. This worship was brought to Britain by the Romans and existed there until the Roman Legions were withdrawn, which occurred late in the fourth century. The members of the Order of Mythra were called "The Sons of Light." This title the Freemasons have inherited. The union of the Sons of Light with the operative Masons, if there was such, must have come at a later date. The historical evidence of this union in Scotland is the subject of a work by Sir Arthur Waite, under the title of "The Secret Tradition of Masonry."

"The Jewels of a lodge are six, three movable and three immovable. The three immovable Jewels are the Square, Level and Plumb. The Square inculcates morality, the Level equality and the Plumb rectitude of conduct. They are said to be immovable because these principles are fixed. The movable Jewels are the rough ashlar, the perfect ashlar and the trestle-board. The rough ashlar is a stone taken from the quarry in its rude and natural state. The perfect ashlar is a stone made ready by the hands of the workmen, to be adjusted by the working tools of the Fellowcraft. The trestle-board is for the Master Workman to draw his designs upon. By the rough ashlar we are *reminded of our own rude and imperfect state by nature. By the perfect ashlar we are reminded of that state of perfection at which we hope to arrive by a virtuous education, our own endeavors and the blessing of God, and by the trestle-board we are reminded that as the operative Mason erects his temporal building agreeably to the designs laid down by the Master Workman upon his trestle-board, so should we, both operative and speculative, endeavor to erect our spiritual building in accordance with the designs laid down by the Supreme Architect of the Universe in the great books of nature and revelation, which are our spiritual, moral and Masonic trestle-board."*

Such is the distribution of the Jewels of a lodge in this country, but in English lodges the reverse is the case. There the rough and perfect ashlars and the trestle-board are known as the immovable Jewels; and the square, level and plumb as the movable Jewels, because the former are always present in the lodge room and the same for all time, while the latter descend from one set of officers to another who may be elected as their successors. Every Mason, whatever his creed, should have some kind of a trestle-board, some rule and guide for his life and conduct. To the Jew it is the Old Testament. To the Christian, the Old and New Testaments, to the Arab it is the Koran, to the Hindu the Rig Veda and to the Parsee the Zend Avesta. The atheist acknowledges no Supreme Master and has no trestle-board and therefore cannot join with us in spiritual, moral and Masonic labor. The so-called precious jewels of a Fellowcraft and Master Mason cannot here be explained, as their meaning is considered esoteric. The jewels worn by the officers of a lodge are as follows:

The Master wears the Square.

The Senior Warden wears the Level.

The Junior Warden wears the Plumb.

The Treasurer wears the Crossed Keys.

The Secretary wears the Crossed Pens.

The Marshal wears a Baton and also carries one in his hand.

The Chaplain wears an Open Book.

The Senior Deacon wears the Square and Compasses on which is a Blazing Sun. He also carries a black rod tipped with a similar jewel.

The Junior Deacon wears the Square and Compasses on which is a Crescent Moon. He also carries a black rod on which is a similar jewel.

The Senior Steward wears a Cornucopia. He also carries a white rod on which is a similar jewel.

The Junior Steward wears the same jewel as the Senior Steward and carries the same rod.

The Tiler wears a sword as a jewel and carries a drawn sword in all processions.

In German lodges each member is presented with a jewel at his initiation. It generally consists of the name of the Deity inscribed on some Masonic device. Masons of the fourteenth and thirty-third degrees of the Scottish Rite wear Rings significant of their rank. The three immovable Jewels are again represented in the expression "right angles, horizontals and perpendiculars"; also by the course of the sun from morning to evening, east to west.

"A lodge is situated due east and west. Because when Moses had conducted the children of Israel through the Red Sea, he by Divine command erected a tabernacle in the wilderness, which he placed due East and West, to commemorate that mighty east wind that had wrought their miraculous deliverance. A pattern of this tabernacle was exhibited to Moses in the Mount."

This due east and west position or situation of a lodge is what is known as its orientation. This was a universal custom of antiquity, as all the notable buildings of the ancients were so located. The length was from east to west and the width from north to south. Then, except in the case of King Solomon's Temple, the entrance was through a porch at the west end, so that the people coming to pay their devotions might have their faces ever towards the rising sun. These customs all originated with sun worship and the place where the sun's rays made their first appearance was held in the greatest reverence. Christian cathedrals were built in the shape of a Latin cross, with the head of the cross towards the east, the foot of the cross to the west and the arms of the cross extending north and south, respectively, as the transepts. The Masonic orientation applies only to the lodge, which is an imaginary thing, and not to the lodge room, so that wherever the Master sits, as the old Scotch story has it, "Wherever McGregor sits, that is the head of the table." Still all Masonic temples, whenever possible without too great sacrifice, ought to be located so that the Master could really have his seat in the east. Even to this day cemeteries are usually so laid out that the foot of the graves should be towards the east, so that if the resurrection trumpet should suddenly call everyone to his feet each corpse would be facing the east. Very little advance can be made in understanding the "whys" of Masonic customs without some knowledge of the Ancient Light religion.

"Lodges were anciently dedicated to King Solomon, as he was our first Most Worshipful Grand Master, but Freemasons of the present day dedicate theirs to St. John the Baptist and St. John the Evangelist, two eminent patrons of Masonry, and since their time there is represented in every regular and well-governed lodge a certain point within a circle embordered by two perpendicular, parallel lines, representing these two saints, and upon the vertex of the circle rests the Holy Bible. The point represents an individual brother, the circle the boundary line of his duty, beyond which he is never to suffer his passions, prejudices or interests to betray him. In going around this circle we necessarily touch upon these two parallel lines, as well as upon the Holy Bible, and while a Mason keeps himself circumscribed within these precepts, it is impossible that he should materially err."

Such is the instruction given in the lodge. The figure here represented is very ancient. It represents the sun surrounded by the circle of the Zodiac and embordered by the summer solstice on the one side and by the winter solstice on the other, with the spring equinox at the top. The summer solstice comes about the 25th of June and near St. John the Baptist's day, as it is appointed in the calendar of the Church of Rome, and the winter solstice comes about the 25th of December, near St. John the Evangelist's day.

It may be worth knowing that the names John and Jonah and Janus are identical. It is also interesting in this connection to know that Oannes, the name of the culture god of the city of Nineveh, is the same name, only varying with the dialect. The great celebrations connected with the worship of Oannes took place at the time of the winter solstice, and at the time when said worship originated the winter solstice happened to be when the sun was in the Sign of the Zodiac, known as "Pisces" or the "Fishes." It may be remembered that the main adventure of the Prophet Jonah was in connection with being swallowed by a fish. The Ninevite god Oannes was always represented on the monuments as half man and half fish. In the Sign of the Fishes there are represented two fishes, one swimming towards the right and one towards the left, as though one looked forward to the new year, while the other looked backward towards the old year just passing out. Among the Romans the god Janus represented the sign of Aquarius, and he was pictured with two faces, one looking forward and one backward.

The symbolism regarding solar worship indicated by the point within a circle has many variations, but one of the most primitive and natural was that the Sun was to be regarded as the male generative power of nature. To the ancient philosopher the origin and creation of life led to the contemplation of only one process, the generative act. The Sun God was certainly the generator of life, light and heat, the male principle, and this was symbolically represented by the Phallus or Lingam, which was some picture, more or less veiled, of the human male generative organ. The most frequent illustration was of a pillar set up in the center of a circle. The circle just as distinctively represented the earth or female principle. The Sun was the Great Father. Under his benign influence all nature germinated, and the earth was the Universal Mother, in whose ample womb all these germs grew to maturity. The great monument of Stonehenge, near Sussex, England, dating far back before Roman times, was a pillar set up in the center of a circle and is evidently the ruins of a vast sun dial.

To the primitive mind there can be only one way to represent the creation of life. In nature it happens in only one manner. So the life-giving power of the Deity, the most important attribute conceived of Him, was always represented by some emblem of this sort. In early times there was no hesitancy in exhibiting these processes just as they actually occurred. In India and in Egypt many temples and shrines are found covered with decorations of this character, which to modern missionaries appear scandalously obscene. Later it was thought proper to veil these processes under some kind of a symbol. It was also more easily hidden from the profane in the work of the mysteries. No matter how moderns may look at these representations there is a great truth buried in it, nevertheless.

The only other natural symbolization of the creation of life that the writer ever saw was exhibited in a carved wooden figure of a man, with an immense number of small human figures sprouting out of his body from every part of it. It was discovered and brought from one of the islands of the Solomon Group. This represents the creation as taking place after the manner of budding, which is not only sensible and true to nature, but has a very lofty ideal connected with it when applied to the soul life as being but a part of the spirit of the Deity in its origin.

The very beautiful lesson which we have from the ritualistic work is modern and the picture that goes with it is modern, but it has other suggestions besides the solar and sexual. Suppose an individual brother were to stand alone at any point on the surface of the earth where his view might be unobstructed. The horizon around him would appear to be circular to his eye, therefore the symbol is not badly chosen for the meaning given it by the ritual. From a Masonic point of view a man's duty is to all the world around him the household of the faithful coming first.

Regarding the matter of the dedication of lodges there is an old tradition that lodges were dedicated to King Solomon until after the completion of the second temple. From that time until the beginning of the Christian Era they were dedicated to Zerubbabel, who erected that edifice. Early in the Christian Era John the Baptist became Grand Master of the Essenes, under which name the Masonic Mysteries of the Jewish people were known. The lodges were dedicated to him after his death, as he had fallen a martyr to his integrity and to his efforts to repress immorality in high places. The lodges continued their dedication to him until after the destruction of the Temple at Jerusalem, and the entire city for that matter. After this event, for a time, the Craft fell much into decay for want of a Grand Master, and many of the Masons went to St. John the Evangelist and besought him to assume that office. Though he was an old man and near his end, he had been initiated in his youth, so that he felt it his duty to accept, and through his instruction the Order flourished so prosperously that it was said of him: "That he completed with his learning the work that St. John the Baptist had begun by his zeal, and in this manner these two saints form a Christian parallel and since that time Freemasons in Christian countries have dedicated their lodges to them."

I will mention some of the curious facts that might have led to Masons having formed the myth that these two saints were real Masons at heart, if not by regular initiation. Of the Baptist there remain but few facts, first of all his asceticism. He dwelt in desert places, clothed in a girdle of camel's hair and lived on locusts and wild honey. There is also a tradition that he resisted the amatory advances of Salome. However that may have been, he lived and died celibate, as did Jesus, and that was also a custom of the Essenes. His ideas regarding morals and the nature of a moral life were strictly Masonic: "Live at peace with your neighbors. Do violence to no man. Be honest. Collect no more than is due you. Be content with your wages. He that hath two coats, let him impart to him that hath none, and he that hath meat, let him do likewise. Repent of your mean acts, turn from them and learn to do good acts." He asked for nothing that the whole world might not do without controverting any of their religious creeds or principles, and he directed the minds and senses of the people to Christ in an expression so strictly connected with the Ancient Mysteries—"Behold the Lamb of God that taketh away the sins of the world"—that it seems hardly possible that it could be a mere coincidence. He also used the Lamb in this connection as a symbol of innocence as well as a zodiacal emblem.

Another indication that this scene of the Baptism referred to a zodiacal mystery, was the expression, "This is my beloved son," which is a translation of a word which many jurisdictions, especially those working under the Scottish Rite, regard as the Master's Word, to be communicated at the raising of a candidate to the sublime degree of a Master Mason.

Regarding St. John the Evangelist, his Gospel starts at the very beginning with the symbolism of the Lost Word, one of the most important symbols of Masonry. The doctrine of the logos was perhaps the most significant and illuminating of all Greek philosophy, and it absolutely pervades John's Gospel. It may be said that the logos was the very flower of the Ancient Mysteries. God, the Ancient of Days, the Ainsoph, was Pure Spirit, unmanifested. The Word was the first manifestation, and by means of the Word or Logos was everything created that was created. And when we come to the apocalypse, which was especially attributed to him, and read his symbolic vision of the New Jerusalem coming down from Heaven, its measurements, Light and Jewels, the numbers seven and twelve that run through the Book, and especially the number of the man, 666, certainly connect the whole subject with the Ancient Mysteries unmistakably, whoever wrote it. The book is an allegory in itself. No one at this day can pretend for an instant to understand it fully. Here is the White Stone with the New Name which no man knoweth, saving him that receiveth it. Here is the Lion, the Ox, the Man and the Eagle. Here is the Lion of the tribe of Judah. Here is the Holy City of the perfect cube. Here is the Alpha and the Omega, the first and the last, the beginning and the end, and hundreds of other allusions, which certainly entitle the writer to the designation of Grand Master.

LECTURE XI
TENETS AND PERFECT POINTS OF ENTRANCE

THE tenets of a Freemason's profession are brotherly love, relief and truth. By the exercise of brotherly love we are taught to regard the whole human species as one common family, the high and the low, the rich and the poor, who as created by one Almighty Parent and inhabitants of the same planet are to aid, support and protect each other. On this principle Freemasonry unites men of every country, sect and opinion and conciliates true friendship among those who would otherwise have remained at a perpetual distance.

"To relieve the distressed is a duty incumbent on all men, but particularly among Freemasons, who are linked together by an indissoluble chain of sincere affection. To soothe the unhappy, to sympathize with their misfortunes, to compassionate their miseries and to restore peace to their troubled minds is the great aim we have in view and on this basis we form our friendships and establish our connections.

"Truth is a Divine attribute and the foundation of every virtue. To be good and true is the first lesson taught in Freemasonry. On this theme we contemplate and by its dictates endeavor to regulate our conduct. Hence, when influenced by this principle, hypocrisy and deceit will be unknown among us, sincerity and plain dealing will distinguish us and heart and tongue join in promoting each other's welfare and rejoicing in each other's prosperity."

PERFECT POINTS OF ENTRANCE—In describing the four perfect points of entrance, we can only give the meaning of the four Latin words here used. Gutta means the throat, pectora means the chest or breast, manus is the hand, while pedes is the feet. These points are to teach us to use care and circumspection over what we eat, drink, say and do and where we go, even what we think in our hearts, and at the same time maintain a noble, sincere and steady purpose of the mind, no matter what the circumstances may be, in which we find ourselves.

The four cardinal virtues seem appropriate to these four points and are usually taught with them for purposes of exemplification.

"Temperance is that due restraint over our passions and our

affections which renders the body tame and governable and frees the mind from all the allurements of vice. This virtue should be the constant practice of every Freemason, for by it he is taught to avoid excess and the contraction of any licentious or vicious habit, the indulgence of which might lead him to disclose some of those valuable secrets which he has promised to conceal and never reveal and consequently subject him to the contempt and detestation of all good Freemasons.

"Fortitude is that noble and steady purpose of the mind whereby we are enabled to undergo pain, peril or danger when prudentially deemed expedient. This virtue is equally distant from rashness as from cowardice and should be deeply impressed upon the mind of every Freemason as a safeguard and security against any illegal attack that might be made upon him by force or otherwise, to extract from him any of those valuable secrets with which he has been so solemnly intrusted.

"Prudence teaches us to regulate our lives and actions agreeably to the dictates of reason, and it is that habit by which we wisely judge and discreetly determine on all things relative to our present, as well as our future, happiness. This virtue should be the peculiar characteristic of every Freemason, not only for the government of his conduct in the lodge, but also when abroad in the world, and it should be particularly attended to in all strange and mixed companies never to let fall the least sign, word or token whereby the secrets of Freemasonry might be improperly obtained.

"Justice is that standard or boundary line of right which enables us to render unto all men their just due without distinction. It is not only consistent with Divine and human laws, but it is the very cement and support of all civil society, and as justice constitutes in a great measure the really good man, so should it be the invariable practice of every Freemason never to deviate from the minutest principles thereof."

In operative Masonry the Entered Apprentice was employed to some extent in bearing burdens, but his first real duty was in drawing and copying plans and in modeling in clay the various designs suggested by the Master. This is the first employment of an architect apprentice at the present day. The materials used at that time, as at the present, were chalk, charcoal and clay, the chalk and charcoal in drawing designs in white and black for light and shadow and the clay in modeling the first designs for sculpture. These are symbolic of the *freedom, fervency and zeal* with which Entered Apprentices should serve their Masters.

"*Entered Apprentices should serve their Masters with freedom, fervency and zeal, symbolized by chalk, charcoal and clay. Nothing is freer than chalk, for the slightest touch leaves a trace behind. There is nothing more fervent than charcoal, to which when properly ignited the most obdurate metals yield, and there is nothing more zealous than clay. Our Mother Earth of all the elements has never proved unfriendly to man. The bodies of water deluge him with rain, oppress him with hail and drown him with inundations. The air rushes in storms, prepares the tempest and the fire lights up the volcano, but the earth, ever kind and indulgent, is found subservient to his wishes. Though constantly harassed, more to supply the luxuries than the necessities of life, she never refuses her accustomed yield, spreading his pathway with flowers and his table with plenty. Though she produces the poison, yet she supplies the antidote and returns with interest every good confided to her charge. And when at last man is called upon to pass through the dark valley of the shadow of death, she once more receives him and piously covers his remains within her bosom. This admonishes him that from it we came and to it we must shortly return.*"

Here we see a hint of the ancient idea that the earth was composed of four elements only, earth, air, fire and water. This notion formed the basis of the ancient pseudo science of alchemy and the art of medicine, as it was studied in those days. The human family was classified into four temperaments to correspond with these four elements respectively. They were known as the phlegmatic or carthy, the nervous or airy, the sanguinous or fiery and the bilious or watery. They also corresponded to the four seasons of the year, the winter to the earthy, the spring to the watery, the summer to the fiery and the autumn to the airy or windy. The four Hebrew words that indicated these four elements were iammim or water, nour or fire, rauach or air and isbeschar or earth, the initials of which I. N. R. I. are significant in Christian philosophy as the initials of the words in the Latin sentence that was placed up over the head of Jesus Christ on the Cross, Iesus Nazarinus Rex Iudiorum, Jesus of Nazareth, King of the Jews. The cabalistic numbers of these initials were 10, 50, 200 and 10 adding up to 270, or the number of days of human gestation.

CHARGE TO THE CANDIDATE—The following charge is very

ancient, certainly more than two hundred years old. It was cut down somewhat by Webb and his followers, but has not been substantially altered in its wording:

"Brother, as you are now introduced into the first principles of Freemasonry, I congratulate you on being received into this ancient and honorable Order, ancient in having subsisted from time immemorial, honorable as tending in every particular so to render all mankind who will be conformable to its precepts. No institution was ever raised on a better basis or more solid foundation, nor were there ever more excellent rules or useful maxims laid down than are inculcated in the several Masonic lectures. The greatest and best men of all ages have been encouragers and promoters of our Art, and they have never deemed it derogatory to their dignity to level themselves with the Fraternity, to enlarge their privileges and to patronize their assemblies. There are three great duties which as a Freemason you are charged to inculcate to God, to your neighbor and to yourself. To God, in never mentioning His Name but with that reverential awe due from a creature to his Creator, to implore His aid in all your laudable undertakings and to esteem Him as the chief good. To your neighbor, in acting upon the square, doing unto him as you would have him do unto you, and to yourself in avoiding all irregularity and excess tending to impair your faculties and degrade the dignity of your profession. A zealous attachment to these duties will secure public and private esteem. In the state you are to be a quiet and peaceful citizen, true to your Government and just to your country. You are not to countenance disloyalty or rebellion, but patiently submit to legal authority and obey with cheerfulness the laws of the country in which you live. In your outward demeanor you are to be particularly careful to avoid censure and reproach. Although your frequent attendance at our regular meetings is earnestly solicited, yet it is not meant that Freemasonry should interfere with your necessary vocations. These are on no account to be neglected; neither are you to suffer your zeal for the Institution to lead you into argument with those who through ignorance may ridicule it. In your leisure hours, that you may improve in Masonic knowledge, you are to converse with well-informed brethren, whom you will always find as willing to give as you will be to receive instruction. Finally, keep sacred and inviolable the mysteries of our Order, as these are to distinguish you from the rest of the community and mark your consequence

among Freemasons. If in the circle of your acquaintance you find a person desirous of being initiated into Freemasonry, be particularly careful not to recommend him, unless you are convinced he will conform to our rules, that the honor, glory and reputation of the Institution may be firmly established and the world at large convinced of its good effects."

I append three other special addresses that have been taken from the work of other jurisdictions, and which it would seem may become frequently appropriate.

CHARGE TO A SOLDIER—"Our Institution breathes a spirit of general philanthropy. Its benefits considered from a social view are extensive. It unites all mankind. In every nation it opens an asylum to virtue in distress and grants hospitality to the necessitous and unfortunate. The sublime principles of universal goodness and love to all mankind, which are essential to it, cannot be lost in national distinctions, prejudices and animosities. The rage of contest it has abated and substituted in its stead the milder emotions of humanity. It has taught the pride of victory to give way to the dictates of an honorable connection. Should your country demand your services in foreign wars, and should captivity be your portion, may you find affectionate brethren where others would find only enemies. In whatever nation you travel, when you meet a Freemason you will find a brother and a friend, who will do all in his power and consistent with his honor to serve you, and who will relieve you should you be poor and in distress to the utmost of his ability and with ready cheerfulness."

CHARGE TO A FOREIGNER—"You, brother, the native and subject of another nation, by entering into our Order have connected yourself by sacred and affectionate ties with thousands of Freemasons in this and other countries. Ever recollect that the Order you have entered into bids you always to look upon the world as one great republic, of which every nation is a family and every particular person a child. When, therefore, you shall return and settle in your own country, take care that the progress of friendship be not confined to the narrow circle of national connections or particular religions, but let it be universal and extend to every branch of the human race. At the same time remember that beside the common ties of humanity you have at this time entered into obligations which engage you to be kind and friendly to your brother Masons of whatever station, country or religion."

CHARGE TO A CLERGYMAN—"You, brother, are a preacher of that religion which inculcates universal benevolence and unbounded charity. You will, therefore, be fond of the Order and zealous for the interests of Freemasonry, which in the strongest manner inculcates the same charity and benevolence, and which like that religion encourages every moral and social virtue which introduces peace and good will among mankind, so that whoever is warmed by the spirit of Christianity must esteem, must love Freemasonry. Here virtue, the grand object in view, luminous as the meridian sun shines refulgent on the mind, enlivens the heart and warms it with sympathy and affection. Though every man who carefully listens to the dictates of reason may arrive at a clear persuasion of the beauty and necessity of virtue, both private and public, yet it is a full recommendation of a society to have those pursuits continually in view, as the sole object of their association, and these are laudable bonds which unite us in one indissoluble Fraternity."

LECTURE XII

DEGREE OF FELLOWCRAFT

AS the degree of Entered Apprentice typifies youth, so the Fellowcraft Degree typifies manhood. The one symbolizes study and theory, the other work and practice. It was evidently the design of the fathers who perfected the organization of our Fraternity that it should be a great college to bring learning and mental discipline to those who, in their early youth, might have been deprived of such advantages.

William Preston, who did more than anyone else to perfect the work of the lodges, as we know it in this country, claimed that the work should cover, in some degree, the entire field of education, at least the seven liberal arts and sciences which are mentioned in the Ancient Charges and manuscripts. And that Masonry should, in very deed, enlighten those who sat in darkness, especially along religious lines.

We find, even to this day, that the student who would go to the bottom of Masonic knowledge must have at his disposal a vast deal of information. At a very early period of this study he discovers that he must know something of Latin, Greek and Hebrew. These as well as Old Saxon are necessary to understand the philology, and Brother Albert Pike, even after he had finished his three-score and ten years, thought it expedient to undertake the study of ancient Sanscrit and Zend sufficiently to translate the Rig Veda and the Zend Avesta. For any first hand information regarding the Ancient Mysteries, a knowledge of ancient Egyptian is necessary, and this simply gives the student a longing to compare this information with ancient Chinese philosophy. Finally the entire subject of folk-lore must be sifted, as well as the primitive initiations of the Men's House, as practiced by all the savage tribes the world over.

My brethren, there is no end to this subject. It is not within the capacity of any one mind to comprehend the whole in the space of the ordinary lifetime allotted to man on this earth. Eventually the student must specialize. The allusions to geometry must take one through the entire range of mathematics and ancient geometry was worked out on a plan quite different from that of modern text books. Astronomy comes next and the student must not be content with having completed the modern science, but he must ascertain what our ancient brethren believed in regard to these things. Astrology and the supposed influence of the planets, the sun and moon upon men's ideas of philosophy and their own destiny, as well as the ancient geography and history, must be included. Then comes architecture and the great buildings which stand to this day, in spite of centuries of wars and devastations, in spite of centuries of inundations and conflagrations, to testify to the patience, the genius, the devotion and the love of our ancient brethren for the Fraternity, and their zeal for the greater glory of God. At every step we must ask, "What does this mean? Whence did this curious custom originate?"

Though to exhaust the various subjects of which Masonry treats may transcend the strongest intellect, yet nearer and nearer approaches to perfection may be made, and the man of wisdom need not check the powers of his ambition in any direction, though his task may appear insurmountable. Perseverance and application remove difficulty after difficulty, as it occurs. Every step he advances new pleasures present themselves to his view and instruction of the noblest kind attends his research. In the diligent pursuit of knowledge the intellectual faculties are truly employed in promoting the glory of God and the general good of man.

Still we would not have the newly-made Mason deceived. Learning is no spade to dig with. It is only capable of throwing light upon our work, so that we may not grope in darkness while we work. A certain old scholar, as he approached his end, gave voice to the following prayer of thanksgiving and triumph: "O Lord, Thou hast sent me into the world empty-headed. I bring it back to Thee stored with useful and elevating knowledge." And if anything which we acquire on earth can go with us to that foreign country, to which we all must soon travel, it is the knowledge and experience we gain and the characters we have built, toiling with the light shining full upon our work.

The first section of the Degree of Fellowcraft is symbolic and resembles the Degree of Entered Apprentice in form, though it differs in substance. The preparation, reception and circumambulation are each appropriate to the new and second step in Freemasonry upon which the candidate is about to enter. The following passage of Scripture is used:

"Thus he showed me and behold the Lord stood upon a wall made by a plumb-line, with a plumb-line in His hand, and the

Lord said unto me, 'Amos, what seest thou?' and I said, 'A plumb-line;' then said the Lord, 'Behold, I will set a plumb-line in the midst of My people Israel. I will not again pass by them any more'." Amos VII—7th and 8th.

In other countries and in other jurisdictions in this country other passages have been preferred. One very appropriate one, it seems to us, is the following:

Luke VI—48th and 49th: "He that heareth these sayings of mine and doeth them, he is like a man that built an house and digged deep and laid the foundation upon a rock, and when the flood arose and the stream beat vehemently upon that house, it could not shake it, for it was founded upon a rock. But he that heareth and doeth not is like a man that, without foundation, built an house upon the sand, against which the stream did beat vehemently and immediately it fell and the ruin of that house was great."

As the great danger of youth comes from the mouth, that he may eat and drink to excess, and talk foolishly and without thought, so upon his reception and afterwards he is warned accordingly. This is not the danger so much to be dreaded in manhood as that he may prove dishonest and have a bad heart. Hence the square is used to remind him of virtuous conduct towards his fellowmen, and to love them and treat them kindly and generously.

How necessary it is to the career of a man that the friendships he may make he shall keep and not drive them away by selfish and deceitful actions. It was the duty of the Fellowcraft to set the stones in the building that had been previously prepared in the quarry and in the workshop. The working tools were therefore the square, the level and the plumb. These instruments also remind the candidate of right angles, horizontals and perpendiculars.

"*The working tools of a Fellowcraft are the square, the level and the plumb. They are thus used: The plumb is an instrument used by operative masons to raise perpendiculars, the square to square their work and the level to lay horizontals. But we as Free and Accepted Masons are taught to make use of ours for more noble and glorious purposes. The plumb admonishes us to walk uprightly in our several stations before God and man, squaring our actions by the square of virtue, ever remembering that we are traveling along the level of time towards that undiscovered country from whose bourne no traveler returns.*"

LECTURE XIII
DEGREE OF FELLOWCRAFT, SECTION TWO

*T*HE *second section of this degree has reference to the origin of the Institution, and views Freemasonry under two denominations, operative and speculative."*

These are separately considered and the principles upon which each are founded are carefully explained. Their affinity is pointed out by allegorical figures and typical representations. The time stipulated for rewarding merit is definitely fixed, and the inimitable moral to which that circumstance alludes is also explained. The creation of the world is described and many other particulars recited, founded upon history and sacred record, all of which have been carefully preserved among Masons and handed down from one generation to another by oral tradition.

"By operative Masonry we allude to the proper application of the useful rules of architecture, whence a structure derives figure, strength and beauty and whence will result a due proportion and just correspondence in all its parts. It furnishes us with dwellings and convenient shelter from the vicissitudes and inclemency of seasons, and while it displays the effects of human wisdom in the choice, as well as in the arrangement of the sundry materials of which an edifice is composed, it demonstrates that a fund of science and industry is implanted in man for the best, most salutary and beneficent purposes.

"By speculative Masonry we learn to subdue the passions, act upon the square, keep a tongue of good import, maintain secrecy and practice charity. It is so far interwoven with religion as to lay us under obligation to pay that rational homage to the Deity which at once constitutes our duty and our happiness. It leads the contemplative to view with reverence and adoration the glorious works of creation and inspires him with the most exalted ideas of the perfections of his Divine Creator."

The speculative Mason is a builder also, not of material edifices composed of wood and stone, but the constructor of a Temple more glorious than that of Solomon, a Temple of honor and virtue and purity and justice. The tools and implements of the operative Mason's art are but to illustrate to him the preparation he is to make, the labors he is to undergo and the dangers he is to encounter in erecting that spiritual building wherein his soul shall at last find peace forever more.

This is, indeed, a more noble and glorious purpose than squaring stones or hewing timbers. It is said that the construction of the great pyramid of Egypt employed the labor of a hundred thousand men for twelve years. The object was apparently to build a monument under whose shadow the mighty dead might repose in imperial magnificence. Freemasons build for the living. King Solomon hoped that the Living God of Israel would descend and dwell within his Temple, so nothing the world could furnish was too good or too expensive to do honor to that Glorious Visitor. Our ancient brethren sculptured and decorated the altars of their vast Gothic cathedrals in the same hope. For to them the consecrated Eucharist was the Actual Presence, so that neither skill nor treasure was spared in the adornment of them to make them worthy of Him who was and is and ever shall be.

We do not wish to belittle these faiths, though we cannot share them. The Shechinah departed from Israel and King Solomon's Temple was destroyed by the Chaldees. The cathedrals even now yield to the devastation of war's artillery, until there scarcely remains one stone resting upon another. The old crumbling Pyramid remains, not as a memorial to Cheops, but rather as a monument to the wickedness, selfishness, extravagance and oppression of a royal fool, whose mortal remains were never destined to rest within its bosom, but to be exposed from nine o'clock to five daily to the curious eyes of a multitude of a different race, in a foreign country ten thousand miles away. Speculative Freemasons are engaged in erecting a structure wherein the Living God may dwell forever. Who shall count the years of immortality, the lifetime of the soul, which is fitted for its place in Heaven? Who can define its outline, or fathom its depth, or measure its journey? It is a stream that grows broader and deeper as it flows onward. An angel's eye cannot measure its length nor an angel's wing travel to its furthest boundary. When earth's proudest monumental piles have crumbled away and their sand been scattered by the desert's wind, and the glory and greatness of the earth have been forgotten, then will the immortal be pluming his wings for loftier flight. It is like a fountain whose sources are in the infinite and whose placid waters flow on forever. The operative Mason builds for a century, the speculative Mason for everlasting years.

"We work in speculative Masonry, but our ancient brethren wrought in both operative and speculative. They wrought at the building of King Solomon's Temple and many other sacred and Masonic edifices. They worked six days in the week and rested on the seventh, for in six days God created the heavens and the earth and rested upon the seventh day. The seventh, therefore, our ancient brethren consecrated as a day of rest from their labors, thereby enjoying frequent opportunity to contemplate the glorious works of creation and to adore their Great Creator."

These six days of creation are technically known among Masons as the Grand Architect's six periods, and these six important periods in the world's history may be more particularly illustrated as follows:

Before it pleased the Great Creator of Heaven and earth to call this vast world into existence, the elements and materials of creation lay blended together without distinction or form (in chaos) and darkness was upon the face of the great deep, and the Spirit of God brooded (moved) upon the face of the waters (over the fluid mass) and the Almighty, as an example to man that all things of moment should be performed with due deliberation, was pleased to be six days in calling it from chaos to perfection. The first instance of Supreme Power was made manifest in that sublime command—"Let there be Light"—and there was Light, and when God saw it, "behold, it was good," and He distinguished it by name, calling the Light "Day" and the darkness he called "Night."

The second day was employed in laying the foundation of the heavens and creating a firmament designed to keep the waters that were in the clouds and those that were beneath them asunder. On the third day He commanded the waters to gather themselves together into one place and bade the dry land appear, and the earth was irregular and barren, and God spoke the word and it was immediately covered with a beautiful carpet of green grass, designed as a pasture for the brute creation. Trees, shrubs and flowers budded and sprang forth that they might thereafter furnish seed to the sower and bread to the eater, and all attained to a due growth, maturity and perfection. On the fourth day He created the two Great Lights, the Sun to rule the day and the Moon to govern the night, and the sacred historian informs us that they were appointed for times and for seasons, for days and for years. On the same day He besprinkled the ethereal concave of the heavens with a multitude of stars, like the sands of the sea, innumerable, so that man, whom He intended thereafter to create, might contemplate thereon and justly admire His majesty and His glory. On the fifth day He commanded the waters to bring forth a variety of fish of every sort, and that He might imprint upon the minds of men a reverential awe for His Divine Omnipotence, He created the other inhabitants of the mighty deep, and they all multiplied exceedingly, each after its kind. On the same day He caused the birds to fly in the air, that man might delight his eyes with their beautiful plumage and his ears with their melodious notes. On the sixth day He created the beasts of the field and the reptiles that crawl upon the earth.

Here we behold the wisdom, power and goodness of the Great Artificer of the universe made manifest throughout the whole of His proceedings. He produced those effects He pleased without the aid of their natural causes, such as giving Light to the world before He had created the Sun and Moon, and making the earth fruitful without the influence of the heavenly bodies. He did not create the beasts of the field until He had provided them with sufficient herbage for their support, neither did He create man until He had supplied him with a dwelling place and furnished it with all things necessary for life and comfort. And then to dignify the works of His hands still more, He created man, who came into the world with more pomp and glory than any creature that had preceded him. All came with but a single command—God said, "Let be" and it "was".

But at the creation of man there was held a consultation, and the Almighty is represented as saying to the assembled hosts of Heaven: "Let us now make man in Our Own Image," and he was immediately formed from the dust of the ground. The breath of Life was breathed into his nostrils and he became a Living Soul. And God gave him dominion over all things that He had made. But God saw that it was not good for man to be alone, so as a last and best gift to man God created a woman (womb-man), and the sacred historian informs us that He caused a deep sleep to come upon the man and, taking a rib from out of his side, under His forming hand the image grew, manlike but of different sex, so lovely fair that what before seemed beautiful in all the earth seemed now mean. Grace was in every step, peace in her eye and every gesture dignity and love, and on she came, led by her heavenly maker, Himself unseen, yet guided by His voice, all in her summed up, in her contained, adorned by all Omnipotence could bestow to make her amiable, taken not from the man's head that she should rule over him, nor from his feet, that he should trample upon her, but taken from his side and next his heart, that .she might be a friend and companion to him through all his chequered career of good and of evil, a help-mate for his labors, a solace for his cares, a comfort for his sorrows, his joy in health and his nurse in sickness, through prosperity and through adversity, for better and for worse, so long as they both should live.

So for that reason it was written that a man should forsake all others and cleave only to his wife, and that they twain should be one flesh. And after commanding them to go forth and multiply and replenish the earth, God finished His six days of labor. And since that time two shall be born, the whole wide world apart, and speak with different tongues and have no thought each of the other's being and take no heed. Yet these o'er unknown seas to unknown lands shall cross, escaping wreck and defying death, and all unconsciously shape every act to this one end, that one day through the darkness they should meet and read life's meaning in each other's eyes.

From the most ancient times and in many different countries and languages these seven days have been named from the seven movable heavenly bodies, the Sun, Moon, Mars, Mercury, Jupiter, Venus and Saturn. Since Christian times and in Latin countries the Sun's day has been called "Dies Dominicus," or "Lord's Day". It was not considered that any important alteration was made in the name, for the analogy between Christ and the Sun had been enlarged upon so persistently by the early Christians, in their efforts to make gentile converts, that they usually spoke of Him as "The Sun of Righteousness" that had arisen with healing in His wings to expel the gloom of death and the grave. They sought out every similarity of adventure and so enlarged upon it that "Dies Solis" and "Dies Dominicus" had come to mean about the same thing.

We now come to the description of the symbolic journey to the Middle Chamber. The portion of the Temple which our ancient brethren thought of as the ground floor was that portion occupied by the space within the propylon or porch and between it and the Temple proper, wherein the two memorial pillars were erected. The Bible describes these pillars very elaborately and further says—I Kings VI—8th: "The door to the

Middle Chamber was in the right side of the house, and they went up with winding stairs into the Middle Chamber and out of the Middle into the Third." The account in the Book of Kings and the account in Chronicles differ in regard to the height of the pillars, Chronicles giving them as thirty-five cubits, fifty-two feet and six inches, with a chapiter or capitol five cubits, seven feet and six inches, on the top of which was a pommel or globe. These were four cubits, six feet, in diameter and these are the dimensions given in our work. This would make the pillars rather more slender than was usually the case and it has been thought by some that this height was intended to include both pillars. However, the account in Kings gives them as eighteen cubits high apiece, twenty-seven feet, exclusive of the capitol.

Kings is the older record, from which the account in Chronicles was doubtless derived. It is said that the Hebrews used three different cubits in their measurements. One for land and exterior measurements, one for internal work and one for jewelry measurement, respectively twenty-one, eighteen and twelve inches each in length. We do not know which to apply in this case, most likely the middle cubit, and this is the one in the estimate here given.

The description in the Bible is somewhat difficult to comprehend exactly, but it is evident that the pillars were made of molten or cast brass and four fingers in thickness. They were cast in the clay ground between Succoth and Zeredatha. The chapiters or capitols were doubtless what are known as lotus capitols, in imitation of the Egyptian capitol of that name and form, the bud serving as the pommel or globe and described as lily-work. The presence of these pillars was an idea derived from the obelisques, so frequently placed in front of Egyptian temples. The pomegranates were, likely, representations of the pomegranate blossom of five petals, somewhat resembling our "rosa canina" or dog rose. The chains were of these flowers, wrought into a network and festooned about the head of the capitol, and joining it with the pommel on the top.

The statement that the constitution, rolls and records were contained within these pillars was doubtless derived from the fact that on the Egyptian obelisques were inscribed, in hieroglyphic writing, many records of the history of that country, the doings of the kings who had erected the pillars, the date and number of years of their reign, and other important par-

ticulars.   There is, in the Ancient Manuscripts, a record of the
ancient pillars of Lamech, the father of Noah.   This record
states that Lamech had a dream or vision that the world was
going to be destroyed either by fire or water, or both, so in
order to preserve the Mysteries of Masonry or Geometry he
engraved the science on two pillars, the one of brass, which
would withstand the effects of water, and the other of laterns
or terra cotta, which would not be injured by fire.   These were
hidden away and after Noah's flood the brass pillar was discovered by one of Noah's sons, and so was transmitted the science
to Euclid and Hermes.   Many have supposed that these pillars
were placed at the entrance of the Temple, that the children
of Israel might be kept in a kind and loving remembrance of
the two pillars that had attended their forefathers in their
journeyings through the wilderness, the pillar of cloud by day,
by which they were hidden from the pursuing hosts of Pharoah,
and the pillar of fire by night, which ever beckoned them on their
journey towards the promised land—"Land of the Behest," as
the old manuscripts speak of it.

The pillar on the left hand was named "Boaz", which denotes
strength.   The one on the right hand was called "Jachin", meaning to establish.   Collectively they denote strength and establishment and are supposed to be alluded to, in Scripture, in God's
promise to David: "In strength will I establish thine house
forever."

*"The globes are two artificial spherical bodies, on the convex
surface of which are represented the countries, seas and various
parts of the earth, the face of the heavens, the planetary revolutions and other important particulars.   Their principal use besides serving as maps to distinguish the outward parts of the
earth and the situation of the fixed stars was to illustrate and
explain the phenomena arising from the annual revolution and
diurnal rotation of the earth around its own axis.   They are
invaluable instruments for improving the mind and giving it
the most exact idea of any problem or proposition as well as
enabling it to solve the same.   Contemplating these bodies we
are inspired with a due reverence for the Creator and His
works, and are induced to encourage the studies of geography,
astronomy and navigation, and the arts dependent upon them
by which society has been so much benefited."*

The symbolism of the globe is a very ancient one.   It is sym-
bolical of the universal extension of the Order and the universal

claim of brotherly love. It is found in the religious system of many countries. Among the Mexicans it was the symbol of universal power. That is probably the idea in the orb presented to the English sovereigns on their coronation. As a Masonic symbol it is probably derived from or at least has an allusion to the winged globe, so common in Egypt, supported by a serpent on either side. This is seen on the entablature of many buildings and over many propylon gates. It was as much the national device of the Egyptians as the eagles of the United States, or the lion of England. Egypt was often called the land of the winged globe. It is believed that the spherical shape of the earth was known to the ancient Egyptians, but it may be just a representation of the sun, or of the egg from which the world was supposed to have been created or hatched, as it was claimed in some of their creation legends. The celestial and terrestrial figures on the globes are of very recent origin and have nothing whatever to do with the Biblical record.

It is recorded in II Chronicles IV—13th: "And four hundred pomegranates on wreaths, two rows of pomegranates on each wreath, to cover the pommels of the chapiters which were upon the pillars."

There is nothing about the pommels in the Book of Kings, but it is said that the chapiters were covered on top with lily-work. If the lodge symbolically represents the world, as it was known to the ancients, the two pillars symbolically represent the two pillars of Hercules, Gibraltar and Ceuta. Astronomically they represent the summer and winter solstices, between which the sun sets at the vernal and autumnal equinoxes, thus indicating the two Saints John, or the two fishes of the constellation, Pisces, in which the sun shows itself at the time of the equinox. They were also astronomical instruments. The ancient geometers drew a chequered floor and erected thereon two pillars. The shadows cast by these pillars gave them an almost exact indication of the position of the sun in its annual journey through the circle of the zodiac.

LECTURE XIV

The Winding Stairs

WE next come to the symbolism of the winding stairs. Here we first come in contact with the philosophy of numbers and their secret meanings and learn of that great system of ancient doctrine made famous by Pythagoras. The Hebrews and Greeks had no special signs to represent numbers, but employed the letters of the alphabet and gave each letter a numerical value. In this way the names of men and countries came to have a connection with certain numbers. For instance, one of the sacred names of Deity, in Hebrew, added up to fifteen. It was the name J. H. probably pronounced "JAH". The "J" or "I" or "Y", all these letters having the same identical sound in that language, was equal to "10" and the "H" to "5". This is likely the reason of there being fifteen steps in the Masonic stairway.

According to all the ancient teachers of magic, there was great efficacy for good and evil in certain numbers. Certain numbers were deemed fortunate and certain others unfortunate. Odd numbers were generally considered favorable, especially three, five, seven and nine. Very few even numbers were thought favorable. Four stood well, for it corresponded with the number of characters in the ineffable name "JHVH." Ten does not appear in Masonry, but with the Pythagorean philosopher it was considered a perfect number because it was the sum of the first four numbers. Twelve also stood high, for it corresponded with the number of signs in the zodiac and was the sum of the three, four and five of the Pythagorean triangle. Twenty-six was the number of the ineffable name, 10 plus 5 plus 6 plus 5. Thirty-six was the number of the sun and twenty-eight the number of the moon, probably because that was the number of days from one new moon to another.

Philolaus says: "Number is great and perfect and omnipotent and the principle and guide of Divine and human life." Fantastical as it may seem there is a truth underlying the statement, for when we think that number is the definite mathematical relation that separates one thing from another, and so, in a sense, it makes them things. Without number and the limitation which number brings, there would be only chaos and the illimitable. Number is the principle of order, the principle by which cosmos and the ordered world subsists. These philosophers found the ground for this position in the regular movements of the heavenly bodies and in the harmony of musical sounds and the dependence of these sounds on regular mathematical intervals. They were apparently the first to discover this fact regarding musical tones and made much of it. They connected these seven tones with the seven planets of the old astronomy and deduced therefrom the theory of the music of the spheres, calling these planets the seven golden chords of the heavenly harp.

Immediately connected with this theory of numbers was their theory regarding opposites, that everything was derived from its opposite, the limited and unlimited, odd and even, right and left, masculine and feminine, rest and motion, straight and crooked, light and darkness, good and evil. This represents a dual system. Unity was considered a thing by itself and was connected with the idea of the unity of God. It was in the union of opposites wherein harmony existed, the neutralization of one with the other, the mystery of the balance, as it was called. In the application of their system to geometry, one symbolized the point, two the line, three the surface and four the cube. Five symbolized marriage, for it indicated the union of the first even number (2) with the first odd number after unity (3). The one was considered the number of the Deity or the Supreme Unity, and therefore left out of consideration in the addition. One was the symbol of wisdom and reason. Two symbolized opinion, because it was unlimited and indeterminate. Four was identified with justice, because it was the first square number, the product of equals. There was in all these ancient systems a very important trinity, which was the object of worship, making three highly considered. Even in the primitive Phallic system the trinity represented the three essential organs of generation, as well the male, the female and the offspring. In the caves of Elephanta may be found a sculptured figure with three faces. This was called the "Trimurti", or Hindu Trinity of Brahma, Vishu and Shiva, which represented the creator, the preserver or form giver and the destroyer or transformer—perhaps the better understood as the builder-up and the tearer-down of the world, the rising, meridian and setting sun, the A. U. M. or Alpha the beginning, Omega or end, and Mem, the middle letters of the alphabet. Again, we

have the famous Egyptian trinity Osiris, Isis and Horus, or
Father, Mother and Child. The Christian trinity of the Father,
Son and Holy Spirit is well known and need not here be dis-
cussed further than to say that the Divine character of the
Virgin Mother was soon regarded very highly, while the char-
acter of the third person seems to have been looked upon more
as an emanation proceeding from the characters of the Father,
Mother and Son. It may also be said that the Hebrew word
"Ruach", translated "spirit", was a feminine noun. It indicated
the "breath" as distinct from the "soul" or "sol", which was the
Divine spark of life, supposed to shine into the foetus in utero
like a ray of light from the sun.

Our ancient brethren employed in the construction of their
cathedrals every sort of numerical symbolism. Our space will
not permit us here to go into this subject very deeply, but we
might say that the cathedrals were erected in the shape of a
cross, the choir and sanctuary towards the east and consisting
generally of five bays. The nave extended toward the west
and generally consisted of seven or nine bays. The transepts
extended to the north and south, generally of three bays each,
and when there were double transepts the eastern pair were of
a single bay. The west end of the nave terminated in two
towers, and the great central tower was over the crossing, nearly
over the high altar. The refectory was at the southern side of
the main building and attached to it, especially in those cathedrals administered by the Monkish Orders. To the north were
the schools, hospitals, workshops, etc. At the extreme east end
and connected with the choir by a passage way was the circular
lady-chapel. If not completely circular it terminated in a semi-
circular aspe divided off into five or seven small altar spaces.
Seven was usually the number intended, though the central
one might be taken up by the passageway. In some of the
continental cathedrals the ground space was insufficient for the
complete plan indicated, so that the transepts would have but
a single bay each. The proportions of the entire cathedral,
height, breadth, height of towers, width of aisles all seemed to
have been arranged on the three, five, seven and nine plan.
Around the crossing four seems to be the prevailing number,
four letters in the name of Deity, four evangelists, four crowned
martyrs of Masonry. Four archangels usually decorated the
pendentives, by which the square of the crossing was reduced
to an octagon for the base of the spire. These archangels were

Michael, Gabriel, Ralphael and Azrael, representing the might of God, or omnipotence; the messenger or herald of God, Omnipresence; the wisdom of God, omniscience, sometimes interpreted as the splendor of God, and Azrael, the angel of death, the sword of God. In St. Sophia, the church dedicated to divine wisdom in Constantinople, these angels appear on the pendentives, though the church has been occupied as a Mohammedan mosque for more than six hundred years. There are many systems of threes in our monitor, three supports of a lodge, three ornaments, three lights, three articles of furniture, three immovable jewels and three movable jewels, three principal officers of a lodge, three degrees in Ancient Craft Masonry, three ancient Grand Masters and three principal tenets of a Mason's profession:

"The three principal officers of the lodge, the Junior Warden, whose station is in the South, the Senior Warden, whose station is in the West, and the Worshipful Master, who presides in the East."

It has been beautifully said of old, that the Worshipful Master opens the lodge at sunrise with solemn prayer, the Junior Warden calls the Craft from labor to refreshment when the sun has attained its meridian height, and the Senior Warden pays the Craft their wages at sunset, when the labors of our ancient brethren had ended. In like manner the great luminary of creation rises in the East to open the day with his mild and genial influence, while all nature rejoices at the appearance of his beams. He attains his meridian in the South, invigorating all things with the perfection of his ripening qualities, but with gradually declining rays he sinks to the West to close the day, leaving all mankind at rest from their labors. This is a fitting type of the three principal stages of human life, youth, manhood and age. The first is characterized by the blush of innocence, clear as the tints that gild the eastern portals of the day. The heart rejoices at the unsuspecting integrity of its own unblemished virtues nor fears deceit because it knows no guile. Manhood succeeds and his ripening intellect appears at the meridian of his powers, but at the approach of old age man's strength decays, enfeebled by sickness and bodily infirmity, his sun is setting in the West, but he lingers on until death finally closes his eventful day. Happy is he if the setting splendors of a virtuous life gild his departing moments with the gentle tints of hope and finally close his short career in peace and harmony and brotherly love.

LECTURE XV

THE FIVE ORDERS OF ARCHITECTURE

*B*Y *order in architecture is meant a system of all the members, proportions and ornaments of columns and pilasters, or it is a regular arrangement of the projecting parts of a building which, united to those of a column, form a beautiful, perfect and complete whole. From the first formation of society, order in architecture may be traced. When the rigor of seasons first obliged men to contrive shelter from the inclemency of the weather, we learn that they first planted trees on end, then laid others across to support a covering. The bands which connected these trees at the top and bottom are said to have given rise to the idea of the base and capital of pillars, and from this simple hint originally proceeded the more improved art of architecture. The five orders may be thus classed—Tuscan, Doric, Ionic, Corinthian and Composite."*

The Tuscan is the most simple and solid of the five orders. It was invented in Tuscany, whence it derives its name. Its column is seven diameters high and its capital, base and entablature have but few moldings. The simplicity of its construction renders it eligible, where ornament would be superfluous.

The Doric, which is plain and natural, is the most ancient. It was invented by the Greeks. It is the best proportioned of the five orders. The several parts of which it is composed are founded on the natural positions of solid bodies. In its first invention it was more simple than in its present state. In after times, when it began to be adorned, it gained the name of Doric, but when first constructed in its primitive and simple form the name Tuscan was conferred upon it. Hence the Tuscan precedes the Doric in rank, on account of its resemblance to that pillar in its original state. The Doric column is eight diameters high and its capital, base and entablature have few ornaments save moldings, though its frieze is distinguished by triglyphs and metopes, and the triglyphs compose the ornaments of the frieze. The solid composition of this order gives it a preference where strength and a noble simplicity are chiefly required. The Parthenon, that beautiful temple of Pallas Athene, the patron Goddess of Athens, contrived and ornamented by Phydias, was of this order.

[119]

The Ionic bears a kind of mean proportion between the more solid and delicate orders. Its column is nine diameters high. Its capital is adorned with volutes and its cornice has dentals. There is both delicacy and ingenuity displayed in this order, the invention of which is attributed to the Ionians, for the great temple of Diana at Ephesus was of this order. It is said to have been formed from the model of a beautiful young woman of elegant shape dressed in her hair, as a contrast to the Doric, which was formed from the model of a strong, robust man.

The Corinthian is the richest of the five orders and is deemed a masterpiece of art. Its column is ten diameters high. Its capital is adorned with two rows of leaves and eight volutes which sustain an abacus. The frieze is ornamented with curious devices and its cornice has dentals and modillions. This column is used in stately and superb structures. The temple of Jupiter Olympus was of this order. This column was invented at Corinth by one Callimachus, who is said to have taken the hint for the capital of this column from the following remarkable circumstance: Accidentally passing by the tomb of a young lady he perceived a basket of toys, covered with a tile, which had been placed over an acanthus root, having been left there by her nurse. As the branches grew up they encompassed the basket, until they arrived at the tile, where they met with an obstruction and bent downwards. Callimachus, being struck with the object, set about imitating the figure. He made the base of the capital to represent the basket, the abacus the tile and the volutes the bended leaves.

The Composite is compounded of the other orders. It was contrived by the Romans. Its column is ten diameters high. Its capital has the two rows of leaves of the Corinthian and the volutes of the Ionic. Its base has the quarter rounds of the Tuscan and Doric. Its cornice has dentals and simple modillions. This order is generally employed where strength, elegance and beauty are sought.

"The ancient original orders of architecture revered by Free-masons are no more than three, the Doric, Ionic and Corinthian, which were invented by the Greeks. To these the Romans have added two, the Tuscan, which they made plainer than the Doric, and the Composite, which was more ornamental, if not more beautiful, than the Corinthian. The first three orders, however, alone show particular character and essentially differ from each other. The others have nothing but what is borrowed and differ

*only accidentally. The Tuscan is the Doric in its earliest state
and the Composite is the Corinthian enriched by the Ionic. It
is to the Greeks, therefore, and not to the Romans, that we are
indebted for all that is grand, judicious and distinct in architecture."*

It may here be said that every race, in the beautiful stone
buildings characteristic of the loftiest type of their civilization,
follow the style which their primitive ancestors adopted when
they first contrived shelter and protection out of the most available materials that could be found close at hand. The vast
temples that housed the gods of ancient Egypt are but granite
imitations of the wattled mud huts which their forefathers
erected on the banks of the Nile. The Semitic Arabs erected
tents of stone and the Greeks imitated their early wooden houses.
The steep and pointed roofs of the Gothic cathedrals tell of a
land of heavy snows and severe rains, and its ever-branching
piers, vaulted and groined, speak of woody paths and deep shade,
where the sun steals through the stained glass as it has ever
done through the leaves of the forest. The rock-bound fortresses
of the Norman conquerors were but elaborated mountain caves,
while the Temple of Solomon, as described in the Bible, aside
from the propylon or lofty watch tower and gateway, was an
attempt to reproduce, in stone, the ancient tabernacle of Moses.

THE FIVE HUMAN SENSES—*"The five steps also allude to the
Five Human Senses, Hearing, Seeing, Feeling, Smelling and
Tasting."*

In the work of the Fellowcraft Degree in the lodges on the
continent of Europe, one of the most prominent symbols was
the mirror or looking-glass, and the lesson drawn was for the
candidate to first seek to know himself. To this was added the
study of the five senses. In our work very little is made of this
portion of the work from a symbolic point of view. In the old
monitors of Webb, they were described as follows:

"Hearing is that sense by which we distinguish sound and are
capable of enjoying the agreeable charms of music. By it we
are able to enjoy the pleasures of society and, reciprocally, to
communicate to each other our thoughts and our intentions,
our purposes and our desires, while thus our reason is capable
of exerting its utmost power and intensity. The wise and
beneficent Author of Nature intended by the formation of this

sense that we should be social creatures and receive the greatest and most important part of our knowledge through the information of others. For this purpose are we endowed with hearing, that by a proper exertion of our natural powers our happiness may be complete.

"Seeing is that sense by which we distinguish objects and in an instant of time, without change of place or situation, view armies in battle array, figures of the most stately structures and all the agreeable variety displayed in the landscape of nature. By this sense we find our way in the pathless ocean, traverse the globe of the earth, determine its figure and dimensions and delineate any region or quarter of it. By it we measure the planetary orbs and make new discoveries in the region of the fixed stars. Nay, more, by it we perceive the temper and disposition, the passions and affections of our fellow-creatures, when they wish most to conceal them, so that though the tongue may be taught to lie and dissemble, the countenance would display its hypocrisy to the discerning eye. In fine, the rays of light which administer to this sense are the most astonishing part of the animated creation and render the eye a peculiar object of admiration. Of all the faculties sight is the noblest. The structure of the eye and its appurtenances evince the admirable contrivances of nature for performing all its external and internal motions, while the variety displayed in the eyes of different animals, suited to their several ways of life, clearly demonstrates that organ to be the masterpiece of nature's work.

"Feeling is that sense by which we distinguish the different qualities of bodies, such as heat and cold, softness and hardness, roughness and smoothness, figure, solidity, motion, extension and viscidity."

"*These three senses, Hearing, Seeing and Feeling, are deemed peculiarly essential among Freemasons.*"

"Smelling is that sense by which we distinguish odors, the various kinds of which convey different impressions to the mind. Animal and vegetable bodies and, indeed, most other bodies, while exposed to the air continually, send forth effluvia of vast subtility, as well in the state of life and growth as in the state of fermentation and putrefaction. These effluvia being drawn into the nostrils along with the air, are the means by which all bodies are smelled. Hence it is evident that there is a manifest appearance of design in the Great Creator having placed the organ of smell on the inside of the canal, through which the air continually passes during respiration.

"Tasting enables us to make a proper distinction in the choice of food. The organs of this sense guard the entrance to the alimentary canal, as that of smell guards that to the canal of respiration. From the situation of both these organs it is plain that they were intended by nature to distinguish that which is wholesome food from that which is nauseous. Everything that enters the stomach must undergo the scrutiny of tasting, and by it we are capable of discerning the changings which the same body undergoes in the different compositions of the art of cookery, chemistry, pharmacy, etc. Smelling and tasting are inseparably connected and it is by an unnatural kind of life that men constantly lead in society that these senses are rendered less fit to perform their natural offices. On the mind all our knowledge must depend. What, therefore, can be more proper as a study for Masons than these senses through which the mind must gain its information? By anatomical dissection and investigation we become acquainted with the body, but it is by the anatomy of the mind alone that we discover powers and principles. We shall add that memory, imagination, taste, reasoning, moral perception and all the active powers of the soul present a vast and boundless field for philosophical disquisition which far exceed human inquiry, and are peculiar mysteries known only to Nature and to Nature's God, to whom we are all indebted for creation, preservation and every blessing we enjoy, and into whose bosom we retire at last—'When the dewdrop slips into the shining sea'."

THE PHILOSOPHY OF THE NUMBER SEVEN—We come now to the philosophy of the number seven. Think of the immense number of groups of sevens that enter into the contemplation of all religious and philosophical questions. In the first place there were seven of the Heavenly bodies that moved freely in the midst of the starry firmament, the other lights never seeming to change their relative positions. Though they passed across the ethereal concave from east to west once every night, they continued their same relative situation as regards each other. These seven took strange journeys, but all seemed to come around to their original positions at regular intervals. Then there was another group of seven stars that every night revolved around the polar star as regularly as the hands round a dial. Another group of seven stars

were found in the Pleiades. The names of the planets gave rise
to the names for the days in the week.

All the temples of the Ancient Magi were seven stories high,
each story being dedicated to one of the planets. These were
painted, each with one of the primary colors which make up the
spectrum of the rainbow, violet, indigo, blue, green, yellow,
orange and red. Then again there naturally appear seven tones
in the musical scale. There were seven wonders of the world,
seven wise men of Greece. Then when one comes to Biblical
record there were seven people saved at the time of Noah's Flood.
The clean beasts were saved by sevens. Then in Pharoah's vision
there were seven fat kine and seven lean kine and there followed
seven years of plenty and seven years of famine, in Joseph's
interpretation of that vision. There were seven lamps on the
candlestick in the tabernacle. There were seven priests with
rams' horns that marched seven times around the doomed city
of Jericho before it fell. There were seven sabbatic years that
made up the full calendar in the Jewish Law, which terminated
in the year of Jubilee, so called. Jesus mentions the number
many times in His teachings and in the apocalypse of St. John
the number seven is employed in a great number of combinations.
In Freemasonry it is directed particularly to the seven liberal
arts and sciences, which are *grammar, rhetoric, logic, arithmetic,
geometry, music and astronomy.* These seven subjects our
ancient brethren considered to comprise all the elements necessary for a liberal education. They were classified into the
trivium, consisting of grammar, rhetoric and logic, which elucidated all the information necessary to the acquirement and
proper use of all forms of language, whether written or spoken,
and the quadrivium, comprising arithmetic, geometry, music
and astronomy, which inculcated all that the ancients knew of
art and science. These seven subjects are mentioned in the
most ancient manuscripts as being particularly essential to
Masonic instruction.

Grammar teaches the proper arrangement of words, according
to the idiom or dialect of any particular people, and that excel-
lency of pronunciation which enables us to speak or write a
language with accuracy and agreeably to accurate and correct
usage.

Rhetoric teaches us to speak copiously and fluently on any
subject, not merely with propriety alone, but with all the advantage of force and elegance, wisely trying to captivate the

hearer by strength of argument and beauty of expression, whether it be to entreat or exhort, to admonish or applaud.

Logic teaches us to guide our reason discretionally in the general knowledge of things and direct our inquiries after truth. It consists of a regular train of arguments, whence we infer, deduce and conclude, according to certain premises laid down, admitted or granted, and in it are employed the faculties of conceiving, judging, reasoning and disposing, all of which are naturally led on from one gradation to another till the point in question is finally determined. This science ought to be cultivated as the foundation and ground-work of our inquiries, particularly in pursuit of those sublime principles which claim our attention as Masons.

Arithmetic teaches the powers and properties of numbers, which are variously affected by letters, figures, tables and instruments. By this art reasons and demonstrations are given for finding out any certain number whose relation or affinity to another is already known or discovered. The greater advancement we make in mathematical science, the more capable we shall be of considering such things as the ordinary objects of our conceptions, and be thereby led to a more comprehensive knowledge of our Great Creator and His works of creation.

"Geometry treats of the powers and properties of magnitudes in general, where length, breadth and thickness are considered from a point to a line, from a line to a superficies—(surface)— from a superficies to a solid. A point is the beginning of all geometrical matter. A line is a continuation of the same. A superficies has length and breadth without thickness—(a continuation of lines). A solid has length and breadth with thickness, which may form a cube and comprehends the whole—(a continuation of surfaces placed one above the other). By this science the architect is enabled to construct his plans and execute his designs, the general to arrange his soldiers, the engineer to lay off grounds for an encampment, the geographer to give us the dimensions of the world and all things therein contained, to delineate the extent of seas and specify the divisions and boundaries of empires, kingdoms and provinces. By it also the astronomer is enabled to make his calculations and fix the duration of times and seasons, years and cycles. In fine, geometry is the foundation of architecture and the root of the mathematics."

An ancient philosopher, no less than the immortal Plato, on being asked the probable occupation of the Deity, replied: "God geometrizes continually." And when we consider the wonderful order and symmetry with which all the works of creation are governed, we cannot but admit that geometry pervades the universe. When, by aid of the telescope, we bring the planets within the range of our observation and with the microscope view particles too minute for the eyes of man unaided to behold, we find all things performing the objects for which they were created in accordance with the strict plans laid down by that all powerful mind. Is there not more truth than fiction in the saying of that ancient teacher in the sacred academy that God geometrizes in Nature? By geometry He rounds the dewdrop glistening on the mountain side, points the conical icicle hanging from the thatched roof, arranges with marvelous exactitude the myriad crystals of the falling snow, bends the foaming cataract into a graceful curve, paints the rainbow on the canvas of a summer shower and forms in the dark fissures of the earth-bound rocks gorgeous caverns, thick-set with starry gems. By geometry He rounds the blushing cheek of beauty and curves the ruby lip and fashions the swelling bosom that heaves in unison with a gushing heart. By geometry He traces in delicate ellipse the opening petals of the budding rose and arrays the simple lily of the field in more wondrous raiment than Solomon in all his glory wore. By geometry He teaches the rugged oak to brace its rootlets to withstand the storm and supports the pliant vine whose gentle tendrils following the journey of the sun climb up its winding stairway to the topmost bough. By geometry He curves the bloom upon the peach and paints in tints of russet and of gold the autumn's mellow fruit. By geometry He forms in mold of perfect symmetry the gentle dove, draws the myriad circles in the peacock's gaudy train and decks the plumage of ten thousand warblers of His praise that animate the mazes of the wooded shade. By geometry He shapes the great leviathan to breast the mighty billows of the angry sea and decks with scintillating scales the silver perch, whose transparent fins cutting the ripples of the placid lake reflect the gorgeous splendors of the king of day, nay even the glassy element in which they dwell when moved by breezy zephyrs, sends its chasing waves in graceful folds by God's own finger traced in parallel. By geometry He teaches the industrious bee to store its honey in prismatic cells, the wild geese to range their triangular passage from the south to north, the noble eagle to wheel and dart upon his prey and the wakesome lark, God's earliest worshipper, to hymn his matin song in spiral flight. By geometry He sank the foundations of the pyramidal mountains that uprear their solid bastions to the sky, on the summit of whose snow-clad peaks blaze sacrificial fires fed by His hand alone. And so around, above, beneath in earth, air and sea, all the manifold workings of His skillful hand go but to demonstrate to him who will pursue the attractive paths of this sublimest science that God geometrizes continually.

"Music is that elevated science that affects the passions through sound. Few have not felt its charms and acknowledged its expressions to be intelligible to the heart. It is a language of delightful sensations far more eloquent than words. It breathes into the ear the clearest intimations. It touches and gently agitates the agreeable and sublime passions. It wraps us in melancholy and elevates us in joy. It dissolves and it inflames. It melts us to tenderness and excites us to war. This science is truly congenial to the nature of man, for by its powerful charms his most discordant passions are quickly harmonized and brought into perfect unison. But it never sounds with such seraphic harmony as when employed in singing songs of gratitude to the Great Creator of the Universe.

"Astronomy is that sublime science that leads the contemplative mind to soar aloft and read the wisdom, strength and beauty of the Great Creator in the heavens. How nobly eloquent of the Deity is the celestial hemisphere spangled with the most magnificent heralds of His Infinite Glory. They speak to the whole universe, for there is no speech so barbarous but their language is understood, nor nation so distant, but their voices are heard among them. The heavens proclaim the glory of God and the firmament declareth the works of His hands. (Day unto day uttereth speech and night unto night showeth knowledge.) *Assisted by astronomy we ascertain the laws which govern the heavenly bodies and by which their movements are directed, investigate the power by which they circulate in their orbs, discover their size, determine their distance, explain their various phenomena and correct the fallacy of the senses by the light of truth."*

The seven-branched candlestick deserves a somewhat more lengthy notice than has usually been given it, especially as to its symbolism. The learned among the Jews probably looked upon it as being emblematical of the seven movable heavenly bodies that were visible to the naked eye and which had supplied names for the seven days in the week. However, our ancient brethren of the Middle Ages were accustomed to regard it as the symbol of the seven essential qualities necessary to sublime architecture. They held that for a building to be truly great and sublime it should be illuminated by seven symbolic lamps, all of which should shine from it as perpetually as did the shechinah from between the cherubim.

LAMP OF TRUTH—The first of these lamps was the Lamp of Truth. The edifice should first of all be genuine, just what it purports to be in all of its parts, no sham in the material, no slights in the workmanship, no elaborate front backed up by useless rubble, but the uncomely parts having the more abundant comeliness.

> In the elder days of Art
>   The Builders wrought with greatest care
> Each minute and unseen part,
>   For the gods see everywhere.

What seems to be gold should be gold and not tinsel. What purported to be cut stone should be cut stone and not moulded plaster of paris. What held out to be solid oak should be solid oak and not grained papier-mache. So in the building of character the sin and fault first to be avoided is hypocrisy. The neophyte should never lose sight of that narrow golden line of veracity which the very virtues and graces that lean upon it bend; that prudence and policy strive to conceal; that kindness and courtesy modify; that courage overshadows with its shield; that imagination covers with her wings and which even charity dims with her tears. Suppose you approach a noble castle which, in the distance, towers the very embodiment of strength and impregnability. You climb its difficult ramp, cower under its frowning battlements and tremblingly step through its lofty portal, to suddenly find yourself in the back yard. Could anything be more disgusting, or can anything detract more from the character of an acquaintance than to shortly find that he possesses nothing save the dignity of outward appearance? His accomplishments all trivial, his learning and ability shallowness personified, his morals weak and his sense of responsibility nonexistent. It has been said that truth is the first lesson taught in Masonry. So should it ever be, for there is no quality more necessary and none whose absence is more sorely felt.

LAMP OF POWER—The second lamp was the Lamp of Power.

The building should be strong and durable and of some considerable size. Size alone lends an important degree of sublimity. The building should be solidly founded on a commanding locality, where every mountain lends its shadow of strength, and its several proportions ought to be such as will successfully support it through centuries of time. So in the building of character natural force and ability count for much. The time and the place count for much more. The word "king" and the word "can" are synonymous. There should be the great mind to plan, the great ambition to desire, the great soul to patiently hope and the strong arm to execute. There is one reason why our ancient brethren insisted upon approximate physical perfection as a requisite for Masonry. They believed there should be the strong mind, well trained and in a healthy body. Men may be good and true and possess many virtues, but unless they have real ability, both mental and physical, they can never be reckoned great. How often we see people, well brought, with fairly good manner, but entirely devoid of character, no resistance to temptation and no ability to accomplish any real good thing, either for themselves or others. They may have a reasonably well-develop wish-bone, but no back-bone. The outer case of the watch may be bright, the movement well jeweled, but the main spring is lacking. Some of these men have sat, in a very dignified manner, on high judicial benches, and have even occupied royal thrones, but they never originated any motion within themselves. Someone else always carried them. One celebrated poet divided the people of the world into two great classes, the people who lift and the people who lean, and claimed that there was only one of the former to twenty of the latter:

There are two kinds of people on earth today,
Just two kinds of people, no more, I say,
Not the evil and just, for 'tis well understood
That the good are half bad and the bad are half good.

Not the humble and proud, for in life's little span
He who puts on vain airs is not reckoned a man.
Not the rich and the poor, for to count a man's wealth
You must first know the state of his conscience and health.

Not the happy and sad, for the swift fleeting years
Bring each man his laughter and each man his tears.
But the two kinds of people on earth that I mean
Are the people who lift and the people who lean.

Wherever you go you will find the world's masses
Are always divided in just these two classes,
And strangely enough you will find, too, I wean,
That there is only one lifter to twenty who lean.

On which side are you? Are you easing the load
Of the overtaxed lifters that toil down the road,
Or are you a leaner, who lets others bear
Your part of the labor, and worry, and care?'

LAMP OF LIFE—The third lamp is the Lamp of Life, as our ancient brethren called it. The building should exhibit the infinite and individual mind and soul of the man that built it. There is one very curious thing about those ancient cathedrals and palaces which adds greatly to their charm. They show the souls of even the humblest Masons that worked upon them. The Master gave his attention to the main plan and assigned the work which each artisan was expected to perform. Further than this he did not go. He did not attempt to place his own mind in the artisan's body and do his thinking for him. He would say to the young Fellowcraft: "Take that small window in yonder chapel and make it as beautiful as you can." The most celebrated artist in the world might compete for the design of the high altar, but his work would show no greater evidence of individual thought than did that of the students. Each had his own ideas of what was perfect and beautiful and each had his opportunity to express it, and the naked spirit of the Craftsman breathed in every rose he carved. The eyes of the beasts and the devils he drew were open and alert, and his angels smiled with real life' and animation. So in character the Lamp of Life stands for individuality and for energy, for fervency, for zeal and for vitality. It means passions, desires and appetites. It means tempted in all things like as we are. It means loves and hates, sympathies and abhorrences, and what is more than all the rest, it means heart and joy in the work itself.

I have heard that in Strasburg Cathedral there stands a tablet erected to the Magister Lapidarium, the translation of which reads as follows: "Erwin Von Steinbach, Grand Master of his Craft, and not him alone, for many generations labored with him, his sons and his sons' sons. Children who came to see these saints of stone, as out of the rocks they rose, grew old and died, and still the work went on, and on, and on, and is not yet completed. The Master wrought his great heart into those sculptured stones. He and his sons with him, as offerings unto God." His heart was in the work.

Once upon a time, back in the Middle Ages, Robert Bruce, King of Scotland, lay upon his dying bed. His old companions in arms gathered about his side, anxious to do something to bring peace to the troubled mind of their old commander. He made them promise that, when his soul should have finally departed from this wicked world, they would open his body, take out his heart and carry it and lay it to rest in the Holy Sepulchre at Jerusalem for whose possession in Christian hands they had so long fought together. During the Great Crusade which followed, when the Christian knights were storming the heights of Acre, the Scottish troops began to waver before the fierce onslaughts of the fiery hosts of Saladin. The Black Douglas is said to have seized the jeweled casket that contained their priceless treasure and hurled it into the very midst of the Saracen foe, crying, "Lead on, O Heart of Bruce, I follow thee." The recreant knights rallied to regain the casket and won a glorious victory. Their heart was in the work.

LAMP OF BEAUTY—The fourth lamp was the Lamp of Beauty. When our ancient masters began to plan for a great and sublime building, they sought out the most perfect and beautiful material and exerted upon it the most accurate and careful workmanship, copying everything that seemed beautiful in nature to adorn the edifice. King David collected for the temple at Jerusalem large quantities of gold and silver and jewels and precious stones and white fine twined linen, and contracted for timber of rare woods and great stones from approved quarries, and Solomon employed a master workman of the most celebrated skill to design the temple and its ornaments. So in the building of character the Lamp of Beauty stands for accomplishments for learning, for skill in art, in poetry, in song and in instrumental music, in painting and in sculpture. It stands for the art of making one's self attractive to those about one. It is an old saying that handsome is as handsome does. It causes as great distress to see these noble graces of character prostituted to ignoble ends as to see Lincoln Cathedral turned into a stable for Cromwell's horses. It is the same as giving that which is holy unto dogs, or casting pearls before swine.

LAMP OF OBEDIENCE—The fifth lamp is the Lamp of Obedience. All great works obey the laws of their being. The tides follow the moon. The earth moves steadily in her path around the sun. The solar system takes the same mathematical journey through the universe. God's laws are invariable and unchangeable, because they are good and perfect as they are, and the more humanity understands them and works in accordance with them, the greater is the sum of human happiness. Great architecture follows the laws of its style in strict conformity to symmetry and order. Obedience in character means orderliness, the subjection to moral principle, the fear to do wrong, the desire to learn the right and to do the right. Many men would rather give charity than do justice. They swell with emotion, weep with sentiment, howl with the mob so long as their own particular little tyranny or injustice is not touched. The Lamp of Obedience also stands for firm will and determination of character, in spite of difficulties and dangers and losses.

> One ship dives east and another dives west,
> With the self-same winds that blow;
> It is the set of the sails and not the gales
> That determines the way it shall go.
>
> Like the ways of the sea are the ways of fate,
> As we voyage along through life;
> It is the set of the soul that determines the goal,
> And not the calm or the strife.

So the Lamp of Obedience stands for self-control, for perseverance and for prudence; in times of peace to prepare for war; when shines the sun to expect the cloud, and in darkness to wait patiently for the coming light. When all the sky is draped in black and beaten by tempestuous gales and the shuddering ship seems all awreck, to calmly trim once more the tattered sails, repair the broken rudder and set again for the old determined course as true as the needle to the pole. He that ruleth himself is greater than he that taketh a city.

LAMP OF SACRIFICE—The sixth lamp is the Lamp of Sacrifice. Every great work in Masonry or any other profession or occupation costs something. Were those vast cathedrals of the Middle Ages, immense in size, covering acres of ground, built of flawless marble, wrought and sculptured on every square inch, from turret to foundation stone, and garnished with gold and crystal, erected without sacrifice? No. They cost labor and blood and tears and starvation and the most strenuous self-denial. For seven years? For seventy times seven, but, finished, they have been the joy and pride and inspiration to untold millions for forty generations. So the greatness in human character is made perfect through suffering. Who will tell of the wearying toil, of the heart-breaking losses, the pangs of ingratitude and disprized love that leave their chisel marks on the character of him who seeks successfully the Higher Light? The Seer of the Apocalypse beheld a happy throng, clad in shining garments, with crowns upon their heads and standing near the throne of God, and asked, "Who are these in bright array?" The voice answered, "These are they who have passed through fiery trials and much tribulation. They have trodden the wine press of great affliction. They endured cruel mockings and scourgings, bonds and imprisonment. They felt the violence of the flame and the edge of the sword. They were stoned and sawn asunder and tempted and slain. They wandered about in sheep skins and in goat skins, destitute, hated and tormented. They dwelt in deserts and in mountains, in dens and caves of the earth, of whom the world was not worthy. But they held faithful, even unto death, as seeing Him, who is invisible. Time was when all forsook them, save the Son of God, who walked with them in the midst of the furnace, but they have washed their garments white. The pure gold of character came up bright out of the assay. And in the strength of it they subdued kingdoms, wrought righteousness, stopped the mouths of lions, quenched the violence of the fire, escaped the edge of the sword and out of weakness were made strong."

LAMP OF MEMORY—The seventh and last lamp on the candelabrum is the Lamp of Memory. The great achievement in architecture, when it was finished, was dedicated to someone or to some purpose worthy of the skill and treasure that had been sacrificed upon it. So the great character should have some great object. The neophyte's endeavor should be to do something, and in doing, to be something. The object must be worth the struggle and it must be unselfish. "Though I sell all my goods to feed the poor, and though I give my body to be burned and have not charity in my heart, I am still but sounding brass and tinkling cymbal." The struggle for higher Light is that men may see by it, and in seeing work by it and live in it. Of the building thus illuminated by these seven lamps, you may say, "They shall perish, but thou remainest," and of character thus illuminated and wrought out you may add, "They shall wax old as doth a garment, and as a vesture shall they be folded up, but Thou art the same, yesterday, today and forever."

At the next stage is introduced an emblem taken from the 12th Chapter of Judges. In the Hebrew language it happens that two words have the same spelling and pronunciation. One is the word meaning "An ear of corn," what we would call a "wheat head," and the other word means "a water fall" or a "small cataract." The tri-literal root is "Sh-B-L" and means "plenty" or "to flow copiously." The force of the emblem lies in the play on words and the differences in pronunciation of the same word in different localities. It is said that in the old days in "Bleeding Kansas" the adherents of John Brown, in order to protect their territory from emigrants coming across the Kaw river from the slave-holding state of Missouri, tied a cow to a tree near the bank of the river at one of the main crossings, and kept her so short of food that any stranger coming across the river was also certain to ask questions regarding her continual bellowing. Their manner of pronouncing the word "cow" showed at once whether they came from the South or the North, and at the same time decided the sort of welcome they were about to receive from the adherents of old "Ossawatomie."

We come now to the explanation of the symbolic significance of the letter "G"—and here we will introduce the substance of an article which appeared in the American Freemason, published by Brother Joseph E. Morcomb, at Storm Lake, Iowa, for the month of February, 1816. The article was written by the Honorable Brother Sir John Cockburn, of England, and is entitled "The Sacred Symbol":

Without symbolism Masonry would lose its distinctive character, and without an interpretation of these symbols the peculiar system of morality veiled therein would be as unprofitable as a hidden treasure. As a rule when a symbol is mentioned in the ritual some explanation is given which proves its fitness to express the underlying idea. But to this rule a striking exception is presented by the most revered and prominent of all our symbols. In the ritual we are told that the letter "G" denoted "God," but not a word is vouchsafed as to the manner in which it fulfills its object. There is no reason why this particular letter of the alphabet should have been promoted to such dignity, nor in what way it illustrates any of the attributes of Deity. Masonic authorities used formerly to maintain that it was selected because it was the initial of the word "God", but this explanation will not bear examination. Masonry was, at any rate until recently, supposed to be universal. It is still to some extent international, while the initial of the name of Deity varies in different languages. In view of this objection more recent writers have held that the letter "G" is called "the sacred symbol," because it resembles in form the Hebrew letter "Jod" or "Yod" or "Iod", the "I", "J" or "Y", the initial of the "Ineffable Name", which we spell "Jehovah" and by which the Most High is known throughout Jewry and Christendom. But admitting that this explanation satisfies the international requirement there still remains the objection that it needs much ingenuity to trace any resemblance between "Jod" and "G". Even if they were almost identical it is inconceivable that, in a system so rich as is Masonry in beautiful and significant symbolism, the device which occupies the highest place should be merely the substitute of a substitute. Moreover, an initial cannot be said to be a symbol at all. It is more an abbreviation which pertains more to short-hand than to geometry.

It is derogatory to the intelligence of our Masonic forefathers that we should think them capable of paying the utmost reverence to a form that bears a false designation. Surely, unless we abandon the attempt to solve the mystery, we should not rest content until we find a solution compatible with the principles of Masonic that is of geometric representation. Some high authorities, in despair of a satisfactory interpretation, have gone so far as to express regret that the unaccountable character was introduced into Masonry and have even wished its deletion. Fortunately the sacrifice is impossible. The letter "G" is too deeply ingrained in Masonry. It occupies a conspicuous place in every lodge and figures alike on clothing and jewelry. It could not be removed without defacing the whole fabric. How poor would be the world if everything beyond our comprehension was destroyed. The easily discovered is not always the most valuable. "For straws upon the ocean float, who seeks for pearls must dive below." So time-honored a feature in Masonry is well worthy of further investigation. Nor will the quest be found hopeless if we start from the beginning and follow clues.

In the second tracing board we are told that certain Hebrew characters, in the Middle Chamber, are depicted by the letter "G" and that it denotes "God". Those characters are the four Hebrew letters read from right to left, "He, Vau, He, Jod", which spell the unutterable Name known to us as "Jehovah". In almost every language, ancient and modern, the name of Deity is composed of four letters, for four has always been regarded as the number of perfection. The sacred symbol is therefore evidently meant to represent the quadrilateral or four-fold name of Deity, called the Tetragammaton for reasons that originally led the Pythagoreans to revere the idea of four under the name of the Tetraktys. So far the coast is clear and without dispute. Now, geometrical representation is the essence of Masonry, and if it can be shown that the sacred symbol geometrically represents the idea of four, the reason for it being regarded with reverence becomes apparent and the problem is solved. But here we encounter the point of difficulty. Between the idea of four and the letter which figures as "G" in our language there is no correspondence. Indeed, there is no letter more devoid of any geometrical form or significance and its presence among geometrical symbols seems anomalous. For the emblems of Masonry are either geometrical or symmetrical, while the ungainly club-footed "G" is markedly deficient in both qualities. It has all the appearance of an intruder among Masonic forms. A glance at the history of the alphabet proves that this must have been the case, for the philosophical system now known as Freemasonry was old before the Roman letter "G" was invented, succeeding the Greek "gamma". Long before the Roman alphabet had traveled beyond the confines of Italy that of Greece had penetrated into many parts of Gaul. The Greek rather than the Roman alphabet was the parent of the letters with which the Anglo-Saxon Masons, working on ecclesiastical structures, were likely to be acquainted. The translation of the volume of the Sacred Law by Ulphilas, the apostle of Christianity to the Gothic race, is the oldest extant monument of the Teutonic languages. This is written in what is known as the Moeso Gothic Script, in which the letter "G" has the shape of the original Greek letter "gamma". This is also the case in the translation of the Sacred Book by Cyril and the Cyeretic or ecclesiastic Slovanic Script is one of the three dominant alphabets of the world. Both the Cyeretic and the Moeso Gothic were missionary alphabets and their influence would, therefore, be far-reaching.

Light now breaks through the obscurity of our problem. When we consider the shape of the letter "G" in these widespread European alphabets there seems no longer any reason to doubt that the sacred symbol is what has happily been called the Greek symbol itself, and the letter "G" was none other than "gamma", the true Masonic Square. The former posture of the square, when worn as a Past Master's jewel, coincides with this view, for it used to be suspended with the short arm horizontal and uppermost. In this attitude it is known as the "gallows square," which is precisely the "gamma". The modern method of suspension, by the right angle, was probably in imitation of the diagram in Euclid's Forty-seventh Problem, under the erroneous impression that this was the method employed by the ancients to prove that in a right-angled triangle the square of the hypotenuse is equal to the sum of the squares of the sides containing the right angle.

Let us now subject the "gamma" to the test with which the substitute "G" did not comply, and inquire whether it can be said, geometrically, to represent the idea of four conveyed by the Hebrew characters of the Tetragammaton. How different is the result. The "gamma" exactly meets the case. The right angle at once suggests and represents the four-sided figure, indeed, the word "square" is indifferently used for either. The cathedral builders, even if illiterate, would be struck with the identity in texts and inscriptions between the square letter and the symbol which was familiar to them in the lodge. It was therefore but natural that they should adopt the name of the letter as a gloss for the symbol which was regarded as both sacred and secret. It not only represented the Ineffable Name, but was also the square which was the key to their mysteries. For it must be borne in mind that the properties of the square, perfect in any desired position, were the practical secrets of a Mason's profession. The square letter was therefore used as a cover to denote and at the same time to conceal that which it was not desirable to mention by the proper name. The practice of substitution would naturally persist, in spite of the change in the name of the letter from "gamma" in Greek to "gebo" in the Mediæval Script, and finally to the letter "G". The fact that the older rituals relate that the Hebrew letters are depicted by the character "G" appears to indicate that this was not always the designation of the symbol. The resemblance of the "gamma" to the square is so close as almost to amount to identity. The swastika, which is composed of four conjoined squares, is often called the "gammedion" and sometimes the "tetragammaton", thus closely approximating in pronunciation to the "tetragrammaton", which is only another spelling of the same word due to handing the word down orally and for which the swastika was frequently used as a symbol. This is all the more probable, as the Deity was sometimes alluded to as the "Square".

Further evidence of the identity of the letter "G" with the square may be found in its association with the Second Degree. "Why were you made a Fellowcraft?" was one of the questions in the old lectures. To which the answer was given, "For the sake of the letter 'G'." The very essence of the degree is the square. Craftsmen will call to mind on what the lodge is closed and on what a candidate is received, by what a Fellowcraft is tried and how the square is applied during the obligation. The significance of the attitude of his arm is disclosed by the statement that it was in such an attitude that he discovered the sacred symbol.

In one account of the exhumation of the body of the slain Grand Master it is said that a slight resemblance of the letter "G" marked on his left breast was discovered. That which is otherwise obscure and meaningless becomes luminous at once, if the letter is regarded as a square. It thus touchingly relates how, even in death, the secret repository retained the impression of the instrument that was once applied, so lately worn and of the four-fold sign. The foregoing considerations appear to prove conclusively the identity of the sacred symbol with the square, and reveal the beautiful and appropriate chain of symbolism by which the letter "G" came to represent the four-fold essence of the God-head and the four Hebrew characters, to which the attention of our ancient brethren was particularly directed.

THE ADVANTAGES OF GEOMETRY—"*Geometry, the first and noblest of sciences, is the basis on which the superstructure of Freemasonry is erected. By geometry we may curiously trace Nature through her various windings to her most concealed recesses. By it we discover the wisdom, power and goodness of the Grand Artificer of the Universe and view with delight the proportions which connect the vast machine. By it we discover how the planets move in their respective orbits and demonstrate their various revolutions. By it we account for the return of the seasons and variety of scenes which each season displays to the discerning eye. Numberless worlds are around us, all framed by the same Divine Artist and roll through the vast expanse, all guided by the same unerring law of Nature. A*

survey of Nature and the observation of her beautiful propor-
tions first determined man to imitate the Divine plan and study
symmetry and order. This gave rise to societies and birth to
every useful art. The architect began to design and the plans
laid down by him, being improved by time and experience, have
produced works that have been the admiration of every age.
The lapse of time, the ruthless hand of ignorance and the de-
vastations of war have laid waste and destroyed many valuable
monuments of antiquity upon which the utmost exertion of
human genius have been employed. Even the Temple of Solo-
mon, so spacious and magnificent and erected by so many cele-
brated artists, has not escaped the unsparing ravages of bar-
barous force. Freemasonry, notwithstanding, still survives.
The attentive ear still receives the sound from the instructive
tongue and the mysteries of Freemasonry are safely lodged
within the repository of the faithful breast. Tools and im-
plements of architecture and symbolic emblems most expressive
have been selected by the fraternity to imprint upon the mind
wise and serious truths, and thus through a succession of ages
are transmitted unimpaired the most excellent tenets of our
Institution."

The following interesting similitude was arranged from some
of the writings of Longfellow, and seems applicable in illustration of the search for Divinity in Nature: "It was a saying
of the ancient Persian, Magi, that the whole world seeketh after
God. That the rivers leap from the mountains and hurry
through all the lands, seeking God in the earth. The vast
Atlantic sends its chasing billows from east to west, from north
to south, deep calling unto deep, seeking God in the caverns of
the sea. The fire, when it is kindled, looks no more upon the
ground, but mounts upward seeking God in the sky. The four
winds hasten from valley to valley and from cliff to cliff, now
stealing softly in a gentle zephyr that scarce moves the aspen's
leaf, now rushing in a mighty tornado that rends the oak
from its strongest foundations, seeking God in the deserts of the
air. The old earth, herself, lifts up the solid bastions of her
hills, whose snow-clad summits far above the clouds peer ever
outward and beyond to see if the Judge of the World comes not.
And so all Nature stands waiting and hoping and yearning
for the unknown God. Whenever the lonely eagle, far up amid
the mists of heaven, looks out through the gray dawn to behold
the coming day; whenever the brooding raven by the mountain

torrent harkens for the footfall of the deer returning from his nightly pasture; whenever the uprising sun calls out the spicy odors of a thousand flowers, then all Nature wakes in expectation and longing for a revelation of God's Majesty. She wakes again, when in the fullness of peace field and forest rest at noon, and through the stillness naught is heard save the whirr of the grasshopper and the hum of the bee, and again at evening when the soaring lark rises up from the sweet-smelling vineyards and Orion puts on his shining armor and marches forth in the fields of heaven. And through all this beautiful and wonderful creation eager, striving life manifests itself in a never-ceasing search, by day and by night, forever surging to and fro. Swifter than a weaver's shuttle it flies from birth to death, from death to birth. From the beginning it seeks the end, but finds it not, for the end is only a dim beginning of a new outgoing and endeavor to find the end. The ice upon the mountain, in the warmth of the summer's breath, melts and divides into drops, each reflecting an image of the sun, so life, which is one and universal in the smile of God's love, divides itself into innumerable forms, each retaining in it and reflecting an image of Him. Into this vast Cathedral of Nature, filled with its sacred scriptures and symbols of deep mysterious meaning, comes the human soul, also seeking its Creator. And here for the first time is this universal longing realized and becomes a certainty, for here in the human soul alone is that image and God-likeness, strongest and most perfect. Here in the human soul alone may the Glory of God made manifest shine on and on and meet its own reflection, clear, steady and firm standing. So at times it is given unto the soul of man the privilege to stand, as it were, on the boundary line between two worlds, his body in the one while his soul is gazing far into the other. From this station he may trace his pathway upward over the manifold landscape of the past and the perishable, while he beholds just beyond the veil the ineffable beauties of the enduring and the true."

The following was taken from Ruskin's description of St. Mark's Cathedral, at Venice: "To our ancient brethren, whether doing well or doing ill, God and Christ were an awful reality, and they wrought as being continually under the scrutiny of an All-seeing Eye and directly inspired by the Holy Ghost. To them a cathedral or a temple was far more than a mere meeting house or place of worship. It was the dwelling place of the Living God, who in the shape of the Incarnate Eucharist rested as perpetually upon the altar as did the Shechinah of old upon the Ark of the Covenant, and the structure itself was not only a symbol of the Bride of Christ, all glorious within and her clothing of wrought gold, but it was the actual Tables of the Law and Testimony, written within and without, and whether it was revered as the Church or as the Bible, it was fitting that neither gold nor crystal be spared in the adornment of it. That as a symbol of the Bride the building of the walls should be of jasper and its foundations garnished with all manner of precious stones, and that as the symbol of the Law its painting and its sculpture should proclaim to the remotest generations the ways of God to men, so that above the crowd, swaying forever to and fro in the restlessness of avarice and the thirst for delight, there might be seen perpetually the glory of that Temple, attesting to them—whether they would hear or whether they would forbear—that there was one treasure that the merchant might buy without price, and that the poorest beggar might enjoy equally with the princes of the earth, and that there was one delight greater than all others in the Word and the Statutes of God. It was not in mere wantonness of wealth, nor in vain ministry to the desire of the eyes, nor yet in pride of skill, that these marbles were hewn into transparent strength and these arches tinted with the colors of the iris, the lily and the rose. There was a story written in the dyes of them, a story that was once written in blood, and a song echoed from their vaults that should one day echo from the vaults of Heaven, that as God the Christ had once dwelt upon the earth, so there He should one day return to do justice and render judgment in the world. For this their skill and treasure gilded every letter and illumined every page, until these Temple Books shine afar off, even unto our day, like the blazing star of the Magi."

CHARGE TO CANDIDATE—*"Brother, being advanced to the Second Degree of Freemasonry, we congratulate you on your preferment. The internal and not the external qualifications of a man are what Freemasonry regards. As you increase in knowledge you will improve in social intercourse. It is unnecessary to recapitulate the duties which as a Freemason you are bound to discharge, or to enlarge upon the necessity of a strict adherence to them, as your own experience must have established their value. Our laws and regulations you are strenuously to support and be ready at all times to assist in seeing them duly executed. You are not to palliate or aggravate the offenses of your brethren, but in the decision of every trespass against our laws you are to judge with candor, admonish with friendship and reprehend with justice. The study of the Liberal Arts, that valuable branch of education which tends so effectually to polish and adorn the mind, is earnestly recommended to your consideration, especially the science of geometry, which is established as the basis of our art. Geometry or Masonry, originally synonymous terms, being of a divine and moral nature is enriched with the most useful knowledge, and while it proves the wonderful properities of Nature, it demonstrates the more important truths of morality. Your past behavior and regular deportment have merited the honor which we have conferred and in your new character it is expected that you will continue to conform to the principles of our Order by steadily persevering in the practice of every commendable virtue. Such is the nature of your duty as a Fellowcraft and to these engagements you are bound by the most sacred ties."*

LECTURE XVI

THE DEGREE OF MASTER MASON

OUR brethren have named this the Sublime Degree of Master Mason. For here is set forth the Great Allegory which lies at the foundation of our Order and which distinguishes it and sets it apart from all other institutions. This is the one and only true Landmark of Freemasonry and without which Freemasonry could not be. It is on this degree that the Grand Lodge meets and all business in any lodge is transacted. Higher degrees there are none. Elaborations there may be of the Legend and the Allegory. Orders with other objects in view may be associated with it, but the real object of Freemasonry is to build character and to teach immortality, and it is here in this Master Mason's lodge that this teaching begins.

This is the only portion of Masonic work which is really aged, that goes back to the skin tents and wattled huts and rock caverns of primitive man. For it was there that the Great Question was first asked, the first conscious question after mere animal wants are satisfied—"If a man die, shall he live again?" was what he asked.

This was the soul and essence of the ceremony of the Men's House. This was the soul and essence of the Ancient Mysteries of Egypt, of Assyria, of India, of China, of Greece, of Rome, of the Druids of Britain, aye! of Mexico and Peru. It is the question of questions asked by all the world. Some men are sufficiently stoical as to seem to have no care for themselves, but when they come to see the earth sift down over the loved and the lost they begin to feel the agony of the ages—"Lo, all the days of my life must I wait, until *my* change comes." Has any man a soul capable of enduring? Is it possible that mentality is only a function of the material brain? Is a universal hope any evidence of reality? Is the wish but the father of the belief? Only faith gives an answer.

> Alas for him who never sees
> The stars shine through his cypress trees,
> Who hopeless lays his dead away
> Nor looks to see the breaking day
> Across the mournful marbles play,

Who has not learned in hours of Faith,
That truth, to flesh and sense unknown,
That Life was ever Lord of Death,
And Love can never lose its own.

The one great analogy on which all tribes and kindreds have built their hope is the phenomena of spring. Henry Ward Beecher once said, "Who can see the leaves fade and come again, fade and come again, year after year, and not learn a lesson of the resurrection?" As the sun sinks in the winter zodiac, death comes to vegetation. The shroud of snow covers its seered remains. The cold winds sing sad requiems over their decay. Yet spring comes, its warm zephyrs play among the dry branches, the sap starts and it buds forth again, and in the place of death is life, beauty and joy. To bring this fact home to every soul with its sermon of triumph has been the mission of the Great Drama of Faith.

The first section of this degree differs from the others which have preceded it, only in such ways as may mark out and distinguish the additional step in Freemasonry. The Scripture readings are taken from the twelfth chapter of Ecclesiastes.

"Remember now thy Creator in the days of thy youth, when the evil days come not, nor the years draw nigh, when thou shalt say, 'I have no pleasure in them.' When the light of the sun and the moon and the stars be not darkened, nor the clouds return after the rain. In the day when the keepers of the house shall tremble and strong men shall bow themselves and the grinders cease because they are few and they that look out of the windows be darkened. And the doors shall be shut in the streets, when the sound of the grinding is low, and he shall rise up at the voice of the bird and all the daughters of music shall be brought low. And he shall be afraid of that which is high and fears shall be in the way and the almond-tree shall flourish and the grasshopper shall be a burden and desire shall fail, because man goeth to his long home and the mourners go about the streets. Or ever the silver cord be loosed or the golden bowl be broken or the pitcher be broken at the fountain or the wheel broken at the cistern. Then shall the dust return to the earth as it was, but the spirit shall return unto God who gave it."

The working tools are all the implements of Freemasonry indiscriminately, but especially the trowel. The trowel is an instrument used by operative Masons to spread the cement that unites a building into one common mass. But we as Free and Accepted Masons are taught to use ours for the more noble and glorious purpose of spreading the cement of brotherly love and affection, that cement which unites us into one sacred band or society of friends and brothers, among whom no contention should ever exist, save that noble contention, or rather emulation, of he who best can work and best agree.

A personage is mentioned in this first section who, from a philological and symbolic point of view, is of some considerable importance in the philosophy of Freemasonry. The traditions associated with this man connect him to some degree, especially as to his occupation, with the hero of the legend of the second section of the degree. In Genesis IV-19th, we read the following passage:

"And Lamech took unto him two wives. The name of one was Adah and the name of the other was Zillah, and Adah bare Jabel. He was the father of such as dwell in tents and of such as have cattle. And his brother's name was Jubal. He was the father of such as handle the harp and organ. And Zillah, she also bare Tubal Cain, an instructor of every artificer in brass and iron, and the sister of Tubal Cain was Naamah."

The ancient manuscripts containing this legend, as connected with Freemasonry, say that this daughter of Lamech was the contriver of the art of weaving and embroidery and that from these four people originated all the science and art of the world. Scholars tell us that the word here translated "instructor" would better be translated "sharpener of tools". The Vulcan of the ancient Semitic mythology was "Bil-Can" or "Baal-Cain". The "Tu" is to be considered only as being the definite article of the Hebrew language, signifying "the", so that the name "Tubal Cain" simply means "The-Tool-Sharpener-of Baal". The words "Baal", "Bell", "Bal" are forms of the word "Bar-Ilu", meaning "Son of Ilu". The words "Ilu", "Al", "El", "Allah" enter into many Hebrew and Babylonish names of men and places. The name of the Deity used in the first verse of Genesis as being the Creator of Heaven and Earth is "ALHIM" or "ELOHIM", which is the plural form of "El" or "Al". It is translated "God" or "The Lord". So that the word "Baal" is equivalent to "Son of God".

The very fact of the father of musicians and the father of tool sharpeners being brothers of the same family reminds us of the same association of Apollo and Vulcan of the Greek mythology. The names "Vulcan" and "Baal-Can" are similar in sound, but the laws of philology fail to connect them, as the Indo-European origin of Vulcan is evidently from "ulga", a fire-brand, and should be associated with "fulmen" and "fulgar", which refers it to lightning and thunder bolts, which Vulcan forged for Jupiter. It is, however, a fact that in connection with names having a cabalistic and cosmic application as these names evidently do have, similarity in sound is fully as much to be relied upon as the so-called laws of philology. The latter is a very late science, while Caballah is a very old one, and in studying Caballah we find the similarity of sound had more to do with the permeation of numerical values through the different languages of the scientifically learned peoples of the world than the laws of philology.

The real object of the Ancient Mysteries was the preservation and inculcation of such scientific knowledge of astronomy and geometry as then existed. This scientific knowledge was common to the learned peoples of all the prominent nations of the world. To keep this knowledge a secret from the common people, and at the same time preserve it and transmit it to succeeding generations, was the object of the Caballah, so we find the same words, or words of as near the same sound and meaning as could be found in the different languages used as carriers of the number philosophy. The idea of the tool sharpener is a very close one to Freemasonry, as a tool sharpener must be a 'very important personage in the eyes of a stone cutter.

Many of our readers will find themselves in remembrance of a certain steel engraving representing a blacksmith sitting on the throne of King Solomon and claiming credit for the building of the Temple, because without him and his trade to sharpen the tools not a single stone could have been fitted for its place in the edifice. In the folk-lore of Britain there is a legend of a secret blacksmith whose anvil and forge are concealed underground. His name is Vollund or Wolland or Wayland. This name can very easily be traced to the Vulcan of the Greeks and Romans. I suppose the number of Wayland Smiths in every city directory would be able to convince any antiquarian that there was some ancient, natural connection or appropriateness between the name "Wayland" and the occupation of a "Smith". Read, for instance, the novel of "Kenilworth", written by Sir Walter Scott. You will there find the old tradition brought down to the time of that romance almost exactly as it exists in myth and legend. The curious workman dwells secretly in the forest and, though apparently friendly to men, he is never seen by them. If any man desires his horse shod he brings the animal and ties him to a certain tree in the forest, places his money on a certain rock, shouts his desire and goes away. When he returns after the usual time he finds his horse shod and the money gone. If he desires a specially good suit of armor or a better sword than can be purchased in the local store, he brings the money and the order and places them on the rock, and in due time he returns to find the articles, whatever they were, completed. The Wayland Smith spoken of in the story of Kenilworth had his forge hidden in a cavern among the rocks, where he could easily hear the conversation of the parties who brought the work, whoever they were. The Masons of the Middle Ages may have gone occasionally to such a person to have their tools sharpened, or, at least, they were sufficiently acquainted with the legend of Vulcan to mention him in their rituals. The connection of Tu-Bal-Cain with modern speculative Masonry was derived from the Ancient Legend of the Craft, which was transmitted to us along with the Ancient Charges and appears in all the old manuscripts.

LECTURE XVII
THE DRAMA OF FAITH

IN the Second Book of Chronicles, XIth chapter and 7th verse, in a letter written by Solomon, King of Israel, to his friend Hiram, King of Tyre, we read the following: "Send me, therefore, a man cunning to work in gold, in silver, in brass and iron, in purple, in scarlet, in blue and in white, fine twined linen, and that can skill to grave with the cunning men that are with me in Jerusalem, whom David my father did provide."

Hiram, King of Tyre, replied to this letter in the following strain, as appears in the 13th verse of the same chapter: "And now I have sent a cunning man endowed with understanding of *Hiram my father*, the son of a woman of the daughters of Dan, and his father was a man of Tyre, skillful to work in gold and silver and in brass and iron, in stone and in timber and in purple and in blue, and in fine linen and in crimson, also to grave any manner of graving, and to find out any device that shall be put to him with thy cunning men and with the cunning men of David, thy father." And in the 11th verse of the 4th chapter of the same book we find a list of the various articles which the aforesaid Hiram made for King Solomon. This bit of Biblical history is a late account taken, most likely, after the return of the Jews from Babylonish captivity, from an earlier account in the 1st Book of Kings, VIth chapter and 13th verse: "And King Solomon sent and fetched Hiram out of Tyre. He was a widow's son of the tribe of Naphtali and his father was a man of Tyre, a worker in brass, and he was filled with wisdom and understanding and cunning to work in all the works of brass, and he came to King Solomon and wrought all his work." Here follows a complete enumeration and description of all the articles that Hiram made, ending in the 45th verse, where it says: "And all these things which Hiram made to King Solomon for the House of the Lord were of bright brass. In the plains of Jordan did the king cast them, in the clay ground between Succoth and Zarthan." It says in Chronicles, written about two hundred years later, that all these vessels were of pure gold. This simply indicates that the ideas of the Jewish writers grew, as they contemplated the vanished glories of Israel, which they themselves had never seen.

The words of the English version, *"of Hiram my father,"* have been translated by Martin Luther in the German version, "Hiram Abiff," as they appear in the Hebrew of Luther's time and as they have always been used in our ritual. That is, employing the word "abiff" as a sort of family or surname. This word "abiff" is equivalent to our word "father" used in the genitive or possessive case as employed in our English version, but it means several other things, especially "master" or "superintendent". This has been, until lately, a very satisfactory interpretation for Masons, as he has always been known as "Grand Master Hiram", reading the Biblical passage, *"I send you Hiram, my master workman,"* using the term "abiff" in its adjective sense, though still employing it as a surname. Recent students have come to believe, however, that the correct form of the Hebrew text is not obtained in this instance without the aid of Caballah, or rather that form of Caballah that is known as "Gematria"; that there has here been a play upon words made for the purpose of concealing the real name, which should have been read "Abib", which is the name of a certain month in which occurs the spring equinox and also the name of a certain brilliant star which appears, at that time in the constellation of the Virgin, right in the middle of the shibboleth or wheat sheaf, which she holds in her hand in all the ancient pictorial maps of the heavens. The name of this month was eventually changed, but it was employed at the time the account was originally written down and becomes of the greatest importance in relation to the adventures which happen to the man in our own particular version of his life and death in Freemasonry.

Literally considered the discrepancy regarding his parentage is of no great importance, as the tribes of Dan and Naphtali were situated very close together and the name "Dan" is also the name of a city, so that any man may have been a son of a woman of the daughters of "Dan", a city, and still be a widow of the tribe of Naphtali at the same time. The two tribes are situated in the extreme northern portion of Palestine on the borders of Phœnicia, the capital city of which was Tyre. This city was situated on an island, a little way out from the main land, for the purpose of better fortification and for the sake of better harbor facilities, as Tyre was a great maritime nation.

Bro. Robert Morris, a Past Grand Lecturer of the Order in this country, visited the Holy Land with a view to picking up all the information possible regarding places and persons mentioned in the ritual of Freemasonry. He furnishes us with a very good picture of the reputed tomb of Hiram, King of Tyre. This ancient piece of Masonry is all that remains in the material world of the great Masonic Trio, whose coalition was the means of erecting the edifice known to us as the Temple of Solomon. Whether the temple builder was old or young, rich or poor, married or single, good or bad in moral character, the Bible does not tell us, though it declares in favor of his skill and cunning and that he could find out any device that might be put up to him. It would appear that above all else he was a cunning jeweler or metal worker, a decorator of somewhat varied qualifications, scarcely more versatile than we know Michael Angelo and Benvenuto Celinni to have been. They were great designers and knew well how to direct others in the carrying out of their more elaborate schemes of decoration. The decoration of the Temple of Solomon must have been limited to some extent by the Jewish law as to the making of any graven image of anything in the likeness of anything in the heavens above or in the earth beneath or in the waters under the earth, which passage, it has been assumed, the Jews took literally. So literally that in modern times Jews have claimed that it was a violation of their law to make any drawing or model of anything at all from nature, and so they invented what is today known as arabesque decoration, which certainly could not be accused of imitating anything. Even the celebrated Cherubim were combinations of four animals, a lion, an ox, a man and an eagle. The lily-work and the pomegranates were doubtless also very conventional in form. We may imagine what we please and draw as good a mental picture as we may from the Biblical description of the temple and its decorations, but all that we know of Hiram Abiff or of the temple, or of anyone connected with its erection, is now written.

The trouble is that this legend resembles what Voltaire said regarding the Babylonish philosopher Zadig: "His name does not appear on any of the tablets of cuneiform writing which have been deciphered up to this date, but what we need from a lamp is that it gives light and shows us the way." It makes no difference whether it is a mere tallow dip, an electric arc or acetylene blow pipe. So it makes no difference to Freemasonry whether the builder, Hiram Abiff, actually lived and passed through the adventures and experiences attributed to him or not. We are not at all certain, but it might embarrass Masonic

philosophers considerably if we should discover a contemporaneous sketch of his life, such as might have accompanied the account of his death in a Jerusalem daily of Dec. 22, A. L. 3000.
Masons do not deal with an historical matter in this instance, but
with a solar myth or allegory, and we know Grand Master Hiram
in the same sense that the readers of Bunyon's Pilgrim's Progress
come to know Great-heart, Miss Much-afraid and the Giant
Despair.

As we have previously remarked, we do not know whether
this legend or how much of it was included in the esoteric work
of the Order at the time of the reorganization of Masonry in
1717, but it seems pretty well conceded by historians that
the dramatization of the legend was first attempted by Dr.
Theophilus Desaguliers about the year 1723. In his version it
seems to have about all the elements of the great solar myth,
as adapted to the purpose of teaching the lesson of immortality
for humanity.

The primitive philosophy or view of Cosmos in which the
solar myth forms the leading or central principle, and which
in some form has dominated thought all down through the ages,
seems to possess, in brief, the following characteristics: In the
beginning God was pure spirit, eternal, immortal, invisible,
unmanifested. In Him was contained all that ever was, is or
shall be. What we know as matter was only a manifestation
of this same spirit. To the Hindus this spirit was "Brahma."
To the Hebrews it was known as the "Ain-Soph." The symbol
by which this was illustrated was that of the "mundane egg",
showing the usual amount of yolk and white. In the yolk a germ
appears which separates the yolk into two equal parts, the one
black and the other white; the one possessing the male and the
other the female principle; the latter the earth and the former
the heavens. This separation was allegorized or symbolized by
the separation of Eve from Adam by drawing a rib from out
of his side. The principal modern symbol is the crescent and
star of the Mystic Shrine. The star stands for the entire
heavens and the sun in particular, and the crescent represents
the rib, which eventually became Eve. We might say that the
same idea is allegorized in the eclipse as the moon's shadow re-
appears from behind the solar disk.

In the Bible story it is represented in the labors of the first
day, where He separated the light from the darkness and day
from night. The old Hebrew zohar or mystery of that nation

represents man and woman as having been created as a single individual with a double body united face to face ("Male and Female created He him") and that God afterwards separated them. It is believed by symbolists that the account refers to the creation of heaven and earth out of chaos, and the creation of the male and female principles in nature. The idea of a firmament was the pet notion of the Ptolemaic Teleo, or earth centralists. In the earlier and, as we believe, the more correct philosophy the word, which in the Greek tongue is the prototype of "ether", is employed in its place. The separation of the light from darkness and the separation of the water from the land is the next process, both of which are spoken of in the Biblical account. As obscurity wanes and light appears, the great lights become visible. The sun, the great father, by his penetrating rays impregnates the earth, the great mother and vegetable and animal life appear, and finally man appears as the child of the earth. Even the name "Adam" means "Red-Earth". In all this system of philosophy these things are not manufactured by the hand of God out of nothing, but appear as emanations from Himself in His desire for manifestation, with His Spirit imminent in them.

As there is a greater amount of white than of yolk in the egg, so in the mundane egg there was the greater amount of light. God was not only imminent, but, in this fact, He appears also to some degree transcendental. In the earlier philosophy the light was God, beneficent, fortunate and powerful. The darkness was but the absence of light and unfortunate. In the later philosophy, and especially in Persia, where these two principles were recognized as directly opposite to each other, light was personified as Ahura Mazda, the all good, while the darkness, as Ahryman, was positive evil. In short, they were personified as God and Devil. This same thought was father to the idea that God dwelt mostly in Heaven, while the devil dwelt under the earth. The sun was the eye of God continually looking down upon the earth and watching all that went on in it.

There are three sorts of symbols employed to represent the Deity. The first sort are used to represent the name of Deity, the second to represent His visible manifestation and the third to represent His attributes and functions, if such a word may be used in such a connection. The first sort is illustrated in the square, the swastika, the cross, the square of a single right angle, the cross saltire, that is the cross of St. George and the cross of St. Andrew combined, thus a cross of eight lines meeting. This was the manner of writing the name of God in old Babylonia cuneiform characters. As we have previously stated the name of God is spelled in most languages with four letters, each represented by a right angle in the square or cross. Thus "J", "I" or "Y", "H" or "E", "O", "U", "V" or "F" and "H" again, combined and read from right to left, "J. H. V. H.", pronounced by us "Jehovah" or "Javeh", was the name of the Deity in Hebrew. This name was not spoken by them at all, being known as the ineffable or unspeakable name. In the Latin "Jove" we see the same name and this probably comes as near to the correct pronunciation as we are likely to get. In Babylonia, the name was "Illu", which has descended to us in the "Allah" of the Arabians. The Greeks used the names "Zeus" and "Theos", the "th" being one letter in their alphabet and known as "theta". Jupiter was equivalent to "Zeus-piter" or Father Zeus. This much for names.

Now the only visible thing that seemed to sort of serve as an image of God and in creation as His deputy and representative was the sun, the eye of the world. This was seen in the shape of a round golden discus. Thus the circle or discus became the shape which the Godhead was supposed to have when He made Himself manifest to man's contemplation. Among many nations this circle was supplied with wings and with a serpent with an erect head on either side of the discus. The serpent, with its tail in its mouth, became the emblem of eternity, neither having beginning nor end. The serpent with the erect head, like, for instance, the hooded cobra, resembled so closely the erect male organ of generation that it came to have the significance of the creation of life.

In the third instance, regarding the attributes or functions of Deity, these were considered to be threefold, that of creation, that of building up or preservation and that of tearing down or destroying a kind of trinity. All that is, being of a Divine substance or concentrated spirit, God could not be the destroyer of Himself, though forms are continually changing, so that in this instance destroyer must be read only as transformer. God is, as regards time, He that was, He that is and He that shall be, past, present and future. He is father, mother and offspring. He is not only the creator of life, but He is life. "I am that I am." These groups of trinities must be represented by the equilateral triangle, the perfect triangle of equal sides and equal angles, each of 120 degrees.

The three ideas which I have shown in regard to mystical philosophy may be summed up as follows: The name is represented by the Greek letter Gamma, or the square. The form is represented by the Greek letter Omikron, or the circle, and the attributes by the Greek letter delta, or the equilateral triangle. It appears thus as a whole or in English letters (GOD). Thus we have represented in this name "God" the three most perfect geometrical symbols.

Again there is something in this word "God" of still more scientific and symbolic importance. The numerical value of these three letters is G-3, 0-6 and D-4, or 364, which is 13 months of 28 days each, or a lunar year of 52 weeks, so that by not counting the day of the Passover we have the length of the Jewish year as reckoned by Sabbaths and new moons. In the old Gothic language they used the word "Go-da" for our word "Year." The word of four "Gs" has been known in symbolic language as the "Tetragramaton", which was originally "Tetragammaton," or word of four gammas.

The ancient record says that the animals passed before Adam and he gave them names. It is believed that this expression refers to the animals of the sky, through which the sun passes on its annual or yearly travels. During the year the sun appears to pass through a kind of circular path around the earth. This circular path was not set exactly level with the flat surface of the earth, that is, just keeping at exactly the same height above the horizon, but it appeared to rise very much higher in the summer and to sink very much lower in the winter, so low that it seemed to lose its life-giving or fructifying powers. In short, it died. Twice during its course the days and nights became equal in length. Thus there was a summer and a winter solstice, or places where the sun stood still for three days and then changed its direction, and twice it stood at equinox. The entire circle was naturally divided into twelve equal parts. How naturally? Ancient geometry was worked upon figures composed of squares. Geometrical work was done upon the square, and that is the origin of the Masonic expression, "upon the square," meaning mathematically honest and true. If you draw a circle inclosed in a large square composed of sixteen smaller squares, or a square which is four equal distances on each side, you will find the compound square thus formed cutting the circle into exactly twelve equal parts. The stars grouped in each of these twelve equal parts of 30 degrees each were given the name of some animal and the whole circle was called a zodiac or zoological garden. This was not on account of the groups of stars, or constellations, as we call them, arranging themselves in the shape of a lion or an ox or a ram, but on account of something in the season of the year that brought these animals to mind, such as the ox being used to plow with in the month of April, the sheep having their lambs in the month of March, the lions coming out of the desert in the hot weather of July, the wheat harvest in the month of August, when the Virgins gathered the sheafs of wheat, etc.

And there was another reason which anyone might observe when one contemplates the shadows made by the sun on certain geometrical figures, which it is impossible to reproduce here. The four special locations mentioned were named first. The lowest point which the sun reached in winter was accompanied by heavy rains and was designated by a man carrying a water jug and known as "Aquarius," or the "water carrier." The highest point was in July, a time of extreme heat and dryness, when the days were longest and the nights shortest. This point was designated by the lion. The vernal or spring equinox was called the "Bull" or "Taurus", while the autumnal equinox was called the Scorpion on account of the early frosts nipping the vegetation. A very brilliant star in this group was "Aquilla" or the "Eagle", so that the grand cross was formed by the lion, the ox, the man and the eagle. The bird more appropriate is the Phoenix that renewed his youth by burning himself to ashes, out of which a worm grew that eventually developed into a new bird that flew away. "He reneweth his youth like the Eagle" or Phoenix. This is the proper season of the year for this phenomenon. So it is the Phoenix and not the true Eagle that we ought to think of in this connection. The year was thought to begin with Aries or the Ram, which occupied the time of year covered by our month of March. The next was Taurus or the Bull; the third was Gemini or the Twins; the fourth was Cancer or the Crab, the astrological house of the moon; the fifth was Leo or the Lion, the astrological house of the sun; the sixth was Virgo or the Virgin; the seventh, Libra or the Scales or Balances; the eighth was Scorpio or the Scorpion, in which was Aquilla, the Eagle; the ninth was Sagittarius, the archer or centaur, the horseman of the Apocalypse, the horse and his rider of the

"Song of Miriam" that was sunk in the sea when the Lord triumphed gloriously. The tenth was the dragon-tailed goat or Capricornus, the eleventh was Aquarius the water carrier, and the twelfth was Pisces or the fishes. The sun seemed to occupy one of these houses for one month, giving origin to the twelve months system of counting time. Counting one degree of the circle per day and 30 days to the month gave a 360-day year, which was soon found to be incorrect by over five days, which resulted in a very unhandy intercalary.

The six other movable heavenly bodies occupied these houses, sometimes alone and sometimes in conjunction with the sun, and sometimes in conjunction with one of the other planets. One alone, almost invariably, occupied the same house with the sun. This was the planet Mercury, which was situated so close to the sun that it rose shortly before the sun or set shortly before it, as it happened to be either a morning or an evening star. As we have before stated, its ancient name was "Hermes", which means "Son of the Sun" or "Son of Light". Next in prominence was the moon, the virgin wife of the sun, as she was known to the ancient philosophers.

Now we have before us the materials or characters for a very fine miracle play or drama, the sun, moon, the planets, especially Mercury, the animal-named constellations of the zodiac, together with the sky and earth. The story of the play runs that Lord Osiris, the King of Kings and Lord of Lords, starts upon his yearly journey as a little child named "Horus". He grows prosperously stronger and older until he leaves the South, where he is attacked by the keepers of the three winter months and is finally slain by Typhon, the dragon-tailed goat, in Capricornus, bringing death into the world. His enemy triumphs over him, cutting his body into little pieces and spreading it all over the sea towards the West. Isis, or the moon, the virgin wife of Osiris, and now widow, takes with her the keepers of the twelve houses of the zodiac and goes out in search of the body. She searches for fifteen days and at last finds a single living fragment in the slender evergreen or sprig of acacia. This she nurses back to life in her own body and from this germ bears a new Horus, who grows up to be the sun of the new year. The death takes place in the last part of the sign of Capricornus and the regeneration begins the sign of Aquarius. His name is "Horus Ammon Abib", which is to say, "Light-Day-Abib". The first name is derived from "ChR" or "HUR" or "KUR".

"ChR" is the reverse spelling of "RCh", which was the Sanscrit or Aryan word for "light" and was written in Greek with an "X" and an "R", the latter letter being shaped like a "P". Doubtless many of our readers have seen this symbol on church garments and altar cloths, for it is frequently used even to this day. The second name "Ammon" is our word "Amen", the Hindu word "A. U. M." and the Hebrew word "I. O. M.", which means "Day". We often hear modern Jews use the expression "Iom or Yom Kipper", meaning "Day of Atonement". The meaning of the word "Abib", we have already explained. He is born of a virgin, and yet at the same time is the son of a widow. His infancy is spent in Pisces, that is to say, he is brought up out of the waters. His youth in Aries leads to his being spoken of as "The Lamb of God, that taketh away the sins of the world", because then vegetation begins again to bloom. He climbs steadily upward, growing stronger as he climbs, until at his culmination he is "The lion of the tribe of Judah". The name "Judah" and the name "J. H. V. H." are of the same numerical value. The letters "D" and "A", one and four, are equivalent to one of the "Hs" in the "J. H. V. H." At this point he can be said to have reached complete manhood, and the next sign is that of the virgin. Here we perceive the meaning of the expression—"The power of the Highest shall overshadow thee." He is now Osiris, and from this point on, his strength begins gradually to decay. Thus "The lion's paw" raises him to the highest Heaven, out of the grave of death. The three winter months have been associated with the name of "The lost word" and with the three Assassins that took his life. We have three characters whose names are very suggestive of this word in its Hindu form of "A. O. M." In this instance the "O" is not "Omikron" or the little "O", but "O-meger" or the big "O", which is equivalent to our "W" or "OO", which was the last letter of the Greek alphabet. The names of these Assassins are explained by some as being a combination of the names of Deity in the three languages of Hebrew, Chaldean and Egyptian, being "Jah", "Baal" and "On". Whether the word "O" was considered as one of the names of Deity in Egypt, we do not know, but it was certainly one of the names of the city of the sun, or Heliopolis, and we read "That Joseph married Asenath, daughter of Potiphira, Priest of On", which likely meant that Potiphira was one of the priests of the sun worshipers at Heliopolis. The connection between the terminal letters of the names of the three Assassins and the Holy Letters "A. O. M." is quite easy to see and needs no explanation. The letters refer to Brahm, Vishno and Shiva, the creator, preserver and destroyer or triune god of the Hindu faith.

Another derivation of the "Jubelum", and which demonstrates the play on words, which our ancient brethren frequently made, unconsciously, while transmitting their instruction by word of mouth to more or less unclassical ears. The Hebrew stone-cutter was a man who resided in the mountains of "Gebal", and a number of these men were spoken of as "Giblim", which is the plural form of the word. This word varied first to "Gib-e-lim", thence to "Gib-e-lum", thence to "Jib-e-lum" and thence to "Ju-be-lum". The difference is that the last-mentioned derivation is certainly natural, while the former is certainly artificial. When a play on words, so closely resembling a pun, is made, generally the natural word is formed first and the artificial word is manufactured to imitate it in sound.

There are many of these solar myth dramas known to history, several of which we have already mentioned. In Samaria, Shamash-On or Samson was the hero of the solar myth. The personal incidents of his story vary somewhat from those in the Egyptian play of Osiris and Isis, but there are the same pertinent allusions. The strength of Samson was in his hair, as the strength of the sun is in his rays. When Samson's hair was shorn by Delilah, his strength departed and he was captured, and his enemies placed him in an underground dungeon, where he turned a mill. Here his hair grew again and the next we know of him he is standing exactly between the two pillars of "Dag-On", which are equivalent to our two parallel lines, on either side of the circle. "Dag" is a word signifying "Fish", and "Dag-On" was a fish god and refers to the constellation of "Pisces". Samson's adventure with the "Lion" is also significant, as was also the allusion to the "jaw bone of an ass", which may allude to the crescent moon.

Coming to Ninevah, we have another solar myth, the hero of which is Oannes, or Jonah, or John. The historic legend of Jonah being swallowed by a mighty fish, who vomited him up again in the space of three days, safe and sound, and the prayer that he uttered while in the whale's belly, are very easily explained as a solar myth among a maritime people, though, as a literal piece of history it is exceedingly trying to credulity. The story of Jonah is a miracle play transformed into a novel or romance for the Eastern story teller. The Oannes cult was a very extended one, and was practiced by a population exceeding that of Israel by twenty times over. We discover upon the decorated and sculptured walls of the old Ninevite palaces and temples priests clothed in garments resembling fish-skins, and also pictures of a man standing in a fish's mouth, and fish bladders, and fish baskets in great numbers, used as symbols. It is likely that the adventures of Jonah are a pretty accurate record of what happened to the candidate during the ceremony of his initiation into the mysteries of Oannes. The journey by ship, the storm at sea, the calling upon God by the men in the boat, the failure of Jonah to do this, his being thrown into the sea, his appearance in the belly of the fish, his prayer after the third day, his resurrection from the dead, his experience with the gourd to show the uncertainty of life, and the final forgiveness of the Gods and his safe return home a better and a wiser man. The nature of this cult would lead the student to believe that its date would be during that period when the sign of Pisces occupied the western or winter solstice.

Another mystery that occupied the attention of the ancient Semitics was what was known as the mysteries of the chariot. This is represented by the story of Elijah, who was borne to Heaven in a chariot of fire. It seems to be connected with the summer solstice, as that of Pisces or Oannes is with the winter solstice. These mystics were known as Mercabores. Some symbolic writings in the first chapter of the Prophet Ezekiel very strongly point to the writer having passed through some such an initiation.

Among the Greeks of Eleusis, the hero was Dionysius, or Adon Yesha, or Bacchus. These were known far and wide as the Elusinian mysteries, and their connection with what was known as the Dionysian school of architects, which fact is alluded to in the Mark Degree, seems to connect them with the hero of the Masonic legend. Grand Master Hiram is there mentioned as being a member of the Dionysian college, and it is also stated that a number of these architects had accompanied the widow's son to Jerusalem and assisted in the building of the Temple. Among the northmen of Scandinavia, the hero was called Balder, the Golden Haired, and we have a romance written by our late Bro. General Lew Wallace, a kind of historical novel, on the conquest of Mexico by Cortez. The story is known as "The Fair God". In Persia the Light God was "Mythras", and the celebrations of his mysteries were kept up by the Romans down to a very late date, perhaps as late as the tenth century.

Many of the ancient lodge halls where the bodies of this Order met have been unearthed. Most of them were situated under ground. The arrangement of these halls was very similar to our modern Masonic Lodge rooms. The great celebration of these mysteries was held at the vernal equinox. The illustrations show a man dressed in a pointed cap, thrusting a dagger into the heart of a bull on which he is mounted. As the blood falls upon the ground vegetation springs up luxuriantly. A small boy is seen trying to catch some of the blood in a cup. The rising of vegetation through the sprinkling of blood is an element in the history of the mysteries of the Holy Graal. The locality of this last-mentioned mystery is near the site of the ancient ruin of Glastonbury Abbey on the coast of Wales. The Order of Mythra comes down to a period as late as that of the origin of English Freemasonry, if we take the statement of the ancient manuscripts regarding the Grand Lodge held by King Athelstane in the ninth century, and seems to have had some connection with it, either through the remembrance of Freemasons or through the learning of Elias Ashmole or Theophilus Desaguliers or some other of the speculative Freemasons of the reorganization, who edited the rituals.

It is difficult to believe that the ancient priests went to all the trouble and expense of maintaining these mysteries for the small purpose of perpetuating the knowledge of so simple an astronomical fact. The solar myth taught something far more important. The sun was the "Son of Man", or mankind in general, and the death and resurrection of the sun was a type of the death and resurrection of human kind. In our Masonic myth, Hiram Abiff not only stands for and represents the sun, but he represents man as well, and especially the candidate.

Space will not permit us to go more exhaustively into the history of this myth than we have already done. If the reader desires to pursue it further he can do so by reading "Morals and Dogma," by Bro. Albert Pike, or Albert G. Mackey's Encyclopedia of Freemasonry. We will add, however, that the X. P. sign is supposed to be the Sign of the Cross that the Emperor Constantine saw in his dream over which was written, "In hoc Signo Vinces." "By this sign ye shall conquer." It is, however, a sign that can be traced back at least a thousand years previous to the time of Constantine. It is the same syllable that forms the root of the name "Christ" and the Greek word for gold "Chris" and the name "Cyrus" and many other names well known in history and philosophy. It was a very pretty conceit of our ancient brethren that the life of the Sun God lingered in the evergreen after all other signs of life in earthly vegetation had ceased. The body of Osiris was found buried in the trunk of an acacia tree in the Elusinian mysteries. It is likely that this portion of the legend is connected with the legend of the two trees that bloomed in the garden of Eden, the "tree of life" and the "tree of the knowledge of good and evil". The fruit of this latter tree was forbidden to our first parents, lest they eat of the former and become like Gods, immortal, so that the flaming sword was placed at the entrance to the garden to keep the way to the "tree of life." The ancient name of the city of Babylon was "Tin-tur-ke" (the place of the tree of life). Sometimes we find the places mentioned as "Gan Dunyash" which is the same as garden of Dionysius, and sometimes as "Gan Eden", or garden of Eden. There are, on the ancient monuments, many representations of this tree of life. It bears twelve manner of fruit or twelve bunches of fruit, and each bunch has thirty buds. Thus one can at once behold the reference to the year with its twelve months and thirty days to each. It is said that Isis sat weeping over Osiris, over the broken acacia tree, and that Horus, her son, came up and consoled her. This scene is represented in the Masonic monument to Hiram Abiff. Time and patience overcome the sharpness of grief for the dead. The scene is differently explained in the lodge.

It would be a wonder if some of the earlier Christian sects should not have illustrated the life and passion of Jesus Christ in a scene very closely allied to our drama of faith. There was abundant need of it on account of the persecution of the early church. It would seem that the followers of Jesus employed every argument to show wherein His career exhibited all the qualifications of a god, in that it resembled the career of Osiris so closely. They pointed out, and even invented the virgin birth, the infant peril, His appellation of "Lamb of God", His twelve disciples or followers. The women seeking His body at the tomb, the resurrection and subsequent ascension are also typical. Again we have the attempt to liken Him to the Prophet Jonah and his career. He said, "As Jonah was three days and three nights in the whale's belly, so shall the Son of Man be three days and three nights in the bosom of the earth." Again we have the three persons implicated in the cause of His death, Judas Iscariot, Caiphas, the High Priest, and Pontius Pilate, the Roman Governor. The three days and three nights could not be made to apply to the time He remained in the sepulchre, as that was only from Friday night until Sunday morning before daylight. The words are, "As it began to dawn towards the first day of the week," which was called the "Sun's Day". The symbol of the fish and the Vesica Pisces or fish bladder on the ring of a bishop, the ceremonial mitre of the bishop, which was undoubtedly taken from the model of the fish's head, was seen upon the dress of the ancient priests of Oannes. The symbolism of the five loaves and two fishes, and the twelve baskets remaining, is also to be connected with this mystery, for it was regarding them that He said, "Unto you it is given to know the mystery of the Kingdom of Heaven, but unto them it is not given." The initials of the Greek words "Iesous Christos Theou Vios Soter", translated, "Jesus Christ, Son of God, the Saviour," spell the word Ichthus, which was the Greek word for "fish". In the moral of our Masonic myth man is bound to be killed sooner or later by accident, disease or old age. He descends into the abode of death, "six feet due east and west and six feet perpendicular," to be raised to a life immortal in the world that is to be, by the paw of the lion and the eagle's claw, as some versions say of the tribe of Judah.

This is the substance of the drama of faith. It may be that the day will come when we shall know how this myth found its way into Freemasonry, but we do not know that now. It is not a proof of a life after death because such proof does not exist, nor has it ever existed. The myth, at best, is only an allegory and an analogy but it deals with high and mighty things and is well calculated to inspire faith in any right-thinking soul.

LECTURE XVIII

THE LOST WORD

THE part played in our ritual by the symbolism of the Lost Word has a history and explanation by itself. It took its origin, some think, in a superstition that if it were possible to call on God by His right Name, He would answer prayer. The failure resulted in not knowing just how His Name should be pronounced.

The ancient Hebrew was written without vowels, all the characters having consonantal value only. The so-called vowel points which at the present time appear in Hebrew writing are of fairly recent origin. For instance, their "H" might be in one place a strongly aspirated "H", while in another place it would appear without the aspiration, as an "E", which we recognize as a vowel. In the Greek written language the "H" is a vowel "Epsilon". In Hebrew the "Chet" is a "Ch", while the same place is filled in the Greek alphabet as "Eta".

Without any written distinction between vowels and consonants the pronunciation must have been entirely fixed by tradition, the sound being taught purely by word of mouth. The Name of God, not being spoken by the people, but having its pronunciation handed down orally from one priest to another, might by the death of one or two priests, more sudden than ordinarily expected, be lost entirely. The reason why the word could not be given without the consent of the three Grand Masters was not so much a matter of consent as it was from the fact that it was likely that each was the custodian of only a portion of the word.

Regarding the secret of the Pythagorean triangle, it is taught that each Grand Master carried one side of the triangle. The Master of the lodge held the side of three cubits, the Senior Warden the one of four cubits and the Junior Warden the side of five cubits. When the three sides were placed together in the form of a triangle the exact square or right-angled triangle would be exhibited.

The instruction which we desire to convey is illustrated by the manner of communicating the Grand Omnific Royal Arch Word. "He that hath ears to hear, let him hear." The idea of the "word of power" is almost, if not quite, as old as King Solomon

himself. It is as ancient as magic. It was supposed to control
the invisible world. The angels and demons, as well, obeyed it.
At the beginning of the Gospel of St. John we read the following:
"In the beginning was the *word* and the *word* was from God
and the *word* was God. The same was in the beginning with
God. All things were made by Him and without Him was not
anything made that was made. In Him was life and the life
was the light of men. And the light shown in darkness and the
darkness comprehended it not." Herein was the doctrine of the
logos or the *word*. If anyone will add the numerical value of
the letters in *logos*—L, 30; O, 6; G, 3; O, 6; S, 300—the sum
will be found to be 345, which are the exact numbers of the
sides of the Pythagorean triangle. The *word* was a sort of
emanation or wave of power from the Deity sent out like the
rays of light from the sun, through which the Deity made Himself manifest in creation.

The great question in magic was how to become possessed of
that *word*. The *word* being lost by the death of the Grand
Master, a substitute was adopted, which was to take its place
until the true one was found. There are many traditions,
especially among the Arabs, regarding this *word*. It could only
be transmitted orally. Only such as had reached the highest
degrees in the Jewish Mysteries ever received it, and they received it in groups of threes. The High Priest alone ever spoke
it aloud, and he but once a year within the sanctum sanctorum
on the great day of Atonement. On that day the sins of the
people were laid upon the "scape goat," and the goat was driven
forth into the wilderness and a lamb was sacrificed without spot
or blemish. It will be remembered that it is in the sign of the
goat that the death of the sun takes place, and in the sign of
the ram or lamb that the resurrection is completed. The space
of time between the nativity, at Christmas and Easter, the time
of the resurrection is apparently unaccounted for in the mysteries, though the sun has been rising in the zodiac for two
months and suffering the perils of the storms of January or
Aquarius and the floods of February in Pisces. The death and
rebirth mark the winter solstice and the resurrection from the
dead is celebrated at the vernal equinox.

It is probable that we have in these traditions a combination
of two different mysteries. Many legends of King Solomon
have come down to us in the stories of the Arabian Nights and
other romances of the same sort. Solomon acquired his knowl-

edge of magic through the possession of the *word*. The Semitic mind in the days of Haroun Al Raschid was romantic in the extreme. The perfection to which they carried the pseudo sciences of astrology and alchemy testify to that, and we have no cause to regret that their investigation and search for the elixia vitae and the stone that should turn all things to gold was unsuccessful, for they at last ended in astronomy and chemistry. These latter have been of a much more substantial benefit to mankind than the things they sought could possibly have been. However, they treasured all that they heard of the magic of King Solomon, his famous seal on which was engraved the Ineffable Name, his possession of the magic worm "Schmir" by whose aid the stones of the temple were cut; his command of the "Jinns", who continued to work on the temple for a long time after the great king's death.

The latter story may be worth repeating. It is told that the king felt that his end was drawing nigh and that yet the temple was not completed. He had himself carried into the temple on a certain morning and had himself placed in a standing position, leaning upon his magic staff in such a way that his body could not fall to the ground, and there yielded up his soul. The Jinns saw him standing there day after day as if watching the work and were unaware of his death. They continued to work on until the day the temple was finished, at which moment the staff upon which he had leaned gave way, having been gnawed by ants until it was honeycombed. The body fell to the ground just as the last jewel was set. The Jinns perceived that they were free and no longer under King Solomon's authority and fled. But the temple was completed.

We often hear in prayers and sermons and theological literature expressions which seem to speak as though the Great Name of God was something in itself. Often we hear a prayer close with this expression, "To the honor of Thy Great and Holy Name." That the user of the expression generally knows the real meaning of what he says we very much doubt, nevertheless it originated in the manner and belief which we have mentioned. It is thought by some writers that the Great Name was comprised in the letters "A. U. M." We will run over some of the many forms which this word takes in different Oriental tongues and it can be easily seen that these writers have some reason for their claim. In Persian and Zend these three letters are found in many words that designate fire, spirit, flame, essence, etc.

It is the root of the name of the Sun-God "Yama" of the Vedas and the "Yang" of the Chinese. In Sanscrit it is "Iama". It is the Chaldean name of the Day-Sun "Ioma". In Hebrew it is the word for day "Iom" or "Yom". It becomes a very early term in Chaldean philosophy as "Aoum" or doubled as "Moum". It is the Hindu word of creation, the word of light "Om" and "AUM", the Sclavonic "Um" or "Oum", meaning Spirit or Soul. "IUM" is the name of the Scandinavian Thunder God; "Ium-Ala", "Ium-jo", "Iumio", the Thunder Goddess; "Ami" or "Ammi" and "Ammi Shaddai"—Hebrew proper names; "Oma", the Holy Fire. "Omannus" or "Ammon" or "AMUN", the Persian Fire God's name. The "Aom" in the Hebrew proper names "Immer" and "Aomar" and the Dorian "Amar" means "day". It appears also in "Mar", the Phoenician word for "Sun", and in "Baal Aum" and "Ah-iam", Hebrew names, also in "Iam", meaning "day" in Egyptian. It is the same as the Egyptian God "Amun", also in the old Germanic Sun God "Am". In Asia Minor it took the feminine form "Amma" and "Ma"; the moon, "Ammia", "Amaia" and "Maia", the earth, and in "Ma" the Egyptian Goddess of Truth. According to the Bactrian teaching "MANU", which is the same as "AMUN" and "NUMA", save that the letters are transmuted, the letters stand for earth, sky and heaven. It is sufficient to say that the same word has come down to us and is used by every religious denomination in the country, and almost in the civilized world as a final invocation. It is the word "Amen".

In a sense this story of the Builder and the Lost Word is repeated constantly in human affairs. The good, the beautiful and the true always suffer under the attacks of the evil, the bad and the false, and for a time evil seems triumphant, but its prosperity cannot endure. "Right is forever on the scaffold and wrong forever on the throne. But the scaffold sways the future and behind dim and unknown standeth God within the shadow, keeping watch above His own." "The all-seeing eye that watcheth over Israel slumbers not, nor sleeps." "Truth crushed to earth shall rise again, the eternal years of God are hers, while error wounded writhes in pain and dies among her worshippers." "Be ye faithful unto death, and I will give thee a crown of life."

LECTURE XIX

Solemn Strikes the Funeral Chime

BROTHER JOSEPH FORT NEWTON has written a marvelously vivid and beautiful sketch and historical exposition of this old hymn so generally used among Freemasons during this part of our ceremonial. We do not believe he would object to our copying it here as it contains a beautiful and impressive lesson:

> Solemn strikes the funeral chime,
> Notes of our departing time
> As we journey here below
> Through our pilgrimage of woe.
>
> Mortals now indulge a tear,
> For Mortality is here.
> See how wide her trophies wave,
> O'er the slumbers of the grave.
>
> Here another guest we bring,
> Seraphs of Celestial wing
> To our funeral altar come,
> Waft our friend and brother home.
>
> Lord of all below above,
> Fill our hearts with Truth and Love,
> As dissolves this human tie,
> Take us to Thy home on high.
>
> Far beyond the grave there lies
> Brighter mansions in the skies,
> Where enthroned the Deity,
> Gives man immortality.
>
> There enlarged his soul will see
> What is veiled in mystery.
> Heavenly glories fill the place,
> And show his Maker, face to face.
>
> God of Life's eternal day,
> Guide us, lest from Thee we stray.
> By some false delusive light,
> To the shades of endless night.
>
> Calm the good man meets his fate,
> Guides Celestial round him wait,
> See he bursts these mortal chains,
> And o'er death the victory gains.

How many tender memories these old familiar words evoke in the mind of a Mason. Often in the open lodge, alas! too often beside the open grave, he has heard them march with slow, majestic step to the measure of the Pleyel's hymn. Never were words and melody more fitly blended and they induce a mood pensive indeed, but not plaintive; rich in pathos, without being poignant, a mood of sweet sadness caught at that point where it stops short of piercing grief. Yet few know where it was written, nor by whom, though many must have paused to muse over the faith of which it sings.

The hymn was written by David Vinton, a lecturer in Masonry and teacher of the ritual in the first quarter of the last century, whose field of labor was in the South, chiefly in North Carolina. Unfortunately, his path through life was dogged by the demon of drink, which left stains upon his character for which he was expelled by a lodge in North Carolina. He died, so Mackey records, in Shakertown, Ky., in July, 1833, but Morris places his death six years earlier and said that it occurred near Russellville, Ky. Morris adds this pathetic fact, "Nor was his own most beautiful hymn sung over his grave on account of his lapse from a life of sobriety."

In 1816 Vinton issued a volume entitled, "The Masons' Minstrel, a Selection of Masonic, Sentimental, Humorous Songs, Duets, Glees, Canons, Rounds, Canzonets, respectfully dedicated to the Most Ancient and Honorable Fraternity of Free and Accepted Masons." An appendix containing a short historical sketch of Masonry and a list of all the lodges in the United States was attached to this work. It was printed for the author by H. Mann & Co., of Dedham, Mass., and more than ten thousand copies were sold to the Craft. This volume contained his funeral dirge set to the melody of Pleyel's hymn. As Mackey remarks: "This collection should preserve the name of Vinton among the Craft, and in some measure atone for his faults, whatever they may have been." From the preface we learn that Vinton was appointed by Mount Vernon Lodge, in Providence, to provide a book of songs for the use of the lodge, and this suggested the book to his mind, the more so when he was unable to find any book to suit his need.

This quaint volume, yellow with age and alternating from grave to gay, from lively to severe, tempts comment, did time permit, but our concern lies with the dirge. Originally it had eight stanzas as written above, but only four generally appear

in our rituals and burial service, and Vinton little thought that
his lines would be sung for a decade, then laid away and taken
up again, and sung whenever a Mason is laid to rest in the land
called America.   Whether we hear this hymn in the tiled recesses of the lodge, or out on the green sward under the sky,
our hearts answer to its appeal. Albeit in more tender tone and
less stately strain, it strikes the note that sounds through the
90th Psalm, that mighty funeral hymn of the human race, with
its chant of the swift death of the morning flowers, or the van-
ishing of man, and the hush of the profound sleep to which all
things mortal decline.

How helpless man is, pursued by time and overtaken by death.
His life is a vapor that melts. His span of years a tale that is
told.   There is here that nameless sorrow, that unutterable sadness which lingers in all mortal music whatsoever, and will linger
in it while we walk in the dim country of this world, where death
seems to divide Divinity with God.   Ever more in hours trivial
or tragic, in moods pensive or gay, solemn strikes the funeral
chime, notes of our departing time as we journey here below
through our pilgrimage of woe.   Touched by the twilight of
time, the singer meditates and prays.   He sees that the vast
machinery of nature carries forward the entire human race and
drops them without fail in one final sleep.   Yet each departs
alone, the father without the child, the wife without her husband,
the maid without her lover, the judge without the court, the
statesman unattended, the babe with no arm about it.

Aye! king and beggar alike and all walk that same dark
inevitable path.   In what solemn dignity they go, their faces all
turned in one direction, following the footprints of a many mil-
lioned multitude into the infinite.   We who are compelled to
watch their moving figures are powerless to detain them, and can
only say farewell and weep.   "Mortals now indulge a tear, for
mortality is here.   See how wide her trophies wave, o'er the
slumbers of the grave."   With all our philosophy and all our
wit, death remains the same old bitter haggard fact, which no
man can either evade or avert.   There is something appalling in
the masterful negation and collapse of the body.   It is profound.
It is pathetic.   Words are futile and there is in that last sad
silence what makes them seem foolish.   What avails it what any
man may say about death?   The real question is, what shall we
say to it, and whether or not we shall let it have the last word?
Not all the preaching since Adam has ever made death other

than death. Heart and flesh fail and the generations come and go, following the forlorn march of dust. Truly for man his days are as the grass and as the flower of the field, so he flourisheth, for the wind passeth over it and it is gone. Suddenly the shadow shifts. Light shineth in the midst of the darkness and we see how true it is, that the soul of man is the one unconquerable thing in this world.

How wonderful is that ancient high heroic faith that refuses to admit that the grave is the gigantic coffin lid of a dull and mindless universe, descending upon it at last. Life tries it, sorrow shadows it, learning deceives it, sin stains it and yet it is victorious. When doubt deepens, that faith becomes still more profound and out of the depths of the blackest tragedy it rises with a song of triumph. So has it been from that far distant day, when the oldest book in the world was written, and so will it be until whatever is to be, the end of things. "Here another guest we bring, seraphs of celestial wing, to our funeral altar come, and waft our friend and brother home." Such a faith is not a mere surrender. It is a force prophetic of its own fulfillment. At its touch a graveyard becomes a cemetery, that is a sleeping chamber, and dark death an all men's tavern, where a fellow-traveler takes a lodging for a night. Those whom we call dead are the guests of God, whose love is the keeper of untold revelations. Also our singer sees that the social life of man, its warmth of sympathy, its sanctity of friendship, its dear love of man for his comrade, has enduring value, and because this is so, because life is brief at the longest, and broken at the best, it must be filled with truth and love.

That so we might bring up to that gate in the mist something too noble to die, hence the wise prayer: "Lord of all below, above, fill our hearts with truth and love. When dissolves this earthly tie, take us to Thy home on high." Oh Death, where is thy victory? Our trust is in God and that He who has made us what we are will finally lead us to what we ought to be. Higher faith there is none. Even so Masonry rests its hope on the ultimate reality. The first truth and the last, and it is therefore that the singer sees amid the fluctuating shadows of this twilight world an august and incomprehensible destiny for man. As a song of triumph the four stanzas which follow the last quoted are worthy of remembrance, but they are seldom if ever used in the lodge.

LECTURE XX
Prayer at the Raising

*T*HOU, O God, knowest our down sitting and our uprising and understandest our thoughts afar off. Shield and defend us from the evil intentions of our enemies and support us in the trials and afflictions we are destined to endure while traveling through this vale of tears. Man that is born of a woman is of few days and full of trouble. He cometh forth like a flower and is cut down. He fleeth also as a shadow and continueth not. Seeing his days are determined, the number of his months is with Thee. Thou hast appointed his bounds that he cannot pass. Turn from him, that he may rest, until he shall accomplish (like an hireling) his day. For there is hope of a tree, if it be cut down, that it will sprout again and that the tender branch may not cease* (and though its stem be dry and its leaves be withered and its root wax old in the earth, yet through the scent of water it shall bud and bring forth flowers like a plant), *but man dieth and wasteth away. He giveth up the ghost and where is he? Like as the water fail from the sea and the flood decayeth and dryeth up, so man lieth down and riseth not up, until the heavens shall be no more. Yet, O Lord, have compassion on the children of Thy creation, administer them comfort in time of trouble and save them with an everlasting salvation. Amen!"* Response by the brethren: *"So mote it be."*

It would seem that if our Masonic forefathers had tried to pick out the most utterly hopeless prayer in the entire field of that sort of literature, the most gloomy and despairing passage in the whole Bible, they could not possibly have succeeded better. In the first place, the Book of Job, while a wonderful epic poem, dealing in a masterly fashion with the problem of justifying the ways of God to men in permitting the righteous to suffer the afflictions which nature brings to all men alike, its faith is not in the hereafter. Whenever this passage is read at a funeral the laity would have abundant excuse for saying that Freemasonry did not believe in a future life at all, when, in fact, its one great purpose of existence is to demonstrate immortality, and that a man's death is not like that of a tree. We believe the prayer distinctly inappropriate and ought never to have been shown to anyone whose faith, in the midst of such a trial as the grave closing over the loved and the lost, needs to be encouraged and supported. It is suitable only for the contemplation of such as welcome death in order to be rid of earthly pain and suffering. Other prayers have been suggested, and we will quote two which we believe to be far more suited to the theme. The following was by Brother Marshall:

"O Sun and all the Gods that give light to men, and Thou Great God who art above all Gods and of whom all other Gods are but names and attributes, Eternal God of nature and revelation! Thou who in Thy world of nature doth raise tree and grass and flower from the death of winter to the life of spring! Thou who in Thy world of revelation doth raise humanity from the winter of death to the springtime of Eternal Life. We come to Thee in this dark hour of grief and gloom, when we call upon one who doth not hear, when hand clasps hand in vain, when doubt is strong and faith is weak and vision dim, when the sting of death is keen and the grave's victory doth seem complete. Thou who hast planted the ever-green and ever-living sprig of faith in every human soul, open Thou our eyes so that we may see the stars of life shining through the night of death. Unstop our ears, so that we may hear Thee say, 'I am the resurrection and the life. He that believeth on Me, even though he be dead, yet shall he live, and he that liveth and believeth on Me shall never die.' Wilt Thou, O God, in these, our mortal years, raise us from evil up to good, from ignorance up to wisdom, from envy, hatred, malice and all unkindness up to brotherhood, and in that world where Thou dost dwell, when time is swallowed up in endless years and all sadness turned to song, wilt Thou raise us up to an immortality that shall outlast eternity. We ask it in the name of that Divine Fatherhood that makes all men brothers. Amen!" Response by the brethren: "So mote it be."

The following was composed by Most Worshipful Bro. C. C. Woods, Past Grand Master of this jurisdiction:

"O Thou Eternal and Omnipotent Judge of the quick and the dead, who turnest man to destruction, yet sayeth, 'Come again, ye children of men.' Thou, in the hollow of whose Almighty Hand weak humanity lives and moves and has its being, and spends its few short years like a tale that is told, enable each one of us to recognize the utter frailty of our own mortality and the hurried coming of the time when for us the grave shall call. Grant that this our brother here, who now lies before us in the dread semblance of death, may realize and deeply realize the

awful solemnity of the symbolism which we exhibit to him this
night, so that looking forward to the future and the reality of
life he may devote himself with full accord of heart and mind
unto the testimony of Thy word. And by the gentle influence of
the pure principles of our art, by the illustrious example of the
celebrated artist he now represents, by the sublime radiance of
the Great Light of Masonry, do Thou raise him up from the
death of sin to a life of righteousness and truth; from the death
of selfishness to a life of charity and love; from the dead level
of everything that is low and mean, from the dead level of
everything that is trivial and vain, from the dead level of everything that is sordid and unclean, do Thou raise him up to a
living perpendicular in the beauty of a high, noble and perfect
manhood. And so may he live, and so may he order his daily
walk and conversation that when the hour of his dissolution shall
draw nigh, when the feeble flutterings of his heart shall cease
and he shall come to lie stark and cold and pale at last, he may
fall asleep in the hope that the strong grip of the Lion of the
Tribe of Judah shall raise him up to the glory of a life eternal,
to the joy and felicity of perpetual youth, in a world without
end. Amen!" Response by the brethren: "So mote it be."

LECTURE XXI
SYMBOLISM OF THE RAISING

A GREAT many different meanings have from time to time been attached to the ceremony of raising aside from the greatest and most important lesson of immortality. As we have already hinted in former pages many have beheld in it a symbolic memorial of the resurrection of Jesus Christ from the dead. It had its origin, as a Masonic ceremony, in Christian times. Freemasonry as an occupation or profession reached its greatest glory in Christian times and under the patronage of Christian monks and priests.

It is entirely within the bounds of possibility that this scene was a miracle play prepared for the Masonic society by some priest or monk of the Middle Ages. We are aware that the early Christians of the Roman Catholic Church were accustomed to illustrate the Passion of Jesus by similar dramas. In the Book of Revelations, fifth chapter and fifth verse, we find these words: "Weep not, behold the Lion of the tribe of Judah, the root of David hath prevailed to open the book and loose the seven seals." It is said that the reason why the grip of an Entered Apprentice could not prevail to raise the body is that natural religion without the aid of revelation has never been able to demonstrate immortality. The reason why the grip of a Fellowcraft could not prevail and was equally unsuccessful, is that the Law and the Prophets are equally silent of any proof of the resurrection of the natural form and semblance of a man after his death and burial. It would seem as though the belief in a life somewhere beneath the surface of the earth was prevalent among the Jewish people. The story regarding the experience of King Saul with the Witch of Endor and the conjuring up of the ghost of the Prophet Samuel, whether the facts are as related in the account or not, thoroughly proves the belief was extant at the time the book was written. The ghost of Samuel was made to appear as though coming up out of the earth. The grip of the lion's paw brings the matter straight down to Jesus Christ and the Christian doctrine.

This was not the doctrine of Jesus Himself, for, so far as the Biblical record goes, Jesus said very little concerning what was likely to take place after death, though He seemed to share the general belief when He said: "In my Father's House are many mansions." His Eternal Life and Kingdom of Heaven were purely ethical conceptions and intended to apply entirely to affairs and conduct on this earth. "He that believeth on Me, even thouth he be dead, yet shall he live," certainly applies to a state of mind and not to place, time or dimensions. But, subsequent to the death of Jesus and founded upon His supposed resurrection from the dead, after lying in the tomb from Friday evening until Sunday morning, St. Paul and the Christian fathers erected their system of doctrine, which assumes the incarnation of the Deity Himself in the body of a man, everlasting life, either in heaven or hell, and the powers of the keys of St. Peter.

If our ceremony is merely memorial, this is what it commemorates. The resurrection from ignorance to wisdom, from intellectual darkness to light, from selfishness to charity and love, from sin to righteousness and all such attributed contraries may be traced into the allegory, if we please to do so. Our favorite impression is the rise from childhood to manhood. A regeneration comes to each man, and at approximately the same period of life. Most of us can well remember the day and perhaps the moment when our whole mental conception of the universe was changed, when our eyes were opened and we began to feel ourselves a part of the great plan. When, previously, we had felt ourselves compelled and obliged by external forces, now we began to realize the power and obligations of duty. When the individual comes to feel the power of duty he is said to be "twice born". He has discovered that perfect "law of liberty" concerning which St. James speaks, when he says: "He that findeth the perfect law of liberty and continueth therein, he being not a forgetful hearer but a doer of the word, that man shall be blessed in his deeds." All other laws are laws of force and compel obedience, the law of liberty is duty.

THE FIVE POINTS OF FELLOWSHIP—In all the old monitors there is represented a five-pointed star, in the center of which are two right hands clasped. This symbol illustrates five principles of conduct that should characterize the attitude of every Master Mason towards his brethren of the Craft. To conformity to these principles the Fraternity holds the brethren to a strict account:

1st. When the necessities of a worthy brother call for my aid and support, I will be ever ready to render him such assistance as within my power, without material injury to myself or family. Indolence shall not cause my footsteps to halt, nor shall wrath turn them aside, but forgetting every selfish consideration I will be ever swift of foot to save, to help and to execute benevolence to a fellow creature, particularly to a Masonic brother.

2nd. When I offer my devotions to Almighty God, I will remember a brother's welfare as my own. Our prayers for others are more likely to be sincere and disinterested than where we ourselves are alone concerned. There is a poem written by Whittier entitled "The Two Rabbis", which every Mason should read in contemplation of this precept. We quote the last passage:

> "Long years afterwards, when his headstone gathered moss,
> Upon the Targum's marge, at Onkelos,
> In Rabbi Nathan's hand these words were read:
> 'Hope not the cure of sin 'till self be dead.'
> Forget it in love's service and the debt
> Thou canst not pay the angels will forget.
> Heaven's gates are shut to him who comes alone,
> Save thou another soul and it shall save thine own."

In this poem two old men, hitherto of blameless life, had suddenly met temptation all too strong to bear and grievously sinned. Miserably repentant, each sought pardon in prayer and humiliation, but with no sense of relief. Finally, believing in each other's piety and wisdom, each sought the other for sympathy and help. Each made confession and besought the other's prayers. They knelt, each praying for the other's pardon, forgetting in the agony and stress of pitying love his own claim of selfishness. Each soon felt his prayers granted in the other's name, and on rising each saw God's pardon shining in the other's face.

3rd. A brother's secrets, when communicated to me and received by me as such, I will keep as I would my own. There is no Masonic obligation compelling one brother to become the unwilling confidant of another brother, but having once received this confidence it should never be betrayed. An exception is made regarding murder and treason. These are left to the election of the brother who receives the secret. Why? A crime in contemplation ought to be prevented if possible. Crime already committed may sometimes, through pity, be concealed. Circumstances alter cases and it can never be our duty to betray one who seeks our protection and aid when in deadly peril. We might be justified in refusing him shelter and help, he being no longer worthy of such assistance, but unless we ourselves are especially bound to a duty as officers of the law we ought to take no further part in his trouble. We as Masons are bound to see that our accused brethren are allowed a fair trial. We are in no way bound to see that guilty brethren are punished, or that our brethren escape from the clutches of the law, whether guilty or not. It is our duty to respect the laws of our country, but it is not our duty to execute them, unless especially so elected or appointed and sworn in. Then our duty as an officer of the law is specified in our instructions and should not be exceeded.

4th. I will support a falling, erring brother. This does not by any means require us to aid him in doing wrong, or in any manner to countenance him in it. Try to reform him if possible. We promise to remind a brother in the most tender manner possible of his failings. This is not a very easy or pleasant proceeding, if one desires to retain his friendship. When the Prophet Nathan went to remonstrate with King David regarding his conduct with relation to Uriah and his wife, Nathan thought up a nice little parable about a certain poor man who had one little ewe lamb, and how a rich man had confiscated it for sacrifice. After David had condemned the act in unmeasured terms, Nathan said, "Thou art the man." It is always a convenient thing to have ready a nice, apt parable to take with you when you go to remind a brother of his failings. About the best way in this day and generation is to set the delinquent brother an example by the rectitude of one's own conduct. Not much is likely to be gained by calling him down or reprimanding him.

5th. A brother's character I will support in his absence as in his presence. I will not wrongfully revile him myself, nor will I suffer it to be done by others, if within my power to prevent it. Give him comforting and consoling words if he is in distress of body or mind, and lead him to feel that you are indeed his brother, and thus will the Fraternity become a family, with God the Father of us all. The following poem has been suggested as appropriate to be employed upon occasion:

Foot to foot, that we should go
Where our help we can bestow,

Pointing out the better way,
Lest our brethren go astray;
Thus our steps should always lead
To the souls that are in need.

Knee to knee, that we may share
Every brother's needs in prayer,
Giving all his wants a place,
When we seek the throne of grace,
In our thoughts from day to day
For each other we should pray.

Breast to breast, to there conceal
What our lips should not reveal,
When a brother doth confide
We must by his will abide;
Masons' secrets, to us known,
We must cherish as our own.

Hand to back, our love to show
To our brother bending low
Underneath a load of care,
Which we may and ought to share;
That the weak may always stand,
Let us lend a helping hand.

Cheek to cheek, or mouth to ear,
That our lips may whisper cheer
To our brother in distress,
Whom our words may aid and bless;
Warn him if he fails to see
Dangers that are known to thee.

Foot to foot and knee to knee,
Breast to breast, as brothers be,
Hand to back and mouth to ear,
That that mystic word we hear
Which we otherwise conceal,
But on these five points reveal.
　　　　　　　　　　　　—N. A. McAulay.

THE MONUMENT—There is here mentioned a monument which is supposed to have been erected to the memory of our Grand Master, Hiram Abiff, who was slain. This was adopted and became a part of the work in American lodges some time very late in the eighteenth century. Its invention is attributed to Cross. It consists of a broken column, a virgin weeping, with a sprig of acacia in her right hand. In her left hand is held a funeral urn, before her is an open scroll and behind her a figure of Time unfurling and caressing the ringlets of her hair. This monument was mounted upon a pedestal of three steps. If there is anything to be taught by it, other than appears in the explanation given in the regular lodge work, it teaches that Masons, as well as other people, should show proper respect for the dead; that funeral ceremonies and funeral appointments should be dignified and significant, not of the pride, ostentation and vanity of the friends and relatives left behind, but what is customary among people of equal rank and fortune and social condition, so that no unfavorable comment may be made, for—

> Neither storied urn nor animated bust
>   Can back to its mansion call the fleeting breath,
> Nor can honor's voice provoke the silent dust,
>   Nor flattery sooth the dull, cold ear of death.

LECTURE XXII
THIRD SECTION OF M. M. DEGREE

THE third section of the degree of Master Mason illustrates certain hieroglyphical emblems and inculcates many useful and impressive moral lessons, and also details several particulars relative to the building of the Temple at Jerusalem.

According to Biblical record that celebrated structure was commenced in the fourth year of the reign of King Solomon, in the beginning of the Hebrew month Zif, the second month of the Jewish sacred year. It was located on Mount Moriah, on the threshing floor of Ornan, the Jebusite. It was also the ground where Abraham had prepared to offer up his son Isaac and it was on the same ground where David had met and appeased the Destroying Angel that had descended in wrath on account of the numbering of the children of Israel. It is supposed to be the spot where now stands the Mosque of Omar and the Dome of the Rock, so called in the modern city of Jerusalem.

This temple was not a large structure, compared with other contemporary temples that are known to history, though it may have been noted for its beauty and cost. It is evident that the wonder and magnificence of the temple increased in the minds of the Jewish people in the generations that followed its destruction. In the two hundred years or more that elapsed between the writing of the Book of Kings and the Book of Chronicles, the material of its decorations changed from bright brass to pure gold. At the dedication, as recounted in Kings, Solomon made his famous dedicatory prayer, turned and blessed the people, ordered a great sacrificial feast, of which all present partook, after which they went to their homes rejoicing, while in the Book of Chronicles the wonder had increased to such a degree that fire descended from heaven and consumed the burnt offering and the sacrifice, and the Glory of the Lord filled the house, in so much that the priests were unable to enter the house, because the Glory of the Lord filled it, and the people fell down on their faces on the pavement.

It would seem that this was a very important phenomenon, if true. Not a single word is said of such a happening in the more ancient account. If a man will take a pencil and paper and sit down and figure for half an hour he will find that the actual bulk of the gold and silver provided by David for the building of the House of the Lord would show a greater cubical contents than the temple itself. Doubtless the temple was a very imposing structure for the size and wealth of the country, and the Jewish people had a good right to feel proud of it. It evidently partook of both the Assyrian and Egyptian styles of architecture and yet it was a true type of neither. Doubtless it was in the minds of the architects to build it as nearly a counterpart of the ancient tabernacle as possible in stone. The interior dimensions were proportioned the same, but on a double scale.

The tower or propylon porch stood in front of it, but was not a part of the building. It was evidently intended as a watch tower principally, but also as a sort of proscenium box, from which the royal family might view the sacrifices which took place at the great altar erected immediately in front of it in the court yard. This tower was a hundred and twenty cubits high (180 feet). Thus it commanded a wide view over the surrounding country and the approach of a hostile force could be easily observed. This tower was occupied by an order or family known as the Sons of Rachab. This order, on account of their special business or duty of watching the neighborhood lest foes approach, was sworn to total abstinence from wine, or any sort of intoxicating liquor.

The temple was sixty cubits long, and allowing eighteen of our inches to the cubit this would make it ninety feet long, thirty wide and thirty high. These were, it is believed, internal measurements. This space was divided into two compartments by the veil, one compartment being a double cube and the other a perfect cube, thirty feet each way. The first was known as the Holy Place and the second as the Holy of Holies (Kadosh Kadoshim), in Latin "Sanctum Sanctorum." The veil was white linen embroidered in blue, purple, scarlet, gold and silver.

It will be noticed that the height of the tower is just twice the length of the building, and it stood thirty feet by fifteen on the ground and was at the east end of the building. This tower was pierced by the entrance to the building, and within it and between it and the building stood the two memorial pillars named Boaz and Jachin. In front of the temple in the courtyard was erected a large brazen altar, thirty feet square and fifteen feet high, with a stairway leading up to its summit. Near this was stationed the large brazen sea or cleansing basin, circular in form, fifteen feet across the top and mounted on the backs of twelve brazen oxen set with their heads facing outward. Against the temple building on either side were erected two tiers of cloisters, which were occupied by the priests and Levites officiating at the temple service.

The entire temple structure with its courts and buildings, together with King Solomon's residence and the House of the Cedars of Lebanon, were erected on a broad platform, so built as to render the uneven top of the mountain level and smooth. This platform alone remains of all the structures connected with the original temple. Such a platform was common to nearly all Assyrian buildings. This was partially to raise the building up above the line of river inundations and to get rid of the swampy emanations and the insect life which becomes such a burden in all towns of the Orient. In building this platform many caverns and deep gullies were walled up and arched over, and many ridges of the hill top must have been cut away. The vaulting of these passages under the great platform stands today, its masonry having endured the unsparing ravages of barbarous force and the changes of heat and cold, sunshine and storm. The stones composing it are, in many instances, quite large, often fifteen feet long by six square, and put together with exceedingly close joints. Large quarries in the immediate vicinity show where the stone was obtained with which the work was done.

The large court formed by this platform was fenced by a lofty wall and on the platform was erected a large arbor built of marble columns and lintels. At the time of the principal festivals this arbor was covered with green boughs so that the people might repose under the shade while eating the meat of the sacrifices. It is supposed that the fourteen hundred and fifty-three columns, and the two thousand nine hundred and six pilasters referred to in our work, were used in the construction of this arbor. There is no mention of any columns in the main structure. The interior was faced with wainscoting carved in lily-work and pomegranates, and as to design, arranged in chains, wreaths and festoons and overlaid with gold and set with precious stones, and the roof was of cedar timbers. The cherubim mentioned were composite animals formed by the union of the figures of the lion, the ox, the man and the eagle, representing the four seasons of the year. This cherub was a sort of national emblem, like the British lion or the American eagle or the Chinese dragon, and is frequently seen as an ornament about most Assyrian buildings. It most likely indicates that in their own eyes the nation possessed the combined characteristics of these four creatures, the intelligence of the man, the swiftness of the eagle, the fierceness of the lion and the strength of the ox.

The wings of these cherubim stretched out so that the wing of one reached the wall on one side and touched the wing of the other in the center, thus overshadowing the Ark of the Covenant. The Ark was the only article of furniture in the Holy of Holies, and that apartment was always kept in thick darkness, save from the light of the Shechinah alone, which burned night and day upon the Mercy Seat on top of the Ark. In the Holy Place there was an altar of incense, a table of shew (show) bread and twelve candlesticks, having each a single light, and a great candlestick having seven lights in one, which had been in the old Tabernacle. The main entrance to the temple was through the porch at the east end, though for some reason this was always kept closed. There was also an entrance in the right side of the house, through which the attendants entered. The winding stairs referred to were probably in the tower and led up to its summit, as there seems to have been no ascent to the building itself and all its floors were on the same level. There was certainly some way of climbing to the top of the tower and from the inside of the building also. There is a story regarding the visit of the Queen of Sheba which indicated "her wonder at the way by which he went up into the House of the Lord". This would seem to indicate that the king had some sort of a private stairway of his own and that the passage that says, "It is for the Prince, the Prince, he shall sit in it, to eat bread before the Lord (sacrifice). He shall enter in by the way of that gate and he shall go out by the way of the same," may probably refer to the same entrance. There is much in the description of the construction of the temple that is difficult to understand or follow, but the facts which we have stated seem to be clear.

The temple was seven years in building, during which time, we are informed by Josephus, it never rained during the daytime, so that the Craftsmen were never interrupted in their labors. *Its chief supports were three Grand Masonic columns, denominated Wisdom, Strength and Beauty. The temple was further supported by 1453 columns and 2906 pilasters, all hewn from the finest Parian marble. There were employed in the building of the temple three Grand Masters, 3300 Masters or Overseers of the work, 80,000 Fellowcrafts and 70,000 En-*

*tered Aprentices or bearers of burdens.   All of these were so
classified and arranged by the wisdom of Solomon that neither
envy, discord nor confusion was suffered to disturb or interrupt
the peace and good-fellowship which prevailed among the workmen.*

Regarding the levees of workmen called to the assistance of
King Solomon, there is room for some difference of opinion,
formed by reading the two accounts, but the Masonic traditions
finally settled down upon the numbers given.   The names Master,
Fellowcraft and Entered Apprentice were supplied by the early
writers of the Fraternity, but were taken from the following
information given in II Chronicles, XI Chapter and 18th verse:
"And he set three score and ten thousand of them to be bearers
of burdens, and four score thousand to be hewers in the mountains and three thousand and six hundred to be overseers to set
the people at work."   I Kings, V Chapter, 15th and 16th verses,
inclusive: "And Solomon had three score and ten thousand that
bare burdens, and four score thousand hewers in the mountains,
beside the chiefs of Solomon's officers which were over the work,
three thousand and three hundred, which ruled over the people
that wrought in the work."   The 17th and 18th verses of the
same chapter say: "And the King commanded and they brought
great stones, costly stones and hewed stones, to lay the foundation of the House, and Solomon's builders and Hiram's builders
did hew them and the stone squarers (giblim).   So they prepared the stones and the timbers to build the House."   And again
it says: "And King Solomon raised a levy out of Israel and the
levy was thirty thousand men.   He sent them to Lebanon, ten
thousand a month by courses.   A month they were in Lebanon
and two months they were at home, and Adoniram was over the
levy."   It is supposed that this last thirty thousand were reckoned in with the others at the numbering.

EMBLEMS—*"The emblems of this degree are of two classes, the
monitorial and the traditional.   The monitorial emblems are the
three steps, the pot of incense, the bee-hive, the Book of Constitutions, guarded by the Tiler's sword, the sword pointing at a
naked heart, the All Seeing Eye, the anchor and ark, the forty-
seventh problem of Euclid, the hour glass and the scythe.   They
are thus explained:*

*"The three steps usually delineated on the Master's carpet are
emblematic of the three prominent stakes of human life, youth,*

manhood and age. In youth, as Entered Apprentices, we ought industriously to occupy the mind in the accumulation of useful knowledge. In manhood, as Fellowcrafts we should apply that knowledge in the discharge of our respective duties to God, our neighbor and ourselves, so that in age as Master Masons we may enjoy the happy reflections consequent upon a virtuous and well-spent life and die in the hope of a glorious immortality."

The Master's carpet here referred to was a piece of tapestry on which were embroidered the emblems of the Fraternity. This method of picture illustration was quite common in the Gothic days, far more so than painting, until the beginning of the sixteenth century, after which time painting came into vogue. Even to this day the most beautiful banners are embroidered in our Order. The entire history of the Norman Conquest of England was illustrated in this manner on the celebrated Gobelin tapestries of the Cathedral of Bayeux in Normandy, the work being done by hand by Queen Matilda and her maids. All sorts of banners, flags and ensigns were made in this way down to the present age. Printed charts and stereopticon views are of a very recent development.

The pot of incense is an emblem of a pure heart, which is always an acceptable sacrifice to the Deity, and as it glows with fervent heat, so should our hearts continually glow with gratitude to the Great, Beneficent Author of our existence for the manifold blessings and comforts which we enjoy.

The bee-hive is an emblem of industry and recommends the importance of that virtue to all created beings, from the highest seraph in heaven to the lowest reptile in the dust. It teaches us that as we came into the world rational and intelligent beings, so should we always be industrious ones, never sitting down content while our fellow creatures around us are in want, when it is in our power to relieve them. When we take a survey of nature we view man in his infancy more helpless and indigent than the brute creation. He lies languishing for days, months and years, totally incapable of providing sustenance for himself, of guarding himself from the attacks of the wild beasts of the field or of sheltering himself from the inclemency of the weather. It might have pleased the Great Creator of Heaven and Earth to have made man independent of all other beings, but as dependence is one of the strongest bonds of society, mankind was made dependent on each other for protection and security, as they thereby enjoyed better opportunity of fulfilling the duties of reciprocal love and friendship. Thus was man made for social and active life, the noblest part of the work of God, and he that will so demean himself as not to be endeavoring to add to the common stock of knowledge and understanding may be deemed a drone in the hive of nature, a useless member of society and unworthy of our protection as Freemasons.

The Book of Constitutions guarded by the Tiler's sword reminds us that we should be ever watchful and guarded in all our thoughts, words and actions, particularly when before the enemies of Freemasonry, ever keeping in remembrance those truly Masonic virtues, silence and circumspection.

The sword pointing at a naked heart demonstrates that justice will sooner or later overtake us, and though our thoughts, words and actions may be hidden from the eyes of man, yet that All-Seeing Eye, whom the sun, moon and stars obey and under whose watchful care even the comets perform their stupendous revolutions, pervades the innermost recesses of the human heart and will reward us according to our merits.

The anchor and ark are emblems of a well-grounded hope and a well-spent life. They are emblematic of that Divine Ark that shall safely waft us over this tempestuous sea of troubles and that anchor that shall finally moor us in a peaceful harbor, where the wicked shall cease from troubling and the weary shall find rest.

The forty-seventh problem of Euclid was discovered by our ancient friend and brother, the great Pythagorus, who in his travels through Asia, Africa and Europe was initiated into the several orders of priesthood and raised to the Sublime Degree of Master Mason. This wise philosopher enriched his mind abundantly with a general knowledge of things and more especially in geometry or masonry. On this subject he drew out many problems and theorems and among the most distinguished he erected this, when in the joy of his heart he exclaimed, "Eureka!" signifying I have found it, and on the discovery of which he is said to have sacrificed a hekatome. It teaches Freemasons to be general lovers of the arts and sciences.

The meaning of the word "Hekatome" is "to cut up a hundred"; that is, he sacrificed a hundred cattle. The word "Eureka" is derived from the Sanscrit root "RCh", which means "light". It is very likely that the joy of Pythagorus was in the fact that in the "3-4-5" of the Pythagorean right-angled triangle lies the connection between all such words as "Logos", "I am that I am", "Al Shaddai", the last syllable of "Her-mes" (Mse) and the first syllable of "Moses" or "Mse-Jah", and all the Semitic and Egyptian words in which the syllable "Mes" occurs, as well as all the words in which the syllable "Ra" occurs, the latter syllable being but the "ChR" reversed, the "E" of the "Re" or "Ra" being the Hebrew of the Hebrew letter "Chet". This demonstration cleared up the problem of the connection of all the languages of the Orient through the word meaning "light". It also connected the Ancient Mysteries as celebrated throughout the world in the closest manner possible, for all these words which we have mentioned, and probably hundreds of others, which during the lapse of time have been lost, read cabalistically 3-4-5, the numbers of the Pythagorean triangle.

The discoverer of this problem or proposition in geometry, whoever it was, whether Pythagorus or Euclid, scientifically discovered the whole process of "triangulation". Herein was a receipt or set of directions for drawing a right angle or square, under any and all circumstances and in any situation. He had discovered that if one takes three lines, in the proportions of three, five and four, and joins them together in the shape of a triangle, it will invariably be a right-angled triangle, with the right angle opposite the longest side. Now the square of three which is nine, added to the square of four which is sixteen, equals twenty-five, which is the square of five. So where we have two sides of a right-angled triangle, if we square these two sides and add these squares together and extract the square root of the sum, we will have the third side; or subtract if one of the two be its hypotenuse. The original problem was always demonstrated by these numbers, 3-4-5.

The figure which we usually have displayed in our lodges in lantern pictures is quite modern, and in some ways makes the problem universal, that is capable of being worked out with other numbers than 3-4-5. We can readily see that any figure bounded by straight lines, no matter what their number or length, can be easily cut up into triangles, and any triangle is naturally composed of two right-angled triangles. It was next shown that even a circle was composed of an infinite number of triangles, the altitude of all and each of them being the radius of the said circle, and the circumference of the circle being equal to the sum of the bases of all the triangles. Therefore, if the area of a triangle was the product of the base by half the altitude, the area of a circle must be the circumference multiplied by half of the radius. In any right-angled triangle, save the 3-4-5 triangle, there will be one unknown side, which will have to be determined by squaring the sides known, as above stated.

Another problem dependent upon the forty-seventh was that the sum of all the angles in a triangle is equal to two right angles, so that when one side and two angles are known, or even two sides and one angle are known, the other dimensions can be determined. This was one of the great secrets of operative Masonry which our ancient brethren carefully kept for many generations. The great secret of the ancient speculative Masons was the "caballah." Had it not been for the sake of the latter our ancient brethren need not have distressed themselves about their secret being discovered. The man that steals a secret in mathematics deserves to be left in full possession of it, for it robs nobody, makes no man poorer in pocket or brain, and one can be very certain that the work that will be necessary to make the stolen property his own will fully equal the value of the possession, and cannot be transferred in any other manner than by that long and painful road by which he himself obtained it.

The hour-glass is the emblem of human life. Behold how swiftly the sands run and how rapidly our own lives are drawing to a close. You cannot, without astonishment, behold the little particles that are contained in this machine, how they pass away almost imperceptibly, and yet, to our surprise, in the short space of an hour they are all exhausted. So wastes man, today putting forth the tender leaves of hope, tomorrow blossoming and bearing his blushing honors thick upon him. The next day comes a frost that nips the shoot, and when he thinks his greatness is still aspiring, he falls like autumn leaves to enrich our mother earth.

The scythe is an emblem of time which cuts the brittle thread of human life and launches us into eternity. Behold what havoc the scythe of time makes among the human race. If by chance we escape the numerous evils incident to childhood and youth and with health and vigor arrive at the years of manhood, yet with all we are soon cut off by the all-devouring scythe of time and gathered into that land where our fathers have gone before us.

The second class of emblems has to do with the tradition of

our Order. Their explanation is secret and can only be obtained within the tiled lodge. They afford subjects of serious and solemn reflection to the rational and contemplative mind.

Thus we close the explanation of the emblems on the solemn thought of death, which without revelation is dark and gloomy. But the good Freemason is suddenly revived by the ever-green and ever-living sprig of faith which blooms at the head of the grave. It reminds him that there is an immortal spark in man, bearing a close affinity to the Supreme Intelligence of the Universe, which shall survive beyond the grave and never, never, never die. This strengthens him to look forward with confidence and composure to a blessed immortality, and he doubts not that on the glorious morn of the Resurrection his body will rise and become as incorruptible as his soul. * * * Then let us imitate * * * in his amiable and virtuous conduct, in his unfeigned piety to God, in his inflexible fidelity to his trust, that we may welcome the grim tyrant, Death, and receive him as a kind messenger sent by our Supreme Grand Master to translate us from this imperfect to that all perfect, glorious and Celestial Lodge above, where the Supreme Architect of the Universe presides.

The ceremonies of these degrees are intended to represent the life of man, through youth and manhood, attended by their various trials, sorrows and temptations, followed by death and the grave, and these by the resurrection and life everlasting.

CHARGE OF A MASTER MASON—*Brother, your zeal for the Institution, the progress you have made in our mysteries and your steady conformity to our useful regulations have pointed you out as a proper object for this particular mark of our favor. Duty and honor now alike bind you to be faithful to every trust, to support the dignity of your character upon all occasions and strenuously enforce by precept and example a steady obedience to the tenets of Freemasonry. Exemplary conduct on your part will convince the world that merit is the just title to our mysteries and that upon you they have not been undeservedly bestowed. In this respectable character you are authorized to correct the irregularities of your less-informed brethren, to fortify their minds with resolution against the snares of the insidious and to guard them against every allurement to vicious practices. To preserve unsullied the reputation of the Fraternity ought to be your constant care, and it becomes your province to caution the inexperienced against any breach of fidelity. To your inferiors in rank and office you are to recommend obedience and submission, to your equals courtesy and affability and to your superiors kindness and condescension. Universal benevolence you are zealously to inculcate, and by the regularity of your own conduct endeavor to remove every aspersion against our venerable Institution. Our Ancient Landmarks you are carefully to preserve, nor suffer them on any pretext to be infringed, or countenance any deviation from our established customs. Your honor and reputation are alike concerned in supporting with dignity the respectable character you now bear. Let no motive, therefore, make you swerve from your duty, violate your vows or betray your trust, but be true and faithful and imitate the example of that celebrated Artist whom you have this evening represented. Thus you will render yourself deserving of the honor which we have conferred, and worthy the confidence we have reposed in you.*

LECTURE XXIII

SPECIAL LECTURES

THE previous chapter closes our comments on the ritual of Freemasonry, as used in Missouri, so far as we may write for the public eye. We have witnessed the work in many other jurisdictions and when all things are considered this work compares very favorably with any rendering that it has been our fortune to see. The following public ceremonies are printed in many monitors, and have their own particular beauties, but possess no esoteric meaning. We will not repeat them here, as the Grand Lodge prints them and sells them in any quantities needed. They are the funeral ceremony, the ceremony of installation of officers, the ceremony for public laying of corner-stones, the ceremony of dedication of halls for lodges, the ceremony for the institution of lodges and the ceremony for a lodge of sorrow or memorial for the dead. These ceremonies are public in their nature and are easily understood by any intelligent man who hears them. They do not differ greatly in the different jurisdictions and some of them are quite ancient.

From time immemorial, in this state, there has existed a mortality lecture which the most celebrated workers have liked to give. They have handed it down from one generation to another, though it was never recognized as a part of the regular ritual. Many of us older members hold it in a good deal of veneration. We believe it should always be given when the candidate seems to be of sufficient intelligence, and sufficiently refined in sentiment, to properly realize and appreciate it, and where the presiding Master has sufficient elecutionary ability to deliver it with solemnity and feeling. There are some narrow minds, ignorant of the history of our ritual, who hold that the slightest deviation from the wording of the ritual, as it came to their ears, either by variation, addition or subtraction, should incur all the anathemas that attend the infringement of an Ancient Landmark, and that the Grand Lodge should punish such an act as a direct defiance of their authority. We hold, and with good Masonic company, that all such rules are impertinent innovations of the most recent character. We are far from believing that an absolutely universal ritual, even if

possible, would be at all desirable. We do believe that the
means of recognition and the determination of Masonic standing ought to be universal, that is the same the world over, but
those addresses and charges with which the Master welcomes
and instructs a candidate are of a different character and should
depend greatly on circumstances. Our own version of the
mortality lecture is as follows:

"We are all born to die. Life is but a span. The death of
others is a solemn reminder of our own mortality. When we
sit at the bedside of a departing friend, we gaze with anxious
solicitude until his last struggle is over and he sinks down into
the fathomless abyss of death, and when we come to stand at
the edge of his open grave, we consciously feel our own feet
crushing the precarious brink upon which we stand, and are
made to realize that e'er long our own throbbing hearts will
have ceased to beat, and that we, too, shall be at rest.

"Generation after generation have felt as we feel now. Their
lives were as active as our own, but they have all passed away
like a vapor, while nature wears the same aspect of beauty
that she wore on the morn when her Great Creator first commanded her to be. The heavens will shine just as brightly above
our graves as they now do about our pathway. The earth will
possess the same attractions for our children's children yet un-
born as it once possessed for us, and now has for our offspring.

"In a little while all will have passed away. Our funeral
cortege will slowly wend its way to the silent city of the dead.
The coffin that contains our last remains will be lowered into
that still and narrow house, six feet due east and west and
six feet perpendicular, and amid the pitiless rattle of the cold
clods of the valley upon our final tenement the last prayer will
be said, 'earth to earth, ashes to ashes, dust to dust,' and when
the sexton's spade shall have rudely shaped the little mound,
which perchance is all that will ever mark the spot, our friends
will turn away and leave us in the chill silence of the tomb.

"It may be, for a little while, our names will be spoken in our
homes, but the cares of the world will creep in and we will soon
be forgotten. Days, months and years will come and go, telling
their life stories in chapters of sunshine and shadow, pleasure
and pain, and even the very room wherein we died will again
resound with laughter and with song. The tears that were
shed for us will be wiped away. The eyes that mourned for us
will again be bright and glisten with new-found joys. Even

our little children will fail to recall our long familiar faces, and the place that knew us once upon the earth will know us no more. Even the stately monuments, erected by sorrowing affection or by worldly vanity, will e'er long have crumbled into clay, the great seal of oblivion will be set upon us and our deeds, be they good, bad or indifferent as they may, will remain recorded only in the book of God's remembrance.

"Thus we close the explanation of the emblems on the solemn thought of death, which without revelation is dark and gloomy, but the good Mason is suddenly revived at the sight of that ever-green and ever-living sprig of faith that blooms at the head of the grave, which reminds him that there is in man a vital spark that bears a close affinity to the Supreme Intelligence of the Universe, that will survive beyond the grave and never, never, never die. This strengthens him with confidence and composure to look forward to a blessed immortality.

"Brother, you and I owe a debt of gratitude to Almighty God and thanks to the Masonic Fraternity that we stopped not, when we had taken the first or the second steps, but that being embued with a sincere desire for more light we pressed forward and have taken the third and have at last been raised to the Sublime Degree of Master Mason; and here in our own persons enacted this symbolic resurrection.

"Freemasonry has many mysteries, but the greatest mystery of all is death. How we shall not always sleep, but we shall all be changed in a moment, in the twinkling of an eye, casting aside the old worthless and corruptible garments, stained with toil and shame and sin, and putting on the glorious and tran-splendent costumes of Eternal Life. And though our last resi-dence here be but this still and narrow house six feet due east and west and six feet perpendicular, there the building of the walls shall be of jasper and its foundations garnished with all manner of precious stones. Though here we travel a rough and rugged road, beset with difficulties and with dangers, there the streets shall be paved with pure gold like unto clear glass, and the wayfaring man, though a fool, need not err therein. Though here we grope in darkness and the valley of the shadow of death, there will be no need of the sun nor of the moon to shine there, for the Glory of the Lord our God shall lighten it and it shall endure forever and ever. And forth from that temple of benevolence and peace there shall flow a river through the midst of the city, beneath whose crystal tide shall be submerged all the sighs and tears and sorrows of this world, and on the banks of the river shall bloom the tree of life, of which the sprig of acacia is the humble symbol, whose leaves and fruit are for the healing of the nations.

"Brother, behold where the Great Light of Masonry sheds its rare and pure effulgence. There breathes the true word of a Master Mason, the word that was once made flesh and dwelt among us. There may you read the truths and promises of revealed religion, and with the eye of faith piercing the dark curtain of the tomb feast your gaze on the ineffable beauties of our Eternal Home, that Temple and Tabernacle that shall endure, that passeth not away, whose builder and whose maker is God.

"Brethren, let us regulate our lives by the plumb-line of justice and square our actions by the square of virtue, so that when the Warden of Heaven shall call for us we may be found ready. Let us cultivate assiduously the noble tenets of our profession. From the square let us learn morality, from the level equality and from the plumb rectitude of life and conduct. Let us imitate in all his varied perfections our * * *, who when assailed by the murderous hands of rebellious craftsmen, maintained his integrity, even unto death, and sealed his principles with his vital blood. Let us emulate his just and amiable conduct, his unfeigned piety to his God, his inflexible fidelity to his trust, and as the little evergreen sprig of acacia blooming at the head of his grave betrayed the place of his interment, so may virtue's ever-blooming loveliness designate us as Free and Accepted Masons. With the trowel let us spread liberally the cement of brotherly love and affection circumscribed by the compass, and let all the energies of our minds and all the affections of our hearts be employed in the attainment of the approbation of our Supreme Grand Master, so that when the hour of our dissolution shall draw nigh, and the cold winds of death come sighing around us and we already feel his chill dew glistening on our brows, with joy may we obey the summons that calls us to go from our labors on earth to everlasting refreshment in the paradise of God, where standing at the right hand of our Supreme Grand Master He will be pleased to pronounce us 'just and perfect Masons'. Then shall we be fitly prepared as living stones for that spiritual building, that house not made with hands, eternal in the heavens, where all that the soul shall experience shall be perfect bliss and all that the soul shall express shall be perfect praise and love Divine, all love excelling shall ennoble every heart and hozannas exalted honor every tongue."

Many of us have felt the need of a short charge to a candidate that had just finished his degrees in Masonry, regarding its effect upon him and the mental attitude in which he was likely to find himself regarding the Institution as the years go on. The following was prepared by Bro. H. B. White, of the Jurisdiction of Iowa:

"Brother, the ceremony of your initiation is now at an end, you have had delivered to you the authorized charge and such parts of the Ancient Charges as relate to your Masonic conduct in the lodge, at home and abroad, and so far all has been carried out in accordance with a prescribed formula that certain invaluable and incomparable landmarks might never be omitted or departed from, but Masonry is so infinite in its application and teachings that it is wisely left to the presiding officer to add anything by way of illustration or admonition that may appear advisable, provided, of course, that in all things the Ancient Landmarks are respected.

"My particular object in thus addressing you is to prevent you leaving the lodge this evening with any of the mistaken impressions frequently entertained by newly-made Masons. I would not have you go away with the idea that you have been fooled, or that any one portion of the recent ceremony is unmeaning or introduced with the mere purpose of mystification. Freemasonry is truly a system of morality, veiled in allegory and illustrated by symbols, and the most apparently trivial incident, both in your preparation and initiation, has its deep and hidden meaning. It is not reasonable to expect that you should, at first sight, penetrate the outer or allegorical symbol, but I trust that you will make it your business as a Mason to arrive at these hidden meanings.

"Another and most fatal delusion I would guard you against is, that of entertaining the idea that the information imparted to you this evening has made you a Freemason. After my efforts to impress you with the importance of the ceremony such a warning from me may create some astonishment in your mind, but what I would imply is, that Masonry is not a mere matter of secret ceremonies. It is something far higher and holier than these. A man may attain to the highest honors that the Craft may offer and be perfectly up in all its lore and working, and yet be far from being a Freemason, as far as he was before his initiation, and unfortunately, there are too many who may be classed in this category.

"The rites and ceremonies of Freemasonry are essential to its existence. They form the outworks where its treasures are and ought to be guarded from the unworthy, and therefore cannot, under any circumstances, be dispensed with, but true Masonry exists in the heart and is composed of brotherly love, relief and truth, and that heavenly consummation of virtues, charity, so beautifully explained in the Volume of the Sacred Law as bearing all things, hoping all things, believing all things, enduring all things and thinking no evil. And it is in the practice of this virtue to which all your Masonic efforts should tend, not only in its common acceptation of pecuniary relief, but as embracing the true brotherly love to the full extent inculcated in the Holy Writings.

"Initiation alone never did and never can make a man a true Mason. It gives the key, but the mere possession of the key does not constitute ownership of the treasure. It sows the seed, but unless the soil be good and carefully cultivated, fruit will not be produced. It opens the portal, but unless the road be traversed the goal cannot be attained. It lays the foundation, but without labor the superstructure cannot be raised. So this evening we have given you the key, we have sown the seed, opened the portal and laid the foundation. It is for you with such assistance, as amongst Masons can always be found by seeking for it in the proper quarter, to complete the work, and I sincerely trust that in this you will not be found wanting.

"Finally, while charging you not to under-value Masonry, I will beg you to remember that it is a human institution and as such necessarily imperfect and liable to error; do not be disheartened (disappointed you naturally will be) if you find some who profess its tenets but do not act up to its teachings. You will probably frequently hear our noble science ridiculed by the unenlightened world and stigmatized as a childish mystery and a pretension to superior excellence, covering only secret revels and excesses. Treat such ridicule with contempt and answer it only by acting up to your profession. A man who ridicules that of which he cannot by any possibility know anything, stultifies himself and is unworthy of notice.

"But alas! you will find unworthy members of the Fraternity, some who abuse its privileges, some who from their own inherent baseness are unable to appreciate its beauties and convert its moments of social relaxation into occasions of debauch; and others who from their mental powers being too dense to enable them to penetrate beyond the exterior consider Freemasonry as mysterious nonsense. If you meet with any such, console yourself with the reflection that there ever has been, and while time lasts there ever will be, such men, in every human institution, and if you are well read in the Great Light of Masonry, you will call to mind instances where holier ordinances have been similarly profaned and misunderstood, and so you will be led to understand that Freemasonry is not to be blamed for the misdeeds and shortcomings of some of its professors.

"I will not detain you with any further observations, but merely in conclusion express the hope that the proceedings of this evening will never be effaced from your memory, and that by your life and actions you will in all things prove to the uninstructed world at large how ennobling, excellent and enlightened an Institution is that of the Ancient Free and Accepted Masons."

The following address on the Holy Bible, to be used in the explanation of the Three Great Lights, was also prepared in the Jurisdiction of Iowa:

"My brother, this Great Light of Masonry, the Holy Bible, is to rule and guide your faith. It is the volume that contains the words of everlasting life and brings immortality to light. It binds our wounds and cements our friendship. It sings in our poetry and chants in our music. It falls on the ear like a story that can never be forgotten. It is a book to take to the heart, to turn to in the hours of joy, to look into in times of sorrow and to accept at all times as our friend, teacher and guide. If we are ignorant it will tell us all that we need to know of God, duty and of the life beyond the tomb. If we are lost it will bring us home. If the inner light burns low it will kindle these poor hearts of ours with a flame from the Altar of God. King and noble, prince and peasant, the rich man and the pauper, are alike students of its pages. Its stories charm and delight the little child as it sits at its mother's knee, its hopes inspire the aged and its promises sooth the bed of pain. The maiden is wedded under its sanction while the grave is covered with its comforting influence. Its lessons are the essentials of religion, the end of philosophy and the principle of morals. No other volume is so frequently quoted, none so often referred to. It contains more true sublimity, more exquisite beauty, more pure morality, more important history and finer strains of poetry and eloquence than can be collected from any other book in whatever language or age they may have been written. May you so read it as to impress upon your heart and mind the truths and words pertaining to the life here, and to that greater, grander, more beautiful life in the Grand Lodge on high, towards which we are all hastening."

LECTURE XXIV
SIDE LINES OF MASONIC STUDY

A N exact knowledge of the questions and answers that go
to make up the lectures of Freemasonry is absolutely
necessary to acquiring a working knowledge of the ritual.
And a comprehensive knowledge of the Bible, the events it
records, the characters in its personnel, the geography of the
countries mentioned, the Jewish law and the Christian doctrine
are all absolutely necessary to the successful study of religious
philosophy in any special line.

This book being old as the oldest, forms a standard of comparison, a measuring wand by which to estimate the value of
the ancient systems of all nations. A hundred years ago it
would not have been necessary to insist upon this information,
for every man who pretended in the least to scholarship was
perfectly familiar with the text of the Bible. It was continuously read in the homes and in the schools, and discussed in every
Sunday gathering. Controversy over its different points of
doctrine was constant. Nearly every one took part in it. Nearly
everybody believed in the verbal inspiration and studied it
entirely from that point of view. People who paid very little
attention to any of its precepts were more familiar with its
literature than many devout churchmen are today.

There is now so much literature extant, so much that is
comical or startling, so much that seems to have money in it, that
people who really love good literature have, in a measure, neglected this great work, but you cannot get anywhere in the study
of the ancient religions, or in the knowledge of the different
systems of philosophy on which they rest, without becoming
familiar with it.

In following the origin of religious traditions we frequently
have to probe to the very bottom of Chaldaic, Assyrian and
Egyptian lore, and also the mysteries through which these
philosophical dogmas were taught and treasured up and transmitted to future generations. In seeking the origin of Jewish
law delivered, according to tradition, by Moses, we can easily
trace it to the Code of Hammurabbi, an Assyrian monarch who
flourished in the days of Abraham and who published his code
on stone pillars set up throughout his dominions. In books

[199]

written subsequent to the Babylonish Captivity, we discover
beliefs and philosophy derived from the Persians and through
them to Iranian and Vedic sources.   This leads us to the study
of Sanscrit and the inexhaustible literature of ancient India.
Hundreds of the holy books of India were carried down from one
generation to another, for three or four thousand years, entirely
by oral tradition.

Later in Christian times the student comes in contact with
the marvelous resources of the Greek mind.   Here is laid out
before us the mental ingenuity of Socrates, Plato, Aristotle and
the Greek Jews of Alexandria.   Following these down to Mohammedan times we come in contact with the literary and philosophical ability that contrived the Cabalah and the Zohair, the
search for the philosopher's stone and the elixir of perpetual
youth, and we may catch some glimpses of the deeper meaning
of those romantic studies that interested the recluses of the
dark ages.   At last we arrive at the great awakening of medieval
art and the origin of our own Society.

No book opens up so many vistas of information.   It is mixed
up with every kind of religious thought in all historical times.
Today very few scholars pay any attention to it unless they
intend taking up the clerical profession.   It is the subject of
all great art in sculpture, painting, architecture, music and
poetry, all that has value, during the last two thousand years.
Any student who expects to accomplish anything along the line
of Masonic lore must begin first by learning the contents of the
Bible.   It is certainly the record of the spiritual experience of
the human race.

The next subject that should interest the Masonic student is
the foundation subject of geometry and its practical application
in trigonometry and its esoteric employment in gematria, which
is only a reconstruction of the title word as it was used in bury-
ing philosophical and astronomical facts so that they might be
hidden from the prying eyes and minds of the uninitiated.   The
pleasure and beauty of pure mathematics does not come to every
scholar, nor to any scholar without work, but when it once arrives there are few that are more entrancing.   Every man that
would be a Master, whatever his occupation, should have felt
this attraction for symmetry, for exactness and for order, which
is its greatest attribute.   No man may become a great
logician, a great orator, a great lawyer, a great economist, and
we very much doubt if he can ever become a strictly honest and

just man, without the mathematical sense.

The very heart and soul of this science is found in the Forty-seventh Problem of Euclid. Space will not permit a more perfect elucidation of this science than has already been given, under its proper head, in the lecture on the third degree, but we have there given enough so that the reader can appreciate our position when we declare that there is no manifestation of the Infinite which is more clearly suggestive of the wisdom and justice of the Deity than geometry. This science is certainly entitled to be counted as the seventh part of a liberal education. Next to the study of this subject in its abstract sense comes its practical application in architecture and engineering.

If there is any satisfaction to be had in living in the memory of one's fellowmen it finds its best reward in the perfection of this art. There is no result of human endeavor so durable or so worthy. To the Freemason who has never read a book on the marvelous work of our ancient operative brethren, we offer a new joy, and for the Past Master of a lodge, who has entirely neglected this, we have something like contempt. He has failed to get an obvious and positive benefit out of the Order, for which he is entirely without excuse. He is not fit to give instruction to his less informed brethren. The books which have been written on the vast Gothic cathedrals yield much information regarding the history of our Order. The Master of a lodge certainly ought to understand the distinguishing marks of the different styles of architecture, the Egyptian, the Assyrian, the old Persian, the Greek, the Roman, the Hindu, the Chinese, the later Mohammedan, and so down to the Gothic of the Middle Ages, which forms the very crown of building science.

Why do we claim that the Gothic was the crown of architectural art? All other forms were composed of the simple column and lintel or hewn out of some solid mountain of rock, whole and complete. These exhibit nice workmanship. The stones are exactly fitted, highly polished and beautifully decorated, but it requires little scientific knowledge to set up a forest of columns near together and lay lintels across them from column to column, and to place flat stones on the top of these to form a roof. In the Gothic our ancient brethren erected an arched structure of small stones, all wrought and fitted in the workshop, and so carefully put together, and the weight of material kept in such delicate balance and equilibrium that the very mass supported adds to its strength. This demonstrates that the plans and designs must have been drawn to accurate scale. The adornment of these buildings with sculpture, mosaic, cameo, tapestry, colored glass and later with oil painting and fresco in distemper, renders each of these forms of ornamentation a study in itself. Our ancient Grand Masters were not only cunning workers in stone and metal, but in blue, purple, scarlet and white fine-twined linen. No one can look upon one of these masterpieces of art without catching some faint glow of a great light that has failed. One cannot even examine a picture of one of these ancient medieval cathedrals and not be at once certified of the presence of a great desire, of some hearts that were once bursting with devotion, of some hands that had been made eloquent with the tender touch of a great love, of a skill that no money could purchase and no fear compel, of a learning no school could teach and no books record, something born of inspiration, nourished in the cradle of romance and poetry, ennobled with great courage and knightly courtesy and burning with the fire of true religion, until we are forced to exclaim, like Nicodemus of old—"Surely no man can do the works that thou doest except God be with him."

In the light of this sublime emotion our ancient brethren wrought miracles in stone. They heaped it up in massive towers that rose on open archways through the lofty roofs of naves and transepts and tapered away in shell-like spires. They carried it over domes of gigantic span. They embroidered it in lace-like tracery. They hung it aloft in foliage vaulting, treated like the gossamer web of nature, scarce capable of sustaining the weight of the stalactite pendants in which their fancy found expression. They cut the granular stone into the thinness of fibrous wood or iron. They sought out the laws of elasticity and equilibrium and reveled in tricks of construction and marvels of workmanship. Here in these stones our ancient brethren told chapter by chapter and verse by verse and incident by incident all the simple wonder stories of the Bible.

Their sculpture was not the exact and finished work, but the rude shaping of a primitive idea. The educated Greek with his cultivated taste and practiced skill carved in order to produce a beautiful and perfect statue. The ancient Freemason carved as well as he could to tell a story or illustrate a mystery. The workmanship was always subservient to the legend to be represented. The Greek often composed a scene in order to exhibit his sculpture. In the classic days of dramatic art the actor employed all his ability to make the scene and literature appear real, to hold the mirror up to nature. Of late years the plays are written to exhibit the special talents of some actor, from the slap-stick variety up, and always with the sole purpose of amusing and startling and never for instructing the patrons, hence the decay of the theatre. The effort to reproduce a story will always be good art, even though the artist be unskillful. The work for the sake of showing off the artist will be bad art, though the sculptor has all the skill of a Phydias or Praxiteles.

The ground plan of a cathedral was, of course, a cross. The main tower was over the crossing. The choir was at the east and the nave at the west of the crossing, and the arms of the cross were made by the transepts extending north and south. The west front or facade usually had a north and south tower, between which were the main entrances. About these entrances and over them were arranged galleries for statuary. Here in the very center of the central porch stood the beautiful Christ as He walked upon the shores of Galilee, and on His right and left prophets and apostles, saints and angels occupied each his appropriate niche. On one side we behold Adam and Eve, accompanied by the Serpent under the apple tree; Cain and Abel at the scene of the first murder; Enoch walking with God in the cool of the evening; Noah with his Ark and the animals going in two by two; Abraham entertaining the angels at the door of his tent; Lot and his family fleeing from the blazing ruins of Sodom and Gomorrah; Jacob wrestling with the Spirit of the Lord or waiting for Rachael at the well; Joseph sold by his brethren into Egyptian slavery, and again wielding the sceptre in the palace of Pharaoh; Moses in his bullrush cradle, again before the burning bush and again receiving the Tablets of the Law from the hand of God on Mount Sinai. Here were Gideon and Barak and Deborah; Jael with her hammer driving the nail into Sisera's skull; Samson walking away with the gates of Gaza upon his shoulders; the youthful David with the gory head of the giant of Gath; Saul in the cave of the witch of Endor; Solomon sitting upon his throne of state entertaining Balchis, Queen of Sheba; Jonah stepping in imperturable serenity from the mouth of the whale; Daniel interpreting the handwriting on the plaster of the wall of Belshazzar's palace, or sitting quietly in the lion's den, and Haman hanging from the gallows that he had prepared for Mordecai. On the other side you may see the shepherds watching their flocks by night on the hills of Judea;

the Wise Men journeying from the East and adoring at Bethlehem; the Venerable Simeon receiving the Holy Child at the Temple's gate; the slaughter of the Innocents; the Flight into Egypt; the Carpenter's shop at Nazareth; the Argument with the Doctors in the Temple. Here is represented the Baptism by John in the Jordan; the Temptations in the Wilderness; the Miracles and the Parables. Here is the Prodigal Son returning home to his father's house; the Wise and Foolish Virgins; the Good Samaritan, and the Sower that went forth to sow. All the different scenes of the Passion; the triumphant entrance into Jerusalem; the Last Supper and the Holy Graal; the Agony in the Garden; the Kiss of Judas; the Atrocious Trial before Pilate; the cruel crucifixion on Calvary; the sad burial in Joseph's tomb; the glorious Resurrection and Ascension, and over the High Altar the awful scene of the last Judgment, the great Assize, when the Shepherd divides the sheep from the goats:

> Not on account of the creeds they had read,
> Not on account of the prayers they had said,
> Not on account of the blood they had shed,
> But just on account of the hungry they had fed,

did the award of that Judgment lay. Here and there wherever he could the workman placed the symbols of his Ancient Craft. Here is the cable-tow entwining about window and doorway, panel and pavement. Here the lion of the tribe of Judah upholds the Broken Column. Here strange beasts and dire monsters, drawn vividly and accurately from the life he knew, tell of temptations unresisted and passions unsubdued.

These were rare buildings, my brethren. It is no wonder that the ignorant of later days believed them to have been erected by magical means. It is no wonder that they speculated upon the wonderful powers of the Lost Word and the Seal-Ring that controlled the services of the fairies and jinns. The walls of these buildings seem to carry no weight. You behold a roof of stone supported on a veil of glass, and such glass! The splendor of all the jewelry of ten thousand Orients blazes before you. The setting sun gilds the halo of the saint, the flames of the martyr, the diadem of the monarch and the corslet of the hero, in one bewildering sheen of glory. Here again we behold the work of the woman's hand. Look at these elaborately wrought Gobelin tapestries that cover the cold gray stone. Here is spread out in imperishable colors all the history of the world, the adventures of kings and queens and knights and ladies, great ceremonies, great sacrifices, great battles and great gifts, all in needle work inimitable and priceless. Here in proudly vaulted chapels hang the ancient swords and shields and armor, and beneath them in richly carved mausoleums sleep the mouldering bodies of the honored great and good who bore these accoutrements worthily in victory and in defeat, their sculptured effigies still testifying to the dignity and universality of death. What grand and solemn pageants brought them hither—

A prince to the fate of the peasant had yielded,
    Dark tapestry waved round the dim-lighted halls;
With scutcheons of silver the coffin was shielded
    And pages stood mute by the canopied palls.

Through the naves at deep midnight the torches were gleaming,
Round the richly carved altars the banners were beaming;
Far down the long aisles sacred music was streaming,
    Lamenting a chief of the people should fall.

But the boast of heraldry and the pomp of power,
    All that beauty, all that wealth e'er gave
Await alike the inevitable hour,
    The path of glory leads but to the grave.

In those old days Christian knighthood marched hand in hand with our Ancient Craft. Sir Launcelot, Sir Bedavere, Sir Parcevale, Sir Galahad, and so on down to Richard of the Lion Heart, Tancred the bravest of the brave, and Bayard without fear and without reproach, went forth from these pictured doorways with the blessings of these altars upon their heads to succor the poor and needy, to champion the cause of the destitute and the oppressed, to set the captive free, to search for the hidden Graal, to reclaim the Holy Sepulchre and do their devoirs as beseemeth men. And all these great deeds did our ancient brethren record in granite, marble and alabaster, for the sake of the greater glory of God and for the most part without the hope of fee or reward. Many of their names have sunk into oblivion, their bones are dust, their working tools are rust, their souls are with the saints, we trust, but their lingering spirits still hover round the work they wrought.

It is related by an aged brother of the Ancient Craft that on one occasion he made a return visit to Rheims, on which cathedral he had labored many years in his younger days. Being weary with his long journey he sat down to rest in a secluded corner of the venerable structure. As he sat meditating on the days he had spent on the work, the companions with whom he had wrought, the stories and legends of the patron saints of the church, the organ began playing for the vesper service, and he lightly dozing, there experienced a very curious vision. He seemed to feel the vibrations of the music communicated to the building itself, and the stones began to sing, the ancient statues and paintings seemed to take on life, the marble saints took up the hymn, the noble army of martyrs followed, the glorious company of the apostles joined, then the goodly fellowship of the prophets, and as he gazed the vaulting of the cathedral melted away and he beheld the church triumphant in heaven, the Cherubim and Seraphim, and heard them chanting over and over again "Te Deum Laudamus."

My brethren, this was but an accidental dream and it may be the story is purely imaginary, but in those old days such a vision was continuous and universal. Its vibrations stirred prince and peasant, king, priest and Mason alike, and have inspired twenty generations since their time to the best there can be in the building art.

It would not be right if we did not here give some suggestion in regard to the bibliography of this portion of our work. We have neither the room nor the funds necessary for the proper illustration of this portion of our subject. Many special works have been written on these ancient buildings which furnish elaborate illustrations. They may be said to begin with John Ruskin, who was obliged to do all his drawing by hand, his work being done previous to the days of dry plate photography. He had one of the finest minds that ever directed a pen. The reader who becomes familiar with his "Seven Lamps of Architecture" and his "Stones of Venice" will finish with a love for Masonry and an appreciation of good architecture which will certainly be a joy and pleasure to him as long as he lives. The student should next take up the "History of Architecture" by Banister and Banister. Here all the ancient cathedrals and other buildings of note are described and illustrated. Their dimensions and ornamentation are shown in such a manner that any ordinary reader may understand the problems which those old builders were required to solve and the way in which they accomplished their results. In addition to these, nearly every cathedral of note has a published history of its own, the structure and the alterations through which it has passed, from its foundation or establishment down to the present day.

There is also another book very interesting to Freemasons known as "The Cathedral Builders" by Leader Scott. This is especially interesting on account of its tracing of the glory of Gothic architecture, extended from the beginning of the tenth century to the end of the fifteenth. We do not say that there were not worthy buildings erected previous to this date, but the influence of the architects of Como in Lombardy and their organization marked the beginning of a great era for cathedral building in Europe, and after the end of the fifteenth century the buildings which the best architects would call good in design, beautiful in workmanship and of sufficient cost and size to make them really worthy to be preserved beyond the present generation, can be counted on the fingers of one's hands.

There have been attempts to restore and even to copy some of the ancient buildings in modern times. In some instances this work has met with some degree of success. Especially is this true of a company of stone workers located in England in the vicinity of the great Cathedral of Exeter. The altar or reredos recently put up in Christ Church Cathedral in St. Louis is an original piece of Gothic work executed by this firm. It is wrought in beautiful white, creamy Caen stone, and in design and workmanship compares very favorably with any piece of ancient work extant. Doubtless more of this style of sculpture could be produced if the demand was sufficient. The fact is that the present rituals of church ceremonial, even in the Roman Catholic denomination, do not call for it, and the Gothic form of building is not adapted to services where preaching is of such dominant importance as it is in all Protestant churches at the present day. Gothic masonry is also very costly compared to other styles of architecture, where only a meeting house is required, as each stone has to be specially designed for the place it is to fill. This has to be accomplished by one mind, and the minds capable of original design are not very plentiful at the present date. A single individual could not expect to erect very many cathedrals in a lifetime, if he was obliged to design every stone in the building with his own hands.

In the old days thousands of Masons worked at this style, as it were, by rule of thumb, and the ornamentation of the work was often extemporaneous. The architect gave them the general idea and the individual workman carved the ornaments according to his own good taste, telling his own story as seemed most proper to himself. We believe the work ought to be much more reasonable in price since the invention of electrical cutting, as a great deal of time can be saved over hand-work. It is the designing and not the cutting that causes the expense. Besides, the stone work is not all the expense that goes to build a Gothic structure. There are the colored glass windows and the mosaic facings, which form a very important element.

It is probable that the most attractive side line of Masonic study for most students will be found in the history of religious philosophy and the origin of religious ideas. This study has led to the writing of such books as "The Great Work" and "Isis Unveiled", the former by an author who styles himself "T. K." and the latter by Madame Henrietta Blavatsky. In these books a serious attempt has been made to attach the esoteric department of Freemasonry to the mystical systems of India. In these books great claims are made for which not one single verifiable fact is advanced. They contain a vast amount of questionable information difficult to verify or disprove, and advanced by authors whom most scholars believe entirely unreliable.

We may freely say that up to the present time no connection has ever been reliably established between any ancient and any modern system. That the various branches of the Brahman religion employ a great deal of mystery and have cultivated to an unusual degree the psychical faculties of the mind is not to be denied. Whether they have employed these faculties and mysteries with any appreciable benefit to humanity in general, or even to that portion that have lived under their particular influence, may be doubted with very good reasons, especially to the modern western point of view. The stories and accounts which have reached the occidental world regarding their achievements along the line of mental suggestion and other so-called occult powers contain so much exaggeration and so much willful falsehood that no dependence whatever can be placed in the reports. We do not believe, at the present writing, that there is any such thing as occult phenomena. In the words of the cowboy scientist—"There ain't no sich animile." Still our minds are open and we are willing to be convinced by satisfactory evidence. We are led to believe that this evidence should not only include the best investigation that our senses can afford, but should also be accompanied by acquaintance with the moral character of the performers for a considerable period of time.

Jesus Christ has given us a pretty good method of judging all such things which appear incomprehensible to our intellects— "By their fruits ye shall know them." They should not only exhibit gifts, but graces also. They must not only perform their miracles in our presence but teach us their art. Even then we cannot agree that such occult powers, supposing them to exist, would be at all desirable. The miracle and the occult belong to an age that has long passed, we sincerely hope, and while the Masonic student may be interested in finding out what our forefathers in their credulity believed, serious investigation of these matters is very likely to result in mental unsoundness, especially if one attempts the study under the tutorship or through the association with modern spiritualistic mediums. It is in such circles as these that the first and only door opens to these supposed mysteries, at least in this country. When a person begins to show an interest in such phenomena he is certain sooner or later to come in contact with these people, and unless he is what is termed a "hard-boiled egg", he regrets the occurrence as long as he lives. The motive is almost never a desire for knowledge, but a craving for adventure. What a combination of hypnotism, suggestion, willful deception, curiosity and credulity will accomplish is the real miracle, and the awakening, if it ever comes, often leaves sensible people with a decided mental twist. Masonry, synonymous with geometry, is the very opposite of all such sort of activity, and ·the Masonry that could be mentioned in the same connection would have to be very "free" indeed.

A very valuable work, but a book very rarely read in these days, is "Draper's Intellectual Development of Europe." We believe this to be the best possible foundation for the study of religious philosophy. When a student has made himself familiar with its contents he can then be trusted with such a book as Volney's "Ruins of Empires", Dr. Otto Wall's book on "Phallic Worship" and Paul Carus's book on the "Devil". We also would have thought our education very incomplete if we had missed reading Plato's "Dialogues" and Pope's "Essay on Man". The general subject of anthropology is a large one, but there is much to be learned in good works on this subject concerning the religious rites of primitive peoples over the earth, their initiations of the youths into manhood, which have a great bearing upon the philosophical phase of Masonic study.

The next line of importance is the history of Freemasonry as an Institution and organization. We have already hinted at many things, as we have gone along, which properly belong to the historical phases of many of our customs and ceremonies. The subject has been profusely written upon, both by those who have made sufficient investigation to give us information in a modest way and by those who have made up an imaginary history of an Institution which existed only in their dreams of what they think Masonry ought to have been.

Scientifically speaking, the history of our Order may be divided into two distinct periods marked by the reorganization of Freemasonry in 1717 and the formation of the Grand Lodge system of government. Since that date the history of our Order is clear and full, though the dates of the introduction of Masonry in some of the countries may still remain somewhat in doubt. At first charters were not granted and lodges were organized without any special authority by members of the Order hailing from lodges connected with this Grand Lodge. Later charters were asked for and granted, though the Grand Lodge of England did not claim any jurisdiction save over lodges organized by them. Still later, territorial jurisdiction was claimed and invasion was discouraged by non-recognition. The literature is voluminous and very uninteresting, at least to the writer of this book. For several years individual Masons were received without regard to the lodge with which they happened to be connected, or whether they were at that time connected with any particular lodge at all. Men were initiated in specially convened lodges wherever a certain number of Masons were congregated together. These Masons were afterwards admitted to regular lodges by signing the by-laws and paying the usual fees and dues.

During the last century all this has been changed. The territorial jurisdiction of the various Grand Lodges in this country has been fixed and may not be invaded without forfeiture of friendly relations and the outlawry of all Masons made under such invasion.

The history of the organization of the first English Grand Lodge in 1717 is worthy of a short exposition in this work. Previous to 1717 there were many operative lodges of Masons scattered over the world. No Grand Lodges, in the modern sense, existed. The Masons in and about the great capital cities were accustomed to hold annual assemblies when they elected the Grand Master to govern the Craft, settled complaints among the brethren and tried offenses against the Ancient Charges and

Landmarks. These lodges had a good many members associated with them who were not Masons by occupation, but were known as Accepted Masons. The Operative Secrets of the Craft were secrets no longer. The days of Gothic Masonry were over and the Institution of Freemasonry had no monopoly over such work as was being done in their line. The Fraternity was in considerable danger of dying out altogether. On September 20, 1714, King George I entered London in magnificent state, and after the Rebellion was over in 1716 the few lodges in that part of London known as Westminster, finding themselves neglected by Sir Christopher Wrenn, the then Grand Master, thought fit to cement under a Grand Master of their own body until such a time as they might have a brother of the nobility who was willing to assume the dignity of that station, thus forming a center of union and harmony. The following lodges were represented:

The lodge that met at the Goose and Gridiron Ale House, in St. Paul's churchyard.

The lodge that met at the Crown Ale House near Drury Lane.

The lodge that met at the Apple Tree Tavern in Charles street, Covent Garden.

The lodge that met at the Rummer and Grapes Tavern, in Channel Row, Westminster.

These representatives together with some old brethren met at the Apple Tree Tavern and, placing the oldest Master Mason then Master of a lodge in the chair, they constituted themselves a Grand Lodge, pro tempore, in due form and forthwith voted to re-establish the Ancient Quarterly Communications of the officers of the lodges called the Grand Lodge. They passed a resolution to hold the Annual Assembly and Feast, and there to choose a Grand Master from among themselves until they could have some noble brother at their head. On St. John the Baptist's Day, in the third year of the reign of King George the First, A. D. 1717, the Assembly and Feast was held at the Goose and Gridiron Ale House. Before dinner the oldest Master Mason then Master of a lodge present, being in the chair, proposed a list of candidates for Grand Master and the brethren by a majority of hands elected Mr. Anthony Sayer, gentleman, Grand Master of Masons, and Mr. Jacob Lamball and Captain Joseph Elliott Grand Wardens. These were forthwith invested with the badges of office and power by the aforesaid oldest Master, and were duly congratulated by the members present, who paid them due homage. The next year, 1718, George Payne was elected

Grand Master and John Cardwell and Thomas Morrice Grand Wardens. At this meeting an order was given by the Grand Master for the brethren to bring all writings in their possession concerning Masons and Masonry in order to show the usages of ancient times. Several old Gothic Constitutions were presented and collated. In 1719 John T. Desaguliers was elected Grand Master and Anthony Sayer and Thomas Morrice Grand Wardens. Some noblemen were made brothers and some new lodges were constituted. In 1720 George Payne was elected Grand Master and Thomas Hubby and Richard Ware Grand Wardens, and in 1721 John, Duke of Montague, was elected Grand Master, with power to choose his own Grand Wardens and Deputies. He requested Dr. James Anderson to compile a Book of Constitutions from the Ancient Constitutions and Charges then in hand.

After this date, the nobility having taken hold of the work of the Institution, the increase of members proceeded by leaps and bounds, many new lodges were constituted and the Order began to spread beyond the limits of the city of London. You will observe that at none of these meetings was there any resolution passed to change in any way the character of the Institution. The change from Operative to Speculative Masonry was gradual and without any expressed intention on the part of any of the members. The proportion of operative members grew less and that of the speculative members increased, until the operative feature was dropped by mutual consent. The Regulations and Charges remain the same to this day as they were before the Grand Lodge was organized. It is a firmly fixed habit of English law that nothing shall be changed unless there is a loud grievance, and then changed only so far as to get rid of the grievance. They invariably patch the old rather than manufacture anything new. This is the custom of Masonry to this day everywhere.

The history of the Institution previous to the organization of the English Grand Lodge in 1717 is of two kinds, documentary and traditional, and is obtained from the following sources:

The Ancient Manuscripts, containing the Ancient Charges and Constitutions of the Order, together with the Ancient Legend of the Craft.

The Records of the Ancient Operative Lodges.

The Statutes adopted by the English Parliament regulating Freemasonry.

The Records of the Construction of Ancient Cathedrals.

The letters, journal and newspaper items where the Order is mentioned.

The oldest of the Ancient Manuscripts that has been discovered up to this date is known as the "Hollowell" manuscript. It is a doggerel poem setting forth the Legend of the Craft and the Ancient Charges. It is written in a language a little more primitive than that in which the poems of Geoffrey Chaucer are written, though it does not differ greatly from the style of English employed by that writer. This "Hollowell" poem is evidently a copy of one older than itself. for it constantly refers to the old book and represents the Institution of Freemasonry as being, at the time this was written, an ancient and flourishing society. Antiquaries place the date of this manuscript between 1350 and 1400, and believe it to be a copy of one derived from German sources. It differs slightly in its account of the events in the Legend of the Craft, from the later prose compositions. It is now in the British museum.

The records of the Ancient Operative Lodges which have been preserved are from Scotch sources mostly, as very few records were kept in English lodges and none save those of recent date were to be had at the organization of the Grand Lodge. Even the records of the Grand Lodge for the first five or six years of its existence are very scant and meagre, and tell scarcely anything of what was done. When Grand Master George Payne ordered manuscripts and records to be brought up to the meetings a considerable number were destroyed by some brethren whose zeal was greater than their knowledge, lest some of the information which they contained might be made public.

It must be remembered that at the accession of George I there were going on many plots and conspiracies in the government for the purpose of reseating the Stuart family on the English throne. It may be that these lodges were frequently used as a cover for Jacobite meetings, and that the records of past meetings were destroyed lest the names of those present at them come to the ears of the officers of the law. Even after King James' death there were two very important wars, those of the "Old Pretender" and "Young Pretender", son and grandson respectively of James Stuart, to secure for them the throne of England, from which James had been driven. From the time of the death of William of Orange to the death of George III the air was dank with Jacobite plots. Large numbers of people in every walk of life from dukes and earls down to the very offscourings of society were involved. Arrests were liable to be made at any time and any list of names might include guilty men and sometimes throw suspicion on those perfectly innocent. It is not strange that any call for ancient records might start a widespread conflagration.

The Statutes mentioned as relating to Masonry are kept on record in the archives of the British Parliament. The earliest of these discovered was passed in 1490 and merely consisted of an article of incorporation of the society or guild.

The records kept of the construction of the old cathedrals are quite voluminous, both in England and on the continent. They were generally kept in the vaults, where they often escaped fires that devastated the upper structures pretty seriously. Leader Scott in her book, known as the "Cathedral Builders," searched through a great many of these old tomes. They tell of the sources and amounts of money appropriated for the work and the names of the Masters who had charge of the construction. The credit was, of course, given to the bishops and abbots who were governing the churches at the time additions and repairs were made. The records at Milan, Cologne, Florence and Pisa are the best and completely demonstrate the existence of the Institution of Freemasonry in Como and Lombardy. These were known over the world as Comocine Masons, because they came originally from those towns in and about Lake Como. The small island in the lake shows some well preserved monuments of their work. There is nothing in these records to show in what manner the Craft was introduced into England, but they do seem to prove pretty conclusively its connection with the Ancient Roman Colleges of Architects.

Many letters and items taken from the journals of such men as Elias Ashmole, the celebrated antiquarian, are valuable in showing the state of the Order during the latter part of the seventeenth century. It is believed that none date further back than the middle of that century. The "Memoires of Benvenuto Cellini" should be read by every Freemason who cares anything about the work of those ancient artists of the Middle Ages. It shows their minds, their beliefs, their superstitions and their habits of life better than all the histories of modern times could possibly show them. Benvenuto was one of these old designers himself. His work is not a novel, but an actual daily record of his work, and shows him at his best and at his worst.

It is our purpose in the next lecture to illustrate what the Legend of the Craft is, as it comes down to us in the Ancient Manuscripts. While the Legend of the Craft is a myth, yet it is possible to learn several things from a myth when rightly studied. The language of the manuscript which we have chosen is not so archaic, but most of the words can be understood without a dictionary, so that the reader of this work may be able to see the sort of story in which our ancient brethren placed their implicit belief. That these brethren really believed these statements to be true, or whether they might have had some cryptogram or cypher buried in them is not positively known, though the latter has been suspected by many students, and not without some evidence for the faith that was in them.

LECTURE XXV

THE LEGEND OF THE CRAFT

THE "Dowling" Manuscript given herewith is in such English as was used about the time of Queen Anne. It resembles very closely the "Travels of Sir John Mandeville", that belongs to about that period.

"The Might of the Father of Kings, with the wisdom of His Glorious Son, through the Grace and Goodness of the Holy Ghost, there bene three persones in One Godheade be with us at our beginninge, and give us grace so to governe us here in this mortall life, liveinge that we may come to His Kingdome, that nevere shall have endinje, Amen!

"Good Breetheren and Fellowes. Our purpose is to tell you how and in what manner this worthy science of Masonrye was begunne, and afterwards how it was favored by worthy Kings and Princes, and by many other Worshipful men, and also to those that be willinge, we will declare the Charge, that belongeth to every true Mason, to keepe, for in good faith and yet have good heede thereto. It is well worthy to be well kept, for a worthy Craft and a curious science. For there be Seven Liberall Sciences, of which seven it is one of them. And the names of the seven sciences bene these. First is Grammere and it teacheth men to speake truly and to write truly, and the second is Rhethoricke and teacheth a man to speake faire and in subtill termes, and the third is Dialectyke and teacheth a man for to diserne or know truth from false. And the fourth is Arithmeticke, and that teacheth a man for to recken and to accoumpt all manner of numbers, and the fifth is Geometrie, and that teacheth mett and measure of the earth and all other things, of the which science is called Masonrye, and the sixth science is called Musick, and that teacheth man songe and voice of tongue and organne, harpe and trompe, and the seventh science is called Astronomye, and that teacheth a man the course of the sunne and moone and starrs.

"These be the seven Liberall sciences, the which bene all founded by one science, that is to say Geometrie, and this may a man prove, that the science of the whole is founded by Geometrie, for Geometrie teacheth a man mett and measure, ponderation and weight, of all manner of things on the earth, for there is no man worketh any science, but he worketh by some mett and measure, nor no man buyeth or selleth, but by some measure or some weight, and all these is Geometrie. And these useth merchants and all craftsmen and all other of the seven sciences, and in especial the plowman and tillers of all manner of grounds, graypes, vynes, flowers and setters of other fruits. For Grammere and Rhethoricke, neither Astronomye, nor none of all other seven sciences can in no manner find mett or measure without Geometrie. Wherefore methinketh, that the science of Geometrie is most worthy and findeth all other. How these worthy sciences were begunne I shall you tell.

"Before Noye's flood there was a man called Lamache, as it is written in the Byble, in the III Chapter of Geneses, and this Lamache has two wives and the one height Ada and the other height Sella. By his first wife Ada he gott two sons and that one Jabell and the other Juball, and by the other wife Sella, he gott a son and a daughter, and these four children founden the beginninge of all sciences in the world. And the elder son Jabell found the science of Geometrie and he departed flocks of sheep and lambs in the field, and first wrought house of stone and tree, as is noted in the chapter above-said, and his Brother Juball found the science of musicke, songe of tongue, harpe and organne, and the third Brother Tubal Cain found Smith-craft of gold, silver, copper, iron and steele, and the daughter found the craft of weaveinge. And these children knew well that God would take vengence for synn, either by fire or by water, wherefore they writ their sciences, that they had founde in two pillars of stone, that they might be founde after Noye's flood, and that one stone was marble, for that would not burn with fire, and that other stone was klepped laterns and would not drown in noe water. (In some of the manuscripts the first pillar was laterns or brick, that would not burn with fire, and the second of marble, that would not drown in water, which is most likely the nearer to good sense.)

"Our intent is to tell you truly how and in what manner these stones were founde, that these sciences were written on. The Great Harmogenes, that was Cuby's son, the which Cub was Sem's son, that was Noye's son. This Harmogenes, afterwards called Hermes, the father of wise-men, he founde one of the pillars of stone and founde the science written there and he taught it to other men. And at the makinge of the Tower of Babylon, there was Masonrye first made much of. And the King of Babylon that height Nimroth was a Mason himself, and loved well the science, and it is said with masters of histories, and when the city of Nyneve and other cities of the East should be made, Nimrothe the King of Babylon sent thither three score Masons at the rogation of the King of Nyneve, his cosen. And when he sent them forth, he gave them a Charge on this manner, that they should be true men, each of them to other, and that they should love truly together, and that they should serve their Lord truly for their paye, so that the Master might have worshippe and all that long to him, and other moe Charges he gave them, and this was the first time that ever Masons had any Charge of his science.

"More over when Abraham and Sara his wife went into Egipt, there he taught the seaven sciences liberall to the Egiptians, and he had a worthy scholar that height Ewclyde, and he learned light well and was Master of all the seaven sciences liberall. And in his days it befell that the Lord and the Estates of that realme had so many sonns that they had gotten, some by their wives and some by other ladies of that realme, for the land is a hott land and plenteous in generacion, and they had not competent livelode, to find with their children, wherefore they made much care. And the King of the land made a great counsell and a parliament, to witt, how they might find their children honestly, as gentlemen, and they could find no manner of good way, and there they did crye through all the realme if there were any man that informe them that he should come to them, and he should be soe rewarded for his travail that he should hold him pleased. After that their crye was made, then came that worthy clarke Ewclyde and said to the King and all his great Lords: 'If ye will take me your children to governe and to teache them one of the seaven sciences wherewith they may honestly, as gentlemen should, under a condition, that you will grant me and them a commission, that I may have the power to rule them, after the manner that a science ought to be ruled.'

"And that the King and all his counsell granted to them anone and sealed their commission. And then this worthy Doctor tooke to him these Lord's sonns and taught them the science of Geometrie in practice for to worke in stones, and all manner of worthy workes, that belongeth to buildinge churches, temples, castills, towers and mannors, and all other manner of buildings and he gave them a Charge in this manner: 'The first was that they should be true to the Kinge and to the Lord that they owe, and that they should live well together and be true eache to other. And that they should call eache other his fellowe or else Brother and not be servant, nor his knave, nor none other foul name, and that they should deserve their paye of the Lord, or of the Master that they serve. And that they should ordaine the wisest of them to be Master of the worke, and neither for love nor great linneage, nor riches, nor no favour to let another that hath little cunnings for to be Master of the Lord's worke, where through the Lord should be evill served and they ashamed. And also that they should call their governors of the worke Master, in the time that they shall work with him, and other many moe Charges that longe to tell.

"And all these Charges he made them sweare a great, great oath, that men used in that time, and ordayned them for reasonable wages, that they might live honestly by. And also that they should come and semble together, every year once, how they might worke best and serve the Lord for his profitt and to their own worshippe and to correct within themselves him that had trespassed against the science. And thus was the science grounded there. And that worthy Master Ewclyde gave it the name of Geometrie and now it is called through all the land Masonrye. Sythin longe after, when the children of Isreal had come into the land of the Behest, that is now called amongst us the country of Jhrlm, King David begunne the Temple that is called Templum Deii, and it is named with us the Temple of Jerusalem. And the same King David loved Masons well and cherished them much, and gave them the manners as he learned of Egipt, given by Ewclyde and other moe charges that ye shall heare afterwards. And after the decease of King David, Solomon that was David's sonne performed out the Temple that his father begunne and sent after Masons into divers countries and of divers lands and gathered them together, so that he had four score thousand workers of stone and were all named Masons. And he chose out of them three thousand that were ordayned to be Masters and governers of his worke, and furthermore there was a King of another region, that men called Iram, and he loved well Kinge Solomon and gave him tymber for his worke, and he had a man that height Aynon, and he was a Master of Geometrie and was chief Master of all his gravings and carvings, and all manner of Masonrye that longed to the Temple, and this is witnessed by the Byble in libro Regnum, the third chapter.

"And then Solomon confirmed both Charges and manners that his father David had given to Masons, and thus was that worthy science of Masonrye confirmed in the country of Jerusalem and many other Kingdomes. Curious craftsmen walked about full wide into diverse countrys, some because of learning more craft and cunninge, and some to teache them that had but little cunninge, and so it befell that there was one curious Mason that height Mamus Grecus, that had been at the making of Solomon's Temple, and he came into Fraunce, and there he taught the science of Masonrye to men in Fraunce, and there was one of the Royal line of Fraunce that height Charles Martell (Charles the Hammer), and he was a man that loved well such a science, and took upon him the Charges and manners and afterwards, by the grace of God, he was elect to be Kinge of Fraunce and when he was in his estate he tooke Masons and did help to make Masons of men that were none, and set them to worke and gave them both Charges and the manners and gave them good paye, as he had learned of other Masons, and confirmed them a Charter from yeare to yeare, to hold their semble when they would and cherished them right much, and thus came the science into Fraunce. England all this season stood voyd, as for any Charge of Masonrye unto Sanct Albones tyme. And in his tyme, the Kinge of England, that was a pagan, he did wall the town about that is called Sanct Albones. And Sanct Albones he was a worthy knight and stewart with the Kinge of his household and had governance of the Masons and cherished them much. And he made their paye right good standing, as the realme did, for he gave them 11s. VId. a week and 11d. to their nunesynches, and before that time and through all that land a Mason tooke but a penny a day and his meate, till Sanct Albones amended it and gave them a charter of the Kinge and his counsell, for to hold a general counsell, and gave it the name Assemble, and thereat he was himself and helped to make Masons and did give them a Charge, as you shall heare afterwards. Right soon after the decease of Sanct Albones there came divers warres into the realme of England of divers nations, so that the good rule of Masonrye was destroyed unto the tyme of Kinge Athelstone's days, that was a worthy Kinge of England, and brought this land into good rest and peace and builded many great workes of Abbys and Toures, and other many divers buildings, and loved well Masons.

"And he had a sonne that height Edwinne, and he loved

Masons much more than his father did. And he was a great practiser of Geometrie and he drew him much talke and to commune with Masons and to learn of them science. And afterwards from the love that he had for Masons and for the science, he was made a Mason and he got of the Kinge his father a charter and commission, to hold every yeare once an Assemble, where that ever they would, within the realme of England, and to correct within themselves defaultes and trespasses, that were done within the science, and he held himself an Assemble at Yorke, and there he made Masons and gave them Charges and taught them manners and commanded that rule be kept forever after and tooke them the charters and commissions to keepe and made ordinance that it should be renewed from Kinge to Kinge, and when the Assemble was gathered he made a crye, that all old Masons and young that had any writings or understandings of the Charges and the manners that were made before in this land, or in any other, that they should bring them and show them forth. And when it was proved, there were founden some in French and some in Greek and some in German and some in English and some in other languages and the intent of them all was founden all one. And he did make a book thereof, and how the science was founded, and he himself bad and commanded that it should be redd and told, that when any Mason was made, for to give him his Charge, and from that day unto this tyme manners of Masons have been keept in that form, as well as men might govern it. And furthermore divers Assembles have been put and ordayned certain Charges, as by the best advice of Masters and Fellowes."

And then follows the Ancient Charges, as they appear in the early part of this book. Many other manuscripts have been found, until there are now about a hundred, but as the one above remarked, in their intent, they have been founden all the same.

Before closing this portion of our work, we would like to say a few words relative to the Hollowell Poem or Manuscript, which dates back to 1390 or thereabouts. It was written in old English letters resembling the present German type of today, and in a very early form of the language, before the union of the Saxon and French dialects of which our tongue is composed was fully cemented, and while the inflection of the nouns and verbs used in the ancient Saxon was still retained. The language is as old, if not more ancient, than the Wycliff Bible, which appeared in the reign of King Richard II of England, the time of the

Watt Tyler rebellion. This speaks of the Fraternity as being then old and in a flourishing condition, and also claims to be a copy of the Charges and Legend of the Craft that had existed from time immemorial. Here we copy one verse of the old poem:

The prevystye of the chamber tell he no man
Ny yn the Logge whatsoever they done;
Whatsaver thou heryst or syste hem do
Telle it no man whersever thou go,
And alle schul swere the same ogth,
Of the Masonus ben they luf, ben they loght
To alle these poyntes hys before,
That hath ben ordeynt by ful good lore.

This manuscript evidently goes back to Roman Catholic days, while all the others date since the Reformation. It is thought very likely that the Hollowell Poem was written by a priest. Attending mass is enjoined, and that they shall be true to God and Mother Church, and that they use no heresy or error by their understanding or teaching of discreet men. Still the sectarian character of the Society was not abandoned until after 1717, when the universal toleration of religion was adopted.

Let us compare the preceding section with a few lines from Chaucer:

A Knight there was, and that a worthy man,
That fro the tyme that he first began
To riden out, he loved chivalrye,
Trouthe and honour, fredom and courtesye;
Ful worthy was he in his Lordes warre
And thereto hadde he riden, no man ferre
As wel in Christendom, as in hethenesse,
And ever honoured for his worthinesse.

Here is another specimen from the Hollowell Poem:

In that tyme through good Gemetry
This foremost Craft of good Maconrye
Was ordayned and made in this mannere
Y-cownterfetyd of thys clerks y-fere,
At these Lordys prayers, they cownterfeyted Gemetry
And gaf hyt the name Maconrye,
For the moste oneste Crafte of alle.

Here is another specimen of Chaucer:

He made the book that height, the house of fame
And eke the death of Blanche the Duchess,
And the parliament of fowles, as I guesse

And all the love of Palamon and Archite
Of Thebes, though the story is knowen lite,
And many a hymne for your Holy days,
That heighten ballads, roundels, virelays.
Hast thou not in a book that lyeth in thy chest
That turned was into a dayeseye.

The comparison of these specimens of Chaucer with the lines of the Hollowell Manuscript would convince any man that the latter was fully as old if not older than the Chaucer verse. The great antiquity of Masonry is not important in itself. It does not add any value to the principles of the Order as taught by the brethren. Its value comes from another direction. The American Masons have a little too good conceit of themselves. They are apt to speak of the people of past ages as being ignorant and savage. Their opinion of the representatives of other races and other countries has come to imply that the latter are greatly inferior to the general average of the present American stock. And it is edifying to learn that no age or race or country can show any monopoly on wisdom or skill, for that matter. The accomplishments of one age may not be necessary to the happiness of another that succeeds it, but it is a good thing to know that some accomplishments did exist. And that back in the far distant past men had hopes and ambitions and aspirations, kind hearts, good manners and true religion, and that they directed their energies in such a manner that success was achieved in the line of their desires.

LECTURE XXVI

MODERN HISTORY OF THE ORDER

THERE have been several important occurrences in the history of the Fraternity since the reorganization of Masonry in 1717, which ought to be noted, because they have given rise to changes and ritualistic features now extant.

The first of these happenings was the secession from the English Grand Lodge of the so-called Grand Lodge of Ancients. This event occurred in the year 1739 and continued up to 1813. The main instigator of the schism was one Lawrence Dermott. He became the Grand Secretary of the body which he formed and in 1764 he published a book, which he called "Ahiman Rezon," or help to all who are or would be Free and Accepted Masons.

Dermott was always a very acrimonious and bitter speaker at the best, nor was he always truthful in speech or writing, but while he was unfair and vainglorious in character, he was undoubtedly far ahead of his opponents in intellectual attainments, and, for that matter, in advance of most thinkers of his age. He was the author of the Royal Arch Degree, or at least he separated the material which composes that degree from the Master's Degree, where it originally appeared.

He and his adherents were dissatisfied with certain actions of the Grand Lodge of 1717, and accusations were made that the Grand Lodge had introduced innovations and altered the rituals and suppressed many ceremonies long in use. As these supposed innovations relate to the esoteric or secret work, orally communicated, we are unable at this late date to ascertain just what they were, but so far as we are able to find out they were trivial. Preston, writing for Dermott's opponents, admits that changes had been made, but claims that they were not introduced until subsequent to the first secession and that they were made necessary on account of certain disclosures of the secret work that had been published, and that these changes applied only to the means of recognition. Preston himself eventually left the Grand Lodge of 1717 and united with the Dermott System.

About the same time, the old Grand Lodge or Assembly at York began to assert its claims, on account of a tradition regarding a set of Constitutions said to have been received in the tenth century from King Athelstone. They held that the antiquity of this code of regulations entitled that body to be considered as Supreme Authority over all matters Masonic in the entire kingdom. This so-called Grand Lodge was weak from the start and in a few years became absorbed into the Grand Lodge of 1717. Dermott, without any authority from the body at York, claimed the title for his Grand Lodge of "Ancient York Masons," and gave the name of "Moderns" to the Grand Lodge organized in 1717, from which it had lately seceded. Dermott gained to his standard many influential persons and went about organizing lodges all over the world and was the first to grant charters to the lodges so organized. This custom was later adopted by the Grand Lodge of 1717.

Many of the lodges in America took their origin from this body, and in several states two Grand Lodges were instituted and for a considerable time worked side by side. The Grand Lodges in New York and Pennsylvania came from this body. The English Grand Lodge of 1717, under the Grand Mastership of John Lord Montague, who, by the way, was a good Roman Catholic, granted authority to a man named Price, in the city of Boston, to organize lodges on the American Continent and created him Colonial Grand Master. Benjamin Franklin, then Grand Master of Pennsylvania, asked for and obtained from Price a charter for his Grand Lodge, though the ritual obtained from the Grand Lodge of Ancients was never changed, even to this day.

In the year 1813, the Duke of Kent, father of Queen Victoria and great-grandfather of the present King of England, was Grand Master of the Ancients, while his own brother, the Duke of Sussex, happened to be at the same time Grand Master of the Moderns. These two men seeing that the differences between the two bodies were very trivial in their nature, eventually succeeded in uniting the two bodies into what is now known as the United Grand Lodge of England, and thus placed England under one authority. The Independent Grand Lodge of Scotland and that of Ireland had both recognized the Grand Lodge of Ancients and it was not then deemed at all impossible for two Grand Lodges to occupy the same territory legitimately.

Since 1813, when the two Grand Lodges of South Carolina united the schism has been forgotten and all the causes great or small that originally led to it. The entire matter has ceased to be of interest, save to the student of Masonic history. It is

simply of importance in accounting for the differences in ritualistic work among the several American Grand Lodges. It has
so nearly passed from remembrance that we often hear it claimed
that no Masonic body can possibly be legitimate that did not
receive its authority in a charter granted by the Price regime.

The next event of importance to be considered is the Antimasonic excitement which grew out of the adventures of one
William Morgan. This member was born in Culpepper, Virginia,
in 1775. At the time he became known in relation to the Masonic
Fraternity he was living in the town of Batavia, Genessee County,
State of New York. The following historical sketch has been
taken from William L. Stone, author of the Antimasonic letters
to John Quincy Adams. Stone says that Morgan was by occupation an operative mason, had been a soldier in the war of 1812,
and had a fair common school education which he had improved
by reading. He was a hard drinker and his associations were
anything but decent and praiseworthy, and his disposition was
envious, vindictive and malicious. Some say that he was a bright
Mason in the first three degrees, but where he obtained his
degrees, or whether he ever obtained them legally, it is impossible to determine. In 1825 he visited lodges and chapters in Le
Roy, a town about fifty miles from Batavia, and did considerable
speaking and writing on the subject of Masonry, but his moral
conduct became so reprehensible that those who had been his
friends were obliged to dispense with his society.

A petition was circulated for a lodge and chapter at Batavia,
and Morgan had taken considerable pains to forward the movement, but as the Masons of that vicinity became acquainted with
him the petition was allowed to drop and another petition, on
which Morgan's name did not appear, was circulated and when
the charter was granted his name was excluded. Morgan was
deeply incensed, and while previously he had been an ardent
friend to the Fraternity, he now became a bitter and relentless
foe. He had visited New York City in 1825 and had there been
very intimate with a man who had been noted as one of the best
informed ritualists in the state, but on account of his bad character had been expelled from the Fraternity.

Whether Morgan ever had any purpose of publishing his
Masonic information at that time is not known, but soon after
the events just related he became associated with one David C.
Miller, a publisher at Batavia, and it was generally given out
that Morgan and Miller were about to publish an exposition of

the secrets of Freemasonry. Miller was of about the same dissolute character as Morgan, and while he had once edited a newspaper in the town of Batavia, its circulation had degenerated, and to such an extent that he had been obliged to abandon it. At first the intended publication attracted but very little attention. They had obtained promises of financial support and had hoped for a great profit from the scheme. The publishers soon saw that unless the book should be violently opposed by the Fraternity the sales would be very small, but if in some way a strong feeling could be aroused on the part of the Masons the curiosity of the public would prove irresistible.

A frame-up was organized and planned that was calculated to bring about the opposition desired. At first, small newspaper articles began to appear, purporting to come from Masons over the country, indicating grave displeasure and criticising the members of the Craft in the neighborhood of Batavia that nothing was done to prevent the publication. These articles were continued by certain indiscrete brethren, and as might have been expected, the more they talked about the matter the more angry they became. Some of the more discreet held conferences with Morgan and expostulated with him. He pretended to relent and turned over to them what purported to be his manuscripts.

Soon it was discovered that he had been doubly treacherous, and that the true manuscripts were in Miller's office, and that the printing was going on as rapidly as possible. In consequence of this, newspaper articles appeared denouncing Morgan as a swindler and impostor. The Antimasons afterwards claimed that in some of these were veiled threats of murder. It seems to have been true that some of the more excitable of the Masons had determined to prevent the publication. They did not know what it was going to contain, but they believed that it was going to expose the secret work of the ceremonial. The creditors of both Morgan and Miller began to press their claims and Miller was arrested and held to bail for debt. Miller also let on to be alarmed for his life and for the security of his office, and took measures for his defense. He claimed that an armed force of forty or fifty, organized from among the Masons of the surrounding country, attacked his office in the night, but when they discovered that it was defended by firearms they disappeared in the gray of the morning.

On the night of Sept. 10, 1826, the stairs leading to Miller's office were found to be on fire. The fire was evidently of incendiary origin, but it was soon extinguished. As Miller had four or five barrels of water at the head of the stairs it is probable that he started the fire himself in order to increase the excitement and arouse the sympathy of the public. The next morning Morgan was arrested for larceny at Canandaigua, a place about fifty miles from Batavia. The articles which he was accused of stealing had been loaned to him, as was shown, so that he was found innocent of the theft. A large posse had accompanied him to Canandaigua, but these were obliged to let him go and return to Batavia, where he was soon arrested for debt and placed in jail there.

The next day, Sept. 12, Miller was informed that an attack was going to be made upon his office. A crowd of sixty or seventy persons did assemble, but they made no demonstration against the office. A constable again took Morgan to Le Roy, but his debt was paid by a man named Dawson and he was released. While in custody his wife appeared and offered his manuscripts to secure his release. These manuscripts had already been put in print and the firm had no further use for them.

No sooner was Morgan released than another creditor appeared from Pennsylvania, and he was turned over to be taken to that state. Morgan's wife stated that a Mason accompanied her home and told her that she was not likely to see her husband again for a year and perhaps longer, but that she and her family would be provided for. She arrived home at Batavia and there found another Mason, who said that he had been appointed to provide for her and her children and that he had made arrangements for her to be boarded at a public house, but she refused both promptly. Several days passed away and as nothing was heard from Morgan she sent some of her friends to Canandaigua to inquire what had become of him. It was reported that after his release from jail on the evening of Sept. 12 he had been seized by a man named Lawson and another man and hurried down the street, crying murder, and though several people had witnessed the seizure none had interfered. He was placed in a carriage and hastily driven away in the direction of Rochester. The carriage reached Rochester about daylight and drove about three miles beyond, where the parties left the carriage and the carriage returned to Rochester. The driver stated that the parties were all unknown to him, but that he had noticed no violence used towards anyone in the carriage.

While there was no direct evidence of Morgan having been

carried away the excitement became intense. Public meetings were held at Batavia, denounced the outrage and demanded the punishment of those engaged in it. Prominent Masons demanded an investigation. The excitement spread like wild-fire. Meetings were held in adjoining counties and committees of investigation appointed. The conduct of some Masons increased the exasperation. All those charged with the abduction were Masons. Some treated the matter lightly and some practically said that it served him right. Remarks of a horrid character, that had not been uttered at all, were imputed to Masons, and reckless and unscrupulous politicians seized upon the excitement to promote their own advantage. The consequence was that while a great many, in fact, a majority of the Masons denounced the crime, they were all equally assailed by fanatics, unless by a public denunciation of the Order they confessed themselves to be either knaves or fools.

The Governor of New York was at that time De Witt Clinton, a very distinguished man and an eminent Mason, Grand High Priest of the Grand Chapter of the state. He offered rewards and did all in his power to discover and bring to justice the guilty parties and to find out the whereabouts of Morgan. It was shown that when the parties left the carriage near Rochester they soon took another, and that by a regular relay of carriages that seemed to appear almost spontaneously they arrived at Niagara. Here they left the carriage and went towards the old fort of Niagara, which was about eighty rods distant.

One of the parties was known to be Eli Bruce. Bruce was immediately arrested, but he was acquitted by the magistrate because it could not be shown that Morgan had ever been abducted and that no violence had been used towards anyone in the carriage. Lawson, Cheesbro, Sawyer and a man named Shelton were indicted for conspiracy against Morgan. They pleaded guilty and were sentenced, Lawson for two years in jail, Cheesbro for one year, Sawyer for one month and Shelton for two months. Shelton was afterwards shown to have been entirely innocent and that he had been mistaken for another man. The judge was denounced for having given so light a sentence and accused of submitting to Masonic influences, though he was not and never had been a Mason.

Governor Clinton addressed letters to the two Canadian governors, asking them to cause search to be made for the missing man, saying it was suspected that he had been carried to Canada.

Courts and lawyers everywhere were accused of being under Masonic influence and the papers urged that they should be declared ineligible for any sort of office or allowed to vote. The wildest stories were told and apparently believed. Morgan had been turned over to old John Brandt, the Mohawk chief. A young Indian had been hired to murder him. He had been taken to Quebec and shipped on board a British man-of-war. He had been found guilty at a Masonic tribunal and executed according to the penalties attached to obligations published in Morgan's book. He had been placed in an open boat and set adrift just above Niagara Falls. Blood had been found in the magazine of the old fort.

The officers who had arrested him at Canandaigua were indicted for murder, but were acquitted because the judge held that they were protected by the warrants. A party named Mann came forward and claimed that a man named Richard Hayward had admitted to him that he was the person who had set fire to Miller's office, and further confessed that Morgan had been murdered and that lots had been drawn to see who should carry out the sentence of death that had been passed against him in the Grand Chapter, and that the lot had fallen to Hayward. Hayward was arrested and indicted for murder, but the proceedings were stopped when it was discovered that Mann was an escaped lunatic, and a few months afterward Mann died in an asylum for the insane, a raving maniac. Hayward left the country. Stone claimed that Hayward was guilty of all that Mann had accused him of.

Stone assumed that Hayward was the party that Avery Allyn, author of Allyn's Ritual referred to in an affidavit published in 1829, to the effect that in March, 1828, he attended a commandery meeting in New York City, and that while there the Prelate had told him that they were certain of Morgan's death, as the person who had executed the penalty of his obligation upon him had visited that very commandery and confessed that he had struck the fatal blow, that another Templar and himself, the former being present and corroborating the story, had furnished him money and placed him on board a ship for Europe. Stone investigated the matter at the time and found that there was not one word of truth in Allyn's affidavit, as a gentleman of his acquaintance who was entirely above suspicion was one of the parties mentioned. It would seem that afterwards Stone came to believe the story true.

In April, 1827, four persons were tried for the abduction, three convicted and one acquitted. In May, 1827, seventeen persons were tried, but all were acquitted under the instruction of the judge that warrants had protected them. Eli Bruce had given the names of Whitney, Smith and Colonel King. Parties were sent to arrest them, but they could not be found. King, however, came in and surrendered himself for trial, and shortly afterward Whitney came in also. Smith was dead and in a short time King died in jail before he could be brought to trial. Whitney was tried and sentenced to two years' imprisonment, as it was impossible to show positively that Morgan had been carried away against his will or that he was dead.

The time for the Presidential election was coming on. The candidates for both the old parties were Masons and Past Grand Masters of the Order, Henry Clay and Andrew Jackson, the former from Kentucky and the latter from Tennessee. A third ticket was nominated, called the Antimasonic ticket. William Wirt was the candidate and Thurlow Weed was the manager of the campaign. The excitement was intense and people spoke of the Masonic Fraternity very much as they spoke of the anarchists immediately subsequent to the murder of President McKinley. Brother was set against brother and father against son and neighbor against neighbor. Even the writer can remember cases where families were broken up as late as 1878 in Vermont because the wife learned that her husband was a Freemason, showing that even then the feeling had not entirely died out. We remember seeing an old sign among the rubbish of our own home bearing the inscription, "Antimasonic Inn", that had formerly been hung over the front door of our house, though previous to the occupancy of our family. The Antimasonic party cast over seventy thousand votes, but carried only one state, Vermont.

A short time before the election a body was found on the beach about forty miles below Niagara. The body was in an advanced state of putrefaction and was entirely unrecognizable. The Coroner's jury brought in a verdict of accidental drowning and the body was buried. In a few weeks the story was circulated that the body of Morgan had been found and that it had been hastily buried for interested motives. It was resurrected and another inquest was held. The jury did not seem to consider that it had been eighteen months since Morgan had disappeared and that no body could have been preserved all that time in the waters of Lake Ontario. There was not one single article of clothing that could be shown to have been worn by Morgan. A dentist appeared who claimed that he had drawn two teeth from Morgan shortly before his disappearance and that these teeth he had kept and that they exactly fitted the jaws of the body in evidence. The body had been shaved and altered considerably since the first inquest, and in all likelihood the teeth had been drawn after the body had been discovered. The jury listened to the identification of Mrs. Morgan and Miller and pronounced it the body of Morgan. Some reporters remarked that "it was a pretty poor imitation of Morgan," but Thurlow Weed, who was present, replied that "it was a good enough Morgan to last until after election."

Two days before the election came off it was shown that a man named Monroe had been lost off of a boat in the Niagara river a few weeks previous to the finding of the body, and that there had been a search for the body without finding it. Monroe's wife and son were present at the third inquest and identified every article of clothing on the body, and also some religious tracts that were in the coat pockets. This inquest found the body to be that of Monroe.

This news was too late to have any effect on the election, but even as it was, General Jackson was elected President without any trouble. It was never shown just what did become of Morgan. Some Masons claimed that they had given Morgan five hundred dollars at the time that they had left him at the old fort, and that he had skipped out, probably to Europe.

The book that had given so much trouble was finally shown never to have been written by Morgan at all, but had been purchased from an Englishman who had been expelled from a lodge in London on account of his bad character. The effect on the Order of all this excitement was, as might have been expected, disastrous. A great many lodges were forced to surrender their charters and the Grand Lodge of Vermont suspended its annual assemblies for several years, but finally the light returned and forty years after Stone had pronounced the Order dead beyond any possibility of resuscitation, it was flourishing with six times as many members as it had on the day of Morgan's disappearance. The Grand Lodges of New York and Vermont suffered the worst, but the effect was felt everywhere.

The worry and sorrow is thought to have caused the death

of Governor Clinton.   Many Antimasons said that it was the
burnings of his conscience.   He would never admit that the
Fraternity at large was in any way responsible for Morgan's
disappearance.   Shortly before his death he wrote as follows:
"I am persuaded, however, that the body of Freemasons, so
far from having any participation in this affair or giving any
countenance to it, reprobate it as a most unjustifiable act, re-
pugnant to the principles and abhorrent to the doctrines of the
Fraternity.   I know that Freemasonry properly understood and
faithfully attended to is friendly to religion, morality, liberty
and good government, and I shall never shrink under any state
of excitement or any extent of apprehension from bearing testimony in favor of the purity of an institution which can boast
of Washington, Franklin and Lafayette as distinguished members, which inculcates no principles and authorizes no acts that
are not in accordance with good morals, civil liberty and entire
obedience to good government and its laws.   It is no more responsible for the acts of its unworthy members than any other
association or institution.   Without intending the remotest degree of comparison or improper allusion, I might ask whether
we ought to revile our holy religion because Peter denied or
Judas betrayed."

LECTURE XXVII

FREEMASONRY AND THE ROMAN CHURCH

THE next series of events which, in a great measure, makes up the history of our Fraternity in its relations with other institutions, has to do with its perennial warfare with the Roman Catholic Church. It is the sole matter of attention with many who think of joining our Fraternity.

It began immediately after the reorganization of Masonry in 1717, and has lasted without compromise down to the present day. We read that, after the reorganization, the Craft of Masonry flourished at a far greater speed than ever before in its existence, and that lodges were chartered all over the continent of Europe and the American colonies, and even invaded Rome itself.

The revolution in England in 1688, which ended in the expatriation of the house of Stuart and the seating of William of Orange on the English throne, had for its main object the preservation of the Protestant religion in that kingdom. James Stuart had, for several years, used his best, or worst, endeavors to change the religion of England back to the Roman Catholic Church. The wars of the old and young Pretenders had just been quieted at the time of the reorganization of Masonry.

As early as 1737, Pope Clement XII issued a bull, forbidding all Catholics from joining or having anything to do with the Society whatever, on peril of excommunication, a ban which could be removed only by the Pope himself, unless the person was in immediate danger of death. Every Pope since that day has renewed the restrictions. Their letters to the bishops and priests under them bristle with the same perpetual enmity.

Let us discuss, for a few pages, the effects of this warfare and the reasons why all efforts to cure the situation have failed to produce any results. This difficulty is not between Roman Catholics and Masons, as individuals. The warfare and controversy is what we have stated it to be, a warfare between the genius of the Roman Catholic Church and that of Masonry. Masons and Catholics may get along very well together, and often do, even in the same family and household. We do not expect our business partner, simply because he happens to be a good Catholic and eats fish every Friday, to put poison in our drinking water or stick a knife into our anatomy the minute our backs are turned; neither does he worry about our treachery in business or any personal affairs. In India good Christian Englishmen frequently enter into business partnerships with Parsees, Hindoos or Mohammedans, without any fretting about their lives or their pounds, shillings or pence.

The warfare does not grow out of the fact that the hierarchy of the church, as many suppose, are essentially bad, selfish or without moral principle, or even because they happen to believe in celibacy or oral confession or, on the other hand, that Masons are irreverent or practice unholy ceremonies. The warfare is between authority in religious matters and liberty in religious matters.

There are several elements that must be considered before any person can thoroughly understand this matter.

In the first place there is the warfare that has always existed between the literalist on the one side and the symbolist on the other. These sides both find their advocates in either system, but it may be said that the laity of the Roman Church are supposed to understand everything in the way of religious dogma in the literal sense, while the priesthood can be symbolists so far as they please, so that they confine it among themselves and never interpret the mystery to the people. Among Masons, and pretty generally among the Protestant religious sects, the ministers and teachers are literalists and the laity symbolists, and, what is more, interpreters of their own symbolism. Then there is the influence of ceremonialism and what might be known as unsystematized worship, or individual worship. There is the question of efficiency in action, through complete organization on the one hand and liberty, at the expense of efficiency, on the other, as well as the question of unity and diversity.

Let us suppose that you have been born a Catholic, or have been converted to Catholicism. Your mind is fitted, or must be made to fit these several propositions and their natural outcome and consequences.

1st. You are a Literalist and must believe in the Fall of Man, Original Sin and Depravity and the Necessity of Redemption.

2nd. You must believe in the so-called plan of Salvation, as taught by St. Paul, that it is not through the life and moral example of Christ, but by His death and resurrection that mankind was to be redeemed.

3rd. That this Redemption was from a literal hell of torture by fire and brimstone, over which a real Devil, almost equal in power with God, presides.

4th. That Christ, while upon earth, organized a Church, and that said Church, at the present time, is represented by the Roman Catholic Church. That Christ, while in full charge, gave the keys of Heaven and Hell to St. Peter and made him and his successors His vicars on earth until He should, literally, return in His glory.

5th. You will believe in the miracles of Christ and the Saints. In fact, all along the line you will believe in the reality of all these things, not in any figurative or mystic sense, but with a full heart and open mind.

The result of such a belief in a man's mind, if he be true and sincere, will be about as follows: This Church will take precedence over all things mortal. The world is God's state. All government is established for the single purpose of carrying out the mandates of the Church. Men and women, their comforts and satisfaction, their loves and their hates, their desires and their aversions count for absolutely nothing where the welfare of that one divine institution is considered. What is the pain of a few men or women burned at the stake when it will prevent a whole nation, or even one person, from burning everlastingly, through all eternity, in a hell of fire and brimstone?

Since Christ has invested St. Peter with the power of the keys, and that power has been regularly transmitted, by accurate and complete apostolic succession, to the Holy Father who presides in the Vatican today, his commands must take precedence over all commands, whether of authority or duty. All this has been frequently announced from the Roman Catholic pulpit and all will admit that the nearer a communicant conforms to these regulations and beliefs, the better Catholic he will be and the more secure he will be of entering Christ's Kingdom after he dies. He can have no opinions of his own and no learning of his own, save what the authorities of the Church mete out to him. The Church, through its priests, assumes all responsibility for the man's soul and its eternal destiny, and all the man has to do is to pay and obey, the former liberally, the latter blindly. Whether great or small, rich or poor, learned or ignorant, the individual counts for absolutely nothing and the institution for everything.

The state of mind is very much the same as of those who believe in the divine right of kings. England, at the time of the Masonic reorganization, was passing through an experience when a considerable portion of her learned men believed in and advocated the divine right of kings. Many men held this opinion to the extreme of its literal meaning, excellent men, too. Obedience was a positive duty, no matter what the king commanded. It was just as obligatory to obey a bad king as to obey a good one. It was a divine right, and if God saw fit to inflict and oppress His people with a false, drunken, lecherous, extravagant villain of a king, they must obey him just the same, even though they are, at that moment, being flayed alive by his orders. No matter what the biography of pope, king or bishop, the obedience on the part of the laity must make their history dignified.

Now to the Freemason, whether in matters of politics or religion, such belief seems the very height of absurdity. The good Freemason looks upon the individual as everything and the Institution as but a means for securing the best happiness and righteousness of the individual members. The various sects of Protestant Christians have tried, ever since such a thing as Protestantism was known, to set up some sort of authority in religion which should be to the Protestant what the power of the keys is to the Romanist. Freemasons have done their best to establish some sort of imitation from which the real power might eventually grow, but without the belief in the literal truth of divine authority behind it, it can never be aught more than an imitation. Protestantism has tried to insist upon the authority of the Bible, and to raise that book, or rather collection of books, to the place of Pope and Council. In this they endeavor to create a diluted reality.

The true Protestant thinks himself at liberty to choose his particular brand of belief embodied in the articles of the sect he prefers, and raise his estimate of their authority to any power he pleases, but when he ceases to please, down they drop. In fact, Protestants have never known what belief is, and until they become willing to kill and be killed for its sake, to live the precepts, to give everything for it and with no reservation whatever, they never will know the meaning of divine right. Protestant authority is and must always be a consummate failure. Every article of Protestant faith is founded upon evidence that for over thirty generations remained in the hands of the Fathers of the Roman Catholic Church, subject to any and all the alterations which the policy of that organization might dictate.

This brings the Freemason down to the solid rock of freedom of religious belief and faith. And all the true faith possible to him is that secured through the practice of the Christian virtues which are recognized by all religions as the virtues revealed by God to men and have the same value in each. Not revealed especially in the holy books of their priests, but in general human experience in every tribe and race. The mental pictures which he may conceive of the future life will be subject to the teaching he has received as child, youth and man. It will be the sum of the impressions he has received of the world around him, a mixture of truth and error, the former or latter predominating, according as his education may have been liberal or the reverse. The religious feeling in him does not depend upon this education in the least, but it must depend entirely upon his desire to act upon the square, to do right by all his neighbors, to love them and bear with them. That such a religion may bring peace to the mind has been proved a thousand times.

The good Catholic may lay all his responsibility, moral and spiritual and temporal, upon the church, and be happy in obedience to his spiritual advisers. The Freemason cannot be satisfied with this; he must find his happiness, if at all, in the practice of the virtues, commonly known as Christian. These virtues were taught by Christ, but they were taught by Buddha, by Confucius, by Mohammed and by every man worthy to lead a religious movement. Their value does not depend in the least upon who taught them, but is intrinsic in them. To the Freemason the Bible is his light, the example of the fathers is his light, music is his light, preaching by someone who has seen the light may help him to see it also, but the light shines brightest when reflected from an altruistic life. In the civil world he must remain free also. He must strive towards the light, and he must strive to spread the light which comes to him. He must give the light its true value, and inasmuch as lieth in him work to increase it among the people around him. He must fight for this freedom of education, to the death if need be. He is by nature a soldier of the people, a soldier of true religion, a soldier of the light, the only religion holding the witness of the Spirit in the heart. Neither preaching, nor long prayers, nor ostentatious ceremony, nor chanting Te Deum

Laudamus is truly worship or religion, but to visit the widow
and the fatherless, to do justice, to love mercy, to walk humbly
and to keep one's self unspotted from the world.

The reason why Pope Clement attacked the new Order so
soon, even before the Institution was fairly organized and before
it came to have the least power or influence as a political force,
was that it was English and owed all its importance to English
Protestantism. Everything English was at that time the object
of extreme hatred on the part of the Roman Church. The
English had just recently driven out their Roman Catholic king,
James Stuart. This king had just been defeated in battle in
Ireland by William of Orange, a Protestant of Protestants and
a Freemason of the old regime. The Jesuits of the house of
Clearmont had attempted to organize a branch of Freemasonry
to be known as the Order of Strict Observance. The "higher
degrees" which they had pretended to discover had for one sole
object the restoration of the house of Stuart. This last attempt
had proved a flat failure, for the young Pretender had failed
more on account of his adherence to the Roman Church than
for any other reason. This did not dispose the fathers of the
Church to look lightly upon any institution, however humble,
that was secret and had its origin on English soil, and had for
its great and important tenet the toleration of all sorts of
religious faith.

The Catholic Church could not then, and cannot now, look with
any sort of complacency upon an institution that receives upon
equal terms Jews, Parsees, Mohammedans, Buddhists and
heretics of every kind. The Spanish Inquisition was not then
dead and many of our members in Latin countries suffered at
its hands. The Church had got along very easily with the
Ancient Operative Craft, and the Craft had done more than
all other things to make the Church great and dignified among
the nations of the world. The great Gothic cathedrals stood
as visible proofs of the devotion of the Craft to her interests.
These marvelous structures covered thickly the continent of
Europe and the British Isles. The change of belief regarding
the dogma of tran-substantiation had done away with their
necessity throughout that portion of the world which had become
Protestant, and even among the Catholics building had become
greatly lessened, both in the number of churches and in the
splendor of architecture. Gothic building had given place to
the new Italian Renaissance. Stained glass had given way to

painting as a means of decoration. The learning in geometry had become common and was no longer confined to the Craft.

The reorganization of the Ancient Fraternity could not appeal in any way to the Catholic Church. It was a mere social club with a strong Protestant leaning, though they made no restriction in their membership against members of the Catholic Church. Even Lord Montague, Grand Master at the time Price was commissioned Deputy for America, was a good Catholic. The heads of the Church could see in the new Institution only an organization likely to grow into a powerful enemy. Time has proved their conjecture to have been well founded. We must say again that this warfare is not a question of individuals. It is a warfare between authority represented by the spirit of the Church and liberty of thought, as represented by the Masonic Fraternity. The victory must ever be on the side of the Masonic Fraternity.

When the Church, as it did at one time, held complete and absolute authority in matters of religion, it selfishness was its ruin. Authority always ends in selfishness as naturally as sparks fly upward. That it might have been a good thing and served the uplift of the world at one time we are not prepared to deny. When every kind of savagery and barbarism was over-running the world it was a good thing that a lonely student might find protection in a monastery. The leading strings that support a child only hinder a strong man. The authority which a parent exercises over child and youth, ignorant of the forces around him, may serve to save its life and enable it to acquire that knowledge without which it might never live to realize its necessity. This same authority will only weaken a grown man and tend to keep him forever a child.

We have no quarrel with the ceremonies of the old Church. As long as the Mass is supposed to be symbolic we can appreciate its strength, but as a literal occurrence we cannot imagine anything more absurd, unless it may be spiritualistic materialization. If it merely signifies a commemoration of an historical event, many Protestants still believe in it implicitly. We have no quarrel with the confessional, though we believe it to be a two-edged sword, powerful for good or evil, according as the priest may be a good and wise or an ignorant and wicked man. In the majority of cases advice so received is beneficial, both in a material and spiritual way. We believe its place should be filled by the parent of the child, and that among those of responsible age the individual had best work out his own problems or obtain such information as he needs from other professional sources. However, we realize that the confessional held a useful place, which cannot be supplied from any other source, providing the belief in the necessity for absolution persists.

During late years there has grown up a large number of people, Catholic in name, whose belief in the efficacy of the church sacraments is very faint. Many are Catholics from heredity. They love the old Church for its associations the same as a man loves the cradle in which he was rocked as a baby, and cares for it and protects it, yet allows it to be covered with dust and would not think of using it for himself or for any of his children. They may have no use for Protestantism either, and find no inclination for resting in any such place. They are inclined to say, "If the old Catholic Church did not see the Risen Lord, nobody saw Him." They no longer look to the Church for its help or fear its excommunication. There are many of the Latin races who are strongly inclined to the latter mental tendency, while the Saxon races are inclined more and more to sectarian divisions and subdivisions.

The safety of our religious liberty does not depend more upon our eternal vigilance than upon the apathy of our opponents. The obedience of the members of the Church depends a great deal upon what she orders them to do and how much it is going to cost them, both in ready cash and in business friendships. If there was anything in the world that would strengthen this obedience it is the bull-roaring of modern Romaphobists, a good many of whom are somewhat ignorant and none too faithful Freemasons.

LECTURE XXVIII

INTERPRETATION OF SYMBOLS

SIR JOHN COCKBURN, in an article which we copied in our discussions of the Fellowcraft Degree, claimed that the letter "G" which appears as a symbol in our lodge rooms was in the Masso-Gothic Alphabet shaped like a square of the gallows variety, made with one arm perpendicular and the other extending horizontally from the top of it, just in the shape of our Past Masters' Jewel as employeod in the degree of Past Master. If this be a fact— and we have no doubt of its truth, for we have verified it as far as the shape of the Ancient "G" is concerned—most of the symbolism of the Fellowcraft Degree shapes itself around the square. Notice the manner of reception into the degree, the answer to the question, "How will you be tried?", the position at the altar, the due-guard, step, etc. All of this seems to us of the greatest interest, because it demonstrates the fact that our ancient brethren were men of exceeding large mental calibre, and not in any sense to be placed in comparison with the ordinary stone-cutter of the present day.

Beyond this, the Freemason of the olden time was an artist by nature, reared among artists from boyhood, usually of lofty religious ideals and free to work them out. Today we have an architect, more or less trained, with every man under him hired, to say the best. Wealth was not so great in the twelfth and thirteenth centuries as at present. Machinery was not as well developed by a thousand per cent. In fact, they had none at all save the tools mentioned in the ritual. But we believe it can be shown, in fact, we believe we have already shown that in philosophy, in culture, in religion and in all the fine arts, the Masters excelled anything we can now show, and that the Fellowcrafts averaged about as skillful as the Masters, because they were free.

The present day produces now and then a genius. He works out his life before the mediocre time servers about him recognize his existence. After he is dead posterity may acknowledge his merit and copy some of his work, but in those days it would have been recognized before he grew up.

The mysteries of Masonic symbolism are to a considerable extent organic. A man may take all the degrees ever practiced and visit the meetings of the society under every conceivable circumstance and never find out any mystery, save the means of recognition and perhaps the ceremonial itself. We have heard Past Grand Masters declare time and again that there was no mystery besides the things mentioned, and glorify the Order because there was not. Such men have eyes and see not, and ears that hear not, and minds that do not understand, neither will anyone else learn from them aught which they themselves do not know already. The entire knowledge of mathematics, be it geometry or algebra, is a mystery to everyone until by diligent search and careful training he finds it out, and we do not need the penalty of our ancient obligations to enforce its secrecy. In ancient times the initiation barely opened the door to the great truths of astronomy and mathematics, and as the neophite toiled under the direction of his Master, he learned not only the science, but what was greater still, the philosophy which had been built up regarding the Great Intelligence that had created and governed the vast universe according to a system of order and symmetry that he was learning. The mystery of mathematics and magic was not buried in the symbolic ceremony, but the great mystery and philosophy of God and the government of His universe was demonstrated and proved in mathematics, applied to the subject of astronomy, as hinted at in a veiled and nebulous manner in the ceremony of initiation.

There are three natural manifestations of the Deity and the Infinite. These are Number, Time and Space. If the human mind, in contemplating these, forms no conception of the eternal, absolute and unlimited Deity, if after this it is necessary to ask him in whom he puts his trust, we must come to the conclusion that he is either an old man in his dotage, a young man in his nonage, a madman, a fool, a mental slave or under some strange suggestion. We believe that our ancient brethren buried their knowledge in the ceremonial and in the sacred books, and made geometry the key by which the knowledge might be unlocked by those who diligently sought it. We also believe, and on no light evidence either, that a large portion of this long hidden wisdom is already extant, and easily obtained by any student who desires, in such modern books on the Cabalah as the "Beginning of Freemasonry," by Frank C. Higgins, of New York, and other works by the same author.

One may say, and many do say, that this symbolism has nothing to do with modern Speculative Masonry, and that at best it is only historical of the Ancient Mysteries. We realize that it is quite possible that such knowledge may be nothing to those whose only ambition is to read the ritual correctly, or repeat it without missing a word by one jot or tittle, and by so doing to be one day elected Grand Master of the Jurisdiction to which he belongs. "Verily he has his reward." To the man who is greatly interested in Masonic relief it may not mean much, for he will often come to that knowledge which Freemasonry desires above everything to teach, through the simple method of obedience to the inner light that every soul inherits. It is nothing whatever to the man who uses Masonry simply for his own selfish motives of personal vanity, aggrandizement or financial profit. But to those who look upon Masonry as a system of morals and a method of teaching morals by means of allegory and symbolism, and that symbolism geometry, we believe it is of vast importance. The importance does not rest in being told about these things, but in the practice and intimate study of them. If the importance does not appear in this last song of Copernicus, it is impossible for us to make it plain:

> Ye golden lamps of Heaven farewell
> With all your feeble light,
> Farewell, ye ever-changing Moon,
> Pale Empress of the night,
> And ye refulgent orb of day,
> In brighter flames arrayed,
> My soul has passed beyond thy sphere,
> And no longer needs thine aid;
> Ye stars are but the shining dust
> Of my divine abode,
> The pavement of those golden courts
> Where I shall reign with God.

We do not believe that an interpretation of an ancient or modern symbol is valueless or foolish, simply because it is unhistorical and was made centuries after the symbol was engraved. Symbolism, as a language, was never capable of lofty literary flight and when first employed as a means of writing or conveying thought other than by voice or some other immediate or corporeal method, its means of expression must have been correspondingly limited. Still that does not contradict the fact that considerable poetic thought may have been orally expressed previous to any writing at all. According to Max Muller, the Vedic hymns and many other Hindu books were transmitted by oral tradition for a good many centuries before they were permitted to be written at all.

What we desire to express is, that many races possessed very elaborate literature before they had any recognized means of writing it down. For instance, we have been nourished in the belief that the American Indians were absolutely ignorant; that they had no such thing as book learning. We know now that this was not the case. We find that they have a good many songs and poems of an epic character, novels or works of fiction composed purely for entertainment, and some legends that pose as historical. They had no written language, but they had a means of refreshing the memory, the most elaborate of which was the wampum and the quippa. Certainly neither of these is by any means a written language. How they were used we do not know, at least the writer does not know. Given an ancient symbol, unless we at one time had heard the story, we could not be expected to make use of the symbol to call the story to memory any more than we can read the wampum, but having learned the story and knowing the meaning, we see the application of the symbol. We are employing these symbols purely for teaching purposes, and it makes no difference whether our ancient brethren or the priests of some primitive religion originally gave them the identical interpretation or not, or even if they employed them for the purpose of cryptographing their scientific knowledge, so that a few small keys might retain it in the limits of a certain caste.

Take the alphabet, for instance. These symbols were not arbitrarily invented in the first place. They were pictures of a whole or a part of something familiar that already existed, that the man employed just because it was familiar and on account of the sound of its name, or what it did, or the noise it made, which seemed to him to resemble the sound he then desired to place in his alphabet. At first the picture is required to show the actors and what they are doing. Next comes the abbreviation of these pictures, the legs of a man, with the feet turned in the direction in which he was supposed to be moving, the hump for the camel, the circle or eight-pointed cross or star for the sun. The hump of the camel might stand for the groaning cry of the animal whenever that sound might be heard in the spoken tongue of the man. The hiss of the serpent might also be represented by the wavy coils of the reptile's body and finally settle down into the sound of the letter "S". In this manner a phonetic system might be built up. The old picture symbols are still there, but in most cases veiled or hidden.

It is interesting to learn how our alphabet was made up, not because we may ever have to make one, or because we expect to find anything valuable that may be translated from some of those ancient inscriptions in which the writing was imperfectly involved, but for the sake of learning thought processes. The man who first invented picture writing and the man who told the stories of the Bible in his rude sculpture on the rocks of some medieval cathedral, were not very far apart. There was a story that went with the picture. The notion of a soul or spirit that was developed from the shadow that followed him during his waking hours, and the dream while sleeping, must have been realized at a very early period, developing soon after the appearance of self-consciousness. Animism, or the belief that everything had a soul, as well as a man, comes immediately, because these cast a shadow and are seen in dreams in the same way that people are. The next question is: How are souls made? Where do they come from? This question is soon answered by the Phallic idea. This answer arrives just as soon as parenthood is recognized in the male. Solar influence is perceived almost as soon as the conditions of light and darkness are consciously recognized, even back in the days of human simianity, if we may use such an expression. Solar parentage of plant life does not require an elaborate knowledge of botany to conceive. It is likely that the notions of soul, spirit, immortality, solar parentage, and it may be of an anthropomorphic Deity were pretty completely developed before any kind of writing was known, and that these primitive people employed signs and symbols, in themselves familiar, simply for refreshing the memory as to the story or incident that seemed to prove the fact.

It is very likely that in the old Gothic Lodge or workshop the Master's square hung up over his head or within easy reach, where he could get it handily whenever he desired to test a piece of work or to draw a design. It is quite possible that the notion of its resemblance to the Deity might not have gained ground until those Masters who invented the Cabalah or the Zohair began to talk about it. Or it may well be until Elias Ashmole and Anderson and Desaguliers and Sayer created the Speculative Craft out of the old Operative Society of Working Freemasons. It may be that they got the idea from the old cornerstone or cubic stein of the German stein metzen, that in some way the square resembled the Deity. It is also possible that the idea came from the Kaaba of the Mohammedan faith. Perhaps it was taken from the idea of the justice of God, that He deals squarely with men and delights in having them deal squarely with each other. It may come from the tetragammaton or four-lettered name of Deity, but when the notion was once established that the letter "G" was emblematic of the Deity, the symbol became sacred and every philosopher could think of a hundred applications of this meaning to the symbol of the square. The central idea is that it is the square and not the "G" which resembles the Deity. This origin was in time forgotten and the initial alone remained. It happened to be the initial of the word "God" and also of the word "Geometry," and when this idea arrived the knowledge that it represented "Geometry" in its practical sense vanished.

There was an old question in the Fellowcraft lecture of a hundred years ago, which seems to have a bearing in some way on this explanation: "Why were you made a Fellowcraft?" The answer was: "For the sake of the letter 'G'." This letter was then mentally adopted as an abbreviation of the four letters in Hebrew, "J. H. V. H", so often mentioned and which has been read "Jehovah". It was used because, as an initial, it was a little more understandable to Masons of the English language. In the German lodges the Bible is employed as the "Haupt Symbol", because it resembles an oblong square when lying unopened on the altar. The four letters written in Hebrew are frequently employed as an architectural decoration. They may be seen in the front of the old Cathedral on Second and Walnut streets in St. Louis.

We do not expect an elaborate mystical system, arranged on purpose, to explain how the square came to represent the Deity. We only need to imagine that the Master hung up his square where it would be most convenient, and that the four-letter name became connected with it and came to be represented by it, not on purpose, but accidentally, in the Masonic consciousness, until a fancied resemblance awoke. Hence we act upon the square. Again, the New Jerusalem that came down from heaven was four square or a perfect cube, and the faces of a cube unfold into a cross of the Latin variety. We do not expect to trace Masonry as an organization back to where T. K. in his "Great Work" so confidently places it. But it did arise in the operative

art. This art did have even then a secret means of recognition
by sign, grip and word. It did have an initiation, in the wording
of which we do find many curious coincidences, and it may be
possible that these coincidences have led to many patchings of
new cloth upon the old garments. Two hundred years ago people
of average education knew nothing at all of philology, and the
knowledge of that science is by no means widespread even to
this day. They also knew very little about history and much of
what they thought they knew was not true. But they knew a
great deal more than anyone knows today concerning the pseudo
science of astrology and alchemy and magic, both black and
white. They had only just ceased believing in the miracle of
transubstantiation. No one doubted that these things were
actual sciences at that date. People might not have very much
faith in their own ability to work magic in any particular case,
or to raise ghosts, but they had not come to doubt that there
actually were people who could perform such supernatural
tricks. Many believe that such things have been done and are
done today in some far-away place, like India, for instance.
Most educated people of the present day are certain that such
things do not now and never did have a reality.

For instance, many people believed that they had actually
seen real devils. Certainly the idea of their shape and semblance
must have arrived before the drawings employed to represent
them, but their cherubim were made up of real animals after
all. One old lady remarked that she knew that there must be
a devil, "Else how could they make pictures that looked so much
like him?" Now we know that devils were a verb, a process, a
sort of conduct, and the shape was created from the personified
idea of what a creature must be to perform such acts and show
such an evil disposition. It is pretty generally conceded that
the most primitive savage has just as good reasoning powers
as the most learned man alive, so far as he possesses a correct
knowledge of the facts. It is no more wonderful that the figures
of speech employed to elucidate sun worship should appear in
the language of our ritual than that they should appear in the
language of St. Paul or the Prophet Isaiah, or in expressions
attributed to Christ: "I am the Light of the world." Again, if
the circle used to represent the sun was, in order to represent
a circle in cuneiform characters, turned into a cross of eight
bars, the cross would in a short time come to represent the sun
by itself without the idea of a circle at all. Again, inasmuch as

the sun was the Deity, the cross would represent the Deity. Even when the minds of people changed in regard to the nature and identity of the Deity, they would by no means necessarily change their manner of representing the Deity and the cross would continue. This would be all the more likely, since the cross was no longer used to represent a circle, as they had acquired much better ways of drawing such a figure, and even cuneiform writing had become a lost art. Now the cross is four square and has four right angles, and if the cross represented the Deity so would the four right angles, thus making a clear connection between the square and the Deity by another method.

On the portrait statue of Tiglath Pilesar, taken from his memorial tablets found in the ruins of the city of Nineveh, there is seen suspended a cross around his neck. It is a perfect copy of what is known as the Maltese cross. The cross is frequently seen as a part of the decorative scheme on the ruined palaces and temples of ancient Mexico and Central America. What its meaning was we do not know, but it most likely signified that the artists were members of a sun-worshipping cult; in short, that they were "Sons of Light." It demonstrates plainly that its signification was recognized by the people of those times. The Crux Ansata, so frequently observed in the hands of the statues of the old kings and gods of Egypt, was evidently both solar and Phallic in signification, and represented a combination of the male and female principles in nature. The tree of life with the serpent entwined around it is also seen, and this symbol also represents the solar and generative processes. There is also found held in the hand of most of the Assyrian Deities the burr of the male date palm. The pollen from this burr was employed to fecundate the blossoms on the female palm and also denotes fecundity as one of its meanings, whatever else they might have ascribed to it. The palm was one of the chief sources of food supply for the desert Arabs, and its importance could hardly be over-estimated. The tree of life has also been handed down to us as the Christmas tree, and in that shape it not only denotes the burning bush mentioned in the experience of Moses, but its angle of 23½ degrees seems also to represent the shape of the universe indicated by the inclination of the axis of the earth to the ecliptic. The Polar Star, being the apex of the tree, the zodiacal circle the base of the tree, with the sun in the center at the roots of the tree, the entire stellar heavens revolving around the trunk in the shape of a cone. Thus when we read of the "Tree of Life" having twelve branches and bearing twelve manner of fruit, we see represented the "Year".

One other sign is worth mentioning. We frequently read of the beast with ten horns and the beast with six horns. These horns are seen represented on the headgear of nearly all the portraits of the Deities. They are arranged on the turban, with the points of the horns turning slightly upward in front. It must be remembered that a large part of the movable wealth of those nations consisted of cattle. The greater the king, the more cattle he possessed and the more horns he was entitled to wear in the ornaments of his turban. In this connection we might mention a verse in Revelations 13th, 18th: "Here is Wisdom. Let him that hath understanding count the number of the Beast, for it is the number of a man; and his number is six hundred, three score and six." Compare this with II Chronicles 9th, 13th: "Now the weight of gold that came to Solomon in one Year was six hundred, three score and six talents of gold."

LECTURE XXIX
THE MANAGEMENT OF A LODGE

HITHERTO, the Book of Constitutions, together with the advice of the Grand Master and District Deputy and District Lecturer, have, in the minds of this Grand Lodge, been deemed sufficient instruction for the management of the lodge. These officers are not always of the same mind, and even if they were they are not at all times present, and while the Book of Constitutions is authoritative and gives many directions, it is not particularly interesting reading and gives no reasons for the procedure required. It has been our intention to write a few lectures on this subject, and on the method of conducting lodge trials, as a kind of practical application of the principles which we have been trying to elucidate in the preceding pages. The general management and responsibility for all the lodge business is intrusted mainly to the Master, *"Whose duty it is to contrive work for the Craft, superintend them during the hours thereof and give them proper instructions for their labors."* The brethren are expected to consent to the expenditure of the funds, as it is they who contribute them. The Master is, however, held responsible by his own lodge, as well as by the Grand Lodge, that the lodge by-laws as well as the statutes of the Book of Constitutions are duly observed. All appeals from his decisions lie first to the District Deputy and through him to the Grand Master, and finally to the Grand Lodge in regular session.

The first element, the very most essential at all times, is the harmony of the lodge, for in the absence of harmony the lodge is not merely useless but a positive harm to its members and to the community in which the lodge is located. The second element is the prudent handling of the funds and other property of the lodge and the management of its financial affairs. The usefulness of that body, especially in cities, depends upon the funds at its command. In country districts personal services in a measure take their place. One great point and one frequently noticed is the tendency to fix the fees and dues at far too small a figure to furnish the amount of money required to conduct the work of the lodge as it ought to be, liberally and without even the appearance of stinginess.

As time goes on and modern manners begin to obtain, personal service grows more and more unacceptable, even in the country, and in the city, so far as our Fraternity is concerned, it cannot be employed at all, in cases of sickness, save in the way of sympathetic visitation, and, speaking from the point of view of a physician, even such visitation does far more harm than good, at least until convalescence has well begun. If the sick brother has any business affair that he would like some brother to attend to for him outside, it is proper that he should make a request for the same. The Master or whoever he may appoint as a committee ought to keep in touch with the family and attendants so as to render such assistance as may be solicited. For this reason the initiation fees should never go into the general living purse of the lodge and should never, under present conditions, be less than fifty dollars for the three degrees. The dues should never be less than ten or twelve dollars per year, according to the style that the membership desires to put on. The initiation fees ought always to be put aside and carefully invested and the income only used exclusively for relief and funeral expenses. The sum mentioned for dues will every cent be needed in the propagation and maintenance of the lodge and Order, rent, paraphernalia, music, service, hospitality, entertainment and the general promotion of friendship and acquaintance among the membership of the lodge.

It has never been denied that the Fraternity ought to be capable of assuming a distinctive, even exclusive, position in society. It would seem as though membership in a Masonic Lodge ought to be worth as much as membership in the Y. M. C. A. or any simply athletic or social club or singing society to any young man, and if it is not so, there is something decidedly wrong, either with the mental or moral quality of the present membership or in the handling of the affairs of the lodge. Freemasonry has a monetary value in its acquaintance and it ought to have a monetary value in the added reputation and the tongue of good report which the member is supposed to bring to the Fraternity, and which the world should know has been tested to the full by that Institution. Of course, the real value of all such things depends upon the integrity and acumen of the human agents which carry them out.

This brings the matter right down to the choice of membership. Every lodge is very much in the situation of a spinster of marriageable age. She cannot, on account of long-established custom, go out and pick and choose whom she would have. She must wait until the right man proposes and then accept. Still there is no harm in her faithfully keeping before the male public the sort of man she finds most agreeable to her. And as the maid who rejects in flirtation a number of nice men on account of trivial faults, no man being perfect, is liable to get a rather scaly fish for a husband at last, so the lodge that rejects a good man a few times on account of trivial jealousies and envious dislikes on the part of some weak brother or brethren, is apt to find that only young boys whose characters are entirely unformed and those of sufficient duplicity to conceal grievous faults can get accepted. In such a lodge there will be ignorance in plenty and the teachers will be few and incapable.

There are few men who live to grow up and obtain any responsible position in society without making an enemy out of some member of a Masonic Lodge. The ambition of the membership of such a lodge as we have mentioned will be settled mainly on offices, jewels and salaries, and the real purposes of the society will be lost sight of. In short, the ambition of the membership, so far as they may be said to have any ambition at all, will be to shine rather than to seek and obtain Masonic light. Here the qualifications of an investigating committee should be, above all things, justice, discretion and industry. To these should be added a certain broad-mindedness that can only be acquired through a wide knowledge of men. It is the duty of this committee to investigate carefully all reports submitted to them regarding the character of a petitioner, and to make inquiry, not only of those likely to reproach, but also those who seem to think well of the man. It is none the less the duty of the members to inform the committee of what they know regarding the character of the petitioner, and when this committee has made the final report to place confidence in it and vote accordingly. It is not to be supposed that any individual brother can have a very high moral reason for casting a black-ball against a candidate, which reason he cannot give to the committee in confidence. And if his dislike grows entirely from personal dealings with him it is quite possible that the brother may have overrated the justice of his own contention. Here the committee are the best judges by far. Men are scarce who have a sufficiently mathematical mind to do exact justice by a man with whom they have had a difference or a quarrel, and are apt to think that a man is necessarily bad or a fool whose interest has in any manner conflicted with their own far enough to cause hard words or a law-suit. Selfishness is still a very serious affliction and anyone who imagines it to be absent among the Craft in their dealings with each other is altogether sanguine, to say nothing with regard to their dealings with the outside world.

The brother who casts a black-ball must not fail to remember that in so doing he is expending out of the lodge funds an amount equal to the initiation fee which would certainly become the property of the lodge in case of the candidate's election to membership. The matter should certainly be considered by him from that point of view, instead of the point of view of his revenge for personal injury which he may think has been done him some time in the past, or against one who he fancies has committed some sin against the caste to which he believes himself to belong.

One of the greatest objects of obtaining Masonic light is "to learn to subdue the passions". And when most of these questions are examined dispassionately there would be few cases where a candidate for Masonry would be rejected by a single ballot and in the face of a favorable report from the investigating committee.

Many Masters of the best judgment have decided on the appointment of a single committee to act for the entire year, except in such cases as the candidate may be a relative or a notorious enemy of some one member of the committee, and thus render him disqualified to act. A permanent committee should have its expenses paid while actually engaged in lodge work. The element most necessary to secure is confidence in the report of the committee and compliance with its recommendations. It is also necessary to continually preach to new members that Freemasonry must not be used as a whip with which to revenge petty spites, but rather as a school wherein universal benevolence may be taught and occasionally learned. Joining a lodge does not make men bad or good any more than joining a church, but example added to precept helps to get men orientated.

The Master should provide a book of registration for his candidates, which should show the date of their proposal in the lodge, the names of the investigating committee and the date at which their report is due, date of the candidate's election or rejection, date of initiation, name and address of some competent brother whose duty it shall be to instruct the candidate in his lecture, date at which the examination is expected, date of examination and vote on proficiency, date of passing and proficiency, date of raising and date of passing final examination on the Master's lecture, so that all the work may be conducted with regularity and each candidate be taken in his turn. When a candidate fails to appear on the night appointed for his reception in any degree, he should lose his turn and his name be placed at the foot of the list, so that no brother should lose his turn on account of another's absence. In case a lodge is so over-burdened with work that special meetings become necessary, it is better to call them than to keep the brethren too late and, in the opinion of the writer, it is better, other things being equal, to use the special meetings for the degrees of Entered Apprentice and Fellowcraft and to confer the Master's Degree on a single candidate at a stated meeting. There is usually too much business for more than one Master's Degree at a stated meeting. At special meetings four or five Firsts or Seconds may be conferred without working too late, or two Thirds. Work should close if possible by 11 p. m.

Regarding his own portion of the ritualistic work the Master may make such appointments as he sees fit for present or future meetings, but it is exceedingly bad taste on his part to make any disposition of the work of the other officers without first obtaining their permission to do so. It is a part of one of the Ancient Charges, "That he who starts a job of work should be responsible for its completion." Besides, some worthy and accomplished officer may be hurt or offended and the Master lose his willing, zealous co-operation. If the Master desires some visitor to assume a certain part of the work on a certain date, he should consult with the officer ordinarily responsible for the part and request him as a favor to invite the person designated to fill the place. These things are small, but they make largely for the popularity of the Master and consequently for the harmony and usefulness of the lodge. Cities should maintain a perpetual Lodge of Instruction, not only for candidates, but for officers as well. A single instructor can lecture several students as well as one and the system makes for uniformity in the lectures. A relay of instructors should be secured from the different lodges in the city, or if the lodges are few, certain nights in the week may be set apart for instruction. The names of all candidates and officers who learn easily and have the best delivery and show the greatest ability in the ritual should be mentioned to the Master, so that there may be some means of knowing who are and who are not proficient and accomplished ritualists.

Upon all ordinary occasions the Master should act as purchasing agent for the lodge, though in some lodges this matter may safely be placed in charge of the finance committee. The Treasurer and Secretary being the conserving and collecting agents of the lodge, never ought to act as purchasing agents if any other brother is competent. It is not by any means advisable for the same man to be collector and distributor, and yet he ought to be one not only familiar with the amount of funds on hand, but also with the future obligations of the lodge. All payments ought to be made by means of a numbered voucher signed by the Master, Treasurer and Secretary. This voucher should be on some bank designated by the lodge as a depository for the funds, and should consist of two parts, one part a regular check for the amount of money to be paid and the other part a regular bill for the goods purchased or service rendered, or debt due to be paid. When this voucher is deposited it serves as a receipt for the amount paid. These vouchers should be duplicated by a stub and the number and amount should be shown in the minutes of the lodge meeting of the same date as having been regularly allowed. At the audit of the books of the Secretary, date, number and title on stub, voucher and minute should all agree. The Secretary should keep another book in which he should keep receipts of the amounts collected by him and turned over to the Treasurer, all of which should be signed by the Treasurer. The difference between these amounts and the amount of the several vouchers ought to show the balance in the hands of the Treasurer. The Treasurer will deposit in the bank these several amounts in separate items, so that his bank book will correspond with this book of receipts. This is a simple system of bookkeeping and as between the different officers of the lodge is not likely to be falsified, neither in their dealings with the outside world, and the audit is very much simplified so that an ordinary mind may grasp it. Concerning the accounts between the lodge and its members we will speak later.

When it may be thought expedient to appoint a special purchasing committee, it ought to be limited to a certain amount and should O. K. all bills contracted. When these bills are presented the Master should invariably say, 'These bills will be paid, unless objections are offered." No objection should be allowed unless the amount exceeds the sum previously fixed, lest the members of the committee be excusably offended. It is presumed that such a committee would act according to its best judgment. If the lodge does not approve of its judgment it should make more suitable appointments in the future. Usually the mistake is made in appointing too many members on the purchasing committee. The result is that the lodge, instead of obtaining the best judgment of the three or more, obtains a mixture of three or more judgments, thus trebling the expense and obtaining an animal like the celebrated Sphinx, that is neither man nor beast nor bird, but a combination of all three.

The Master should enjoy perfect authority to distribute relief among needy members at his discretion, though it is always prudent when possible for him to consult with the two Wardens, the Treasurer and Secretary. If the initiation fees are kept and invested for this purpose only, there will generally be sufficient income for all necessary expenditures along this line. It might be permissible to invest these funds in a hall property for the use of the lodge, but aside from this the surplus ought to be invested in government bonds or savings bank deposits. The lodge and other bodies meeting in this hall should pay a reasonable rent to this fund for its use, and in this manner furnish an income that may be applied for the relief of distressed worthy brethren, as the necessity occurs. Again, it is not well for the deserts of a needy brother to be discussed in open lodge. The Master and Wardens are the best men to make all necessary investigations of this sort and may have their discussion privately. If every man was equally successful in obtaining a job, equally industrious, equally wise in his expenditures, and equally careful in investing his money, there would be very little need, but this is notoriously not the case and it must not be forgotten that need is the question to be discussed and not desert at all. Humanity is prone to error, some of one sort and some of another, and there come unforeseen accidents and calamities in the lives of all men. Moral perversities are always accompanied by mental inadequacies. As a rule, small amounts frequently repeated give the best satisfaction in relief work.

In the opinion of the writer every lodge should provide a certain amount for the build-up of a lodge library of Masonic literature. And in case there happens to be no public library in the place there should be added as many as possible of the classic books on general subjects other than Masonic. Masonry is primarily an educational institution, rather than a strictly charitable or relief society, and this is a fact that ought to be made prominent, as many approach the Order with the contrary idea. Again, a lodge ought to be of use to a community, a power of good influence in the town and capable of bringing united support to a good cause. This cause should be entirely public and not sectarian.

It may be very proper for a Mason to support a sectarian object or cause, but hardly so for the Order at large, but it ought to be kept generally known that the Order is on the side of every good work, be it political, moral, religious or merely social. And it ought not to hesitate for an instant to use its united influence when wisdom, patriotism or good judgment dictates. The question ought to be, first, "Is it right?", second, "Is it just?", third, "Is it possible of accomplishment?", fourth, "Is it kind?", fifth, "Is it necessary?". Great foresight should be used in allowing the discussion of such questions in open lodge, that no criticism of motives be permitted. It is quite proper at any time to discuss the effects of a proposition or a contemplated measure in the lodge, but the motive of any brother in bringing the proposition before the lodge, or in taking one side or the other in an argument, should never be questioned, even by implication or suggestion. Any remark made calculated to reflect in any way on the personal integrity of a brother should at once be called to account by the Master and turned aside. Such remarks are very dangerous, even in joke. If the Master interrupts the speaker and says, "Brother —————, you do not mean, in your last remark, to question the good character or integrity of Brother —————?", undoubtedly he will say that he did not and disclaiming all unfriendly intention will beg the pardon of the brother mentioned. If the remark be left unquestioned, and the brother thinking himself disparaged be allowed to reply, he would most likely say something that could not on any account be permitted in the lodge, and if the discussion, perchance, be continued outside the lodge, its harmony will most certainly be broken.

It is desirable that the lodge room be suitable and as attractive as can be obtained. Its furniture should be orderly and in keeping with the styles in the best homes of the community, and it is usually wise, as soon as the lodge can afford it, to have two sets of collars and aprons, nice, clean banners, flags and paraphernalia, one of which, like a gentleman's full dress suit, should be kept for public display and gala occasions, while at ordinary times their working clothes are good enough, on which the stains of labor do not look dishonorable. There ought to be portraits of all Past Masters and Wardens and such as have served the lodge faithfully in any capacity, either fine oil paintings or framed photographs to be hung in the lodge room, that new members may learn the names and faces of those who have worked in building up the Order and lodge into which they have been permitted to enter. Hospitality to visiting brethren and to the families and friends of the members of the lodge is enjoined in the Ancient Charges and serves also as a proper advertisement, keeping the Order in the public eye. For this reason a suitable dining room is always a great convenience and almost a necessity in modern lodges. It would seem to the writer that at the beginning of the year a survey of the probable revenue of the lodge for the ensuing year should be made and a budget prepared, apportioning this revenue to the following purposes:

1. Rent of lodge rooms.
2. Salaries of Secretary, Tiler, Stereoptician, Organist and Librarian.
3. Hospitality and entertainment of brethren and visitors.
4. Public observances, parades, church services, etc.
5. Paraphernalia, repairs, additions, laundering, etc.
6. Masonic Directory and advertising of meetings.
7. Grand Lodge taxes.
8. Expenses of Representatives and Past Masters to Grand Lodge meetings.
9. Postage, stationery, sundries for Secretary's office.
10. Board of Relief taxes.
11. Employment Bureau taxes.
12. Lodge of Instruction.
13. Master's contingent fund.
14. Master's jewel, apron, hat and portrait.
15. Library special fund.
16. Funerals and relief special fund.

It must not be forgotten that as the lodge grows older the average age of the members increases with it, and the amount of sickness and distress becomes much greater and funerals more frequent. When the lodge has increased in size up to five or six hundred members, the suspensions and deaths will often more than keep pace with the legitimate increase. This is the main argument for the careful investment of surplus funds while the lodge is young. A pretty close calculation of the amounts that can be devoted to each of these several channels should be made, and unless the revenue exceeds the amount estimated these disbursements ought not to be passed by the Master in his appropriations for the year, though by vote of the lodge it should be possible in cases of emergency to transfer small amounts from one appropriation to another.

In the opinion of the writer the by-laws of the lodge should be few, stating only the following points:

1. The name of the lodge.
2. The place or location where the lodge is to meet.
3. The night of stated meetings.
4. The hour of stated meetings.
5. The fees for the several degrees and when payable.
6. The amount of the regular annual dues and when payable.
7. The salaries of paid officers when payable.
8. The amounts to be set apart for special purposes, when and to whom payable.
9. The date of annual election of officers.
10. The manner of alteration of the by-laws.

All other matters should be settled by resolution, changeable at any time by the ordinary majority vote of the lodge members present. It is a good plan to set the hour for opening of stated meetings early, as early as 7:30 p. m., so that as soon as a quorum of seven are present the Master or one of the Wardens may open the meeting and get through with those necessary ceremonies by the time the majority of the members have assembled. The lodge can then be ready to set to work at once and save a great deal of time, the routine business being got out of the way.

The time required for the opening of the lodge in an orderly and dignified manner in this Jurisdiction is considerable. Indeed, it takes nearly an hour, especially if there are examinations of candidates for proficiency in the different degrees. When the lodge is once open for business in the third degree, the regular order should be called, and any item coming up either disposed of or postponed to some definite date. It is an easy matter for the Secretary to have his work arranged so that it can be disposed of rapidly. When any matter comes up and the Master has determined the best manner of disposing of it, instead of saying to the lodge, "What will you do about it?", he should say, "Unless objections be offered it will take the following course." This method of dealing with unimportant business will save a great deal of time in useless discussion. If the matter is of importance the Master should call upon some well-posted brother for his opinion and offer the floor for discussion. We have frequently seen hours consumed in discussion, motion upon motion and amendment upon amendment offered upon questions about which no brother cared a penny, and which might have been decided in one minute in the manner we have stated. The regular order of business should be about as follows:

1. Minutes of preceding meetings.
2. Petitions.
3. Reports of committees.
4. Correspondence.
5. Bills.
6. Ballotting on candidates.
7. Voting on proficiency.
8. Reports of sickness and distress.
9. General business relative to the welfare of the lodge. Introduction of resolutions and action thereon.

If committees are to be appointed other than investigation committees on candidates, one member is generally sufficient. A committee composed of several members has the following characteristics: Each member expects some other member to do all the work, and when the time for report arrives it is frequently discovered that no one has attended to the matter. When a single brother is appointed to attend to any matter he generally does the work promptly. When the business calls for the making of a contract for the expenditure of money, one man will feel free to exercise his best judgment the way he would act in case of his own personal affair, but when several be on a committee all must be satisfied. This invariably costs more than when there is one alone. Again, one man may have a clear and comprehensive idea of the work on hand and be able to construct a plan for carrying it out, while the different ideas of three or five may be utterly impossible of combination in any manner that would be workable.

Immediately on the opening of his term of office the Master should appoint an auditing committee to examine the books of the financial officers of the lodge, the Secretary, Treasurer and the Trustees, if such there be. This is due to the new officers, so that they may start with a clean record. This is just as important where the same men are continued in office from year to year. Where this is possible an expert accountant, not a member of the lodge, should be hired to open the set of books and do the auditing. Most ordinary members are incompetent for the purpose and they are often too easily influenced by the officer whose books they are auditing, not so much because they mean to be influenced, but because so much explanation is necessary to make them understand the simplest matter in bookkeeping. A regular accountant is likely to be impartial and will be under no man's influence. Again, all the financial officers should be bonded in a regular bonding company. The bond of a brother of the lodge or a relative ought never to be allowed. In the first place an officer is not near as apt to handle the funds carelessly, or keep the books carelessly, or embezzle the funds of the lodge, if a regular bonding company is looking after him. These are matters into which friendship ought not to enter. The lodge should pay out of the general funds of the lodge for this bond and the company will inform the lodge when the bond expires. It is no reflection on the character of an officer to insist upon his being bonded, or that his books shall be frequently, at least annually, audited. The brother who assumes such an office ought to insist upon it himself.

The books necessary for the Secretary seem to be as follows:

1. A minute book.
2. A cash receipt book, in which he notes down all items of cash received.
3. A receipt book, in which the Treasurer receipts for all items of cash turned over to him.
4. A receipt book with stub, from which the Secretary issues receipts to each member for dues paid. These are generally procured from the Grand Secretary of the Jurisdiction and bear his certificate that the lodge is regular and in good standing under seal of the Grand Lodge.
5. A voucher, check and warrant book combined with stub, numbered.
6. A classified expense book, in which are entered all items of expense, with number of voucher.
7. A membership ledger, loose leaf, so that the names can be arranged alphabetically.
8. A roster, with dates of petitions received, elected or rejected, initiated, proficiency examination; passed, proficiency examination; raised, proficiency examination; dimitted, suspended, expelled, died, funeral. The last five items may be classed under one, membership terminated.

THE MINUTE BOOK OF PROCEEDINGS—It is the duty of the Secretary to carefully observe the proceedings of the lodge and record all things proper to be written. As a general proposition we might say that a note should be made of every item of business that is governed in any way by a statute of the Grand Lodge or a by-law of the particular lodge. A few of them may be mentioned as follows:

1. The date of the meeting, stated or special.
2. The place of meeting.
3. The Master or Warden presiding.
4. The names of the officers filling the different chairs. At least seven must be mentioned by name, as they demonstrate the necessary quorum.
5. If a stated meeting, the regular successive opening in each of the three degrees in due form and the business transacted in each.
6. In all action on petitions the record must show that the petition was in due form, full name, residence, age, occupation, length of residence in the jurisdiction, date of previous rejections and lodge where rejected, if any, appointment of investigating committee and names. If the petition is objected to the minutes should so state, but without mentioning the name of the brother or brothers objecting, or designating him further than to state whether he was a member of the lodge. It must also be shown that the usual fee accompanied the petition and any other requirement covered by statute.
7. In all action on candidates it must be shown in the case of the first degree that the candidate had been regularly elected to receive the degrees, and in case of the second and third degrees, that he had been examined and declared proficient in the preceding degree. It must also be shown that the fee for the degree had been paid. A note must also be made of the member having passed examination in the lecture of the third degree on the date when such examination was held.
8. In all reports of investigating committees on petitions the minutes should simply show that the committee reported and were discharged, or allowed further time, but should not show whether the report was favorable or unfavorable.
9. In matters of balloting it should simply be noted that the ballot was spread on such a name and that he was declared elected or rejected. In cases where a single blackball appears and it is necessary to take a second ballot, the minutes should state that the ballot was spread a second time and the result. In case of a reballot at some future time, the minutes must show the order from the Grand Master and state that the resident members were notified to be present.
10. All resolutions requiring the expenditure of money, the amount authorized must be shown and in whose favor the voucher was drawn, so that the auditor of the books may

find the authorization. Also when the final account was presented and the amount paid. It is the custom to have a certain place in the records of the meeting where all financial items are separately exhibited, with number of voucher, which must correspond with the title, number and amount in the voucher book.

11. In case of the suspension of a brother for non-payment of dues, the minutes must show the date, the name or names were reported to the Master as being delinquent and the ordering of the final notice. At the expiration of the legal notice the minutes must show that the necessary summons was issued to come up and show cause why he should not be suspended on a certain date. At the expiration of the summons there ought to be some proof exhibited that the summons had been delivered either by personal service or by registered letter receipt, or that a copy of the summons had been left at his last known place of residence. All these must appear in the minutes previous to the vote being taken on his suspension.

All these points should appear in the minutes to show that the statutes of the Grand Lodge have been carried out in the manner and form directed in the Book of Constitutions in case the matter should ever be made a cause for review by the Grand Master or his Deputy. We have not taken up all matters made the subject of statutory legislation, but we have mentioned enough of them to illustrate the manner in which the book ought to be kept. When the minutes are finally read and approved by the lodge, the Master should sign the record.

CASH RECEIPT BOOK—The cash receipt book should be ruled to show the following headings:

1. Name or source of income.
2. Date of receipt.
3. Degree fees, first, second and third.
4. Dues and year for which paid.
5. Income from investments.
6. Income from other sundry sources.
7. Totals from each and all sources.

EXPENSE BOOK—The Secretary's expense book should be ruled to classify expenses as follows:

1. Name or title of voucher and number.
2. Fees for degrees, returned.
3. Rent, janitor's services, insurance on hall, repairs.
4. Salaries of officers.
5. Postage, stationery, advertising meetings.
6. Hospitality and entertainment.

7. Parades and public observances.
8. Paraphernalia, repairs, additions, laundry, insurance on same.
9. Grand Lodge tax and other board taxes.
10. Sundries.
11. Relief, gifts to members and their dependents.
12. Funerals, carriages, flowers, etc.
13. Vouchers to Trustees for permanent investment, bonds, certificates of deposit, etc.

In fact, the expense book should have a space for each class of expense made in the original budget of appropriation, previously shown, with totals for each and all varieties of expense.

The Secretary's ledger should include no accounts save dues of members. The fees for the degrees are supposed by law to have been paid before the degrees were received and before dues are chargeable, and are shown in the Secretary's receipt book, while the ledger is posted from this cash receipt book and shows the accounts of each individual member. As we have said, this ledger should be kept on the loose leaf plan, so that the accounts may be shown in alphabetical arrangement. In time the accounts of suspended or deceased or expelled members may be removed, showing only the live accounts. The dead accounts may be preserved in a separate binding. Under the present law dues are payable in advance. It is no kindness to a member to keep him on the roll after he has become delinquent. He should be immediately suspended, unless he is unable to pay, and if he is unable to pay from sickness or any good cause, his dues ought to be remitted. To keep him on the roll after he has become delinquent necessitates the paying of the Grand Lodge tax for him, and the less he owed the lodge when he was suspended the easier will it be for him to reinstate himself to good standing. In auditing the books the Secretary should furnish the committee with a list of members who have become delinquent, have died or become suspended or expelled, and also those who have paid in advance. The auditing committee should send a letter to each member reported delinquent, informing him of his standing and telling him their understanding of the state of his account with the lodge and asking him to show his receipt for dues, if he is dissatisfied with the account as it stands. This will enable the committee to fix the amount of money that ought to have been paid to the Secretary during the year. These lists should be verified in the ledger and on the stub of the book of receipts for dues. The dues of all not on these lists should be accounted for. This will render the audit complete and what it is expected to be. It will not only show that the dues with which the Secretary has credited himself have been properly accounted for, but also what he ought to have received. The number of members multiplied by the amount of annual dues will show the total, with the following exceptions:

1. Dues paid in advance.
2. Dues still owing, according to list of delinquents.
3. Dues of members who have come in during the year and consequently only charged for a part of the year.
4. Dues for a part of year in cases where the member has dimitted during the year and a portion of his dues has been paid over to the lodge with which he has affiliated. The portion paid over will be accounted for by voucher. In case of death during the year it would be right that the portion of unearned dues still remaining to the brother's credit be returned to his family or estate.

Every member should be cautioned to see that he gets his receipt and immediately signs it on the margin. In nearly all jurisdictions a visitor is required to show his receipt for dues for the current year, and he should certainly be able to exhibit a receipt for the year just past, so he should invariably carry his receipt with him when traveling in localities where he is not known as a Mason.

It must not be forgotten that when a member pays for the current or any former year, his Grand Lodge tax must be included and sent in to the Grand Secretary when the annual returns are made. The Grand Lodge tax is found by multiplying the number of members by the amount of the tax per capita charged by the Grand Lodge. This amount plus the tax for any delinquent reinstated will be the amount due the Grand Lodge. The Grand Lodge requires that the lodge shall pay the tax for any member whose dues have been remitted by vote of the lodge for inability to pay same. It would seem to be better to credit such member with having paid his dues in full and draw a voucher in favor of the Secretary for the amount, charging the same to the relief department.

We have already advised that a regular accountant not a member of the lodge be paid to do the auditing. An auditing committee appointed from among the brethren of the lodge fails to prove efficient at the very time when the books have been cooked to hide a shortage. They always start with full confidence in the officers and when they fail to understand any matter in the books they assume that the explanation given by the officer is correct. The disinterested expert only looks to the books themselves to show the exact financial condition of the lodge.

Again, it is a very unwise method of assisting some needy, unfortunate, incapable brother to give him charge of the finances of the lodge, simply because he needs the amount of the salary to get along. Next to the Master the financial officers should be capable of keeping straight books and handle money. In ninety-nine cases out of a hundred, where the Secretary or Treasurer is found short in his accounts, it is due to the incapacity of the officer as a bookkeeper and his careless handling of the money of the lodge, along with his own, and his failing in memory to make a record of some collection or disbursement, or to give or take a receipt. Conscious theft of the lodge funds is not a frequent occurrence, but borrowing out of the funds of the lodge in order to make change, or to save a trip to the bank and forgetting to replace it, frequently leads to small shortages, which the officer might find it exceedingly difficult to replace when the amount is shown to him by the auditing committee, and sometimes he is unable to account for the amount in his own mind and comes to believe that the auditing committee is wronging him. So it is easy to see why the auditing committee should have no possible interest in friendship to shield any delinquent officer, or to throw any unjust suspicion upon any individual whatever.

The Secretary's voucher book is also the Master's voucher book and the Treasurer's voucher book, and is about all the record of disbursements necessary, save the Secretary's expense book, and both must agree.

We have also mentioned the Secretary's book of receipts for dues. The stub of this book is very important. The date on the stub should always agree with the date on the receipt given in case of a dispute. When the amount of dues received does not agree with the number of members, certain receipts should be called in and verified with the stub and with the member's account in the ledger.

A frequent method of cooking accounts is to give a member a receipt for the amount paid, properly dated, and to write a date on the stub showing the previous or some former year, still leaving the member apparently delinquent, or to place a lesser amount paid on the stub and on the ledger than was mentioned in the receipt. Sometimes it will be found that the register shows a less number of members than the lodge really has, so that considerable searching may be necessary to show the real state of things where the Secretary or Treasurer has been a long time in office. The Treasurer needs only his bank deposit book and this should in all cases possible show the items separately, as he has receipted for them to the Secretary. In addition there will be the small items of interest allowed by the bank on daily balances. These amounts should be reported to the Secretary and entered by him in the department of sundry receipts. It would also be well, where possible, to have these items agree with the minute book where the Secretary reports the amount received since the last meeting, so as to show that the money has been regularly paid over to the Treasurer by the Secretary and the money deposited promptly. The amounts deposited less the vouchers drawn show the amount on deposit. The only possible discrepancy will be the interest allowed on daily balances.

An item of exchange on outside checks paid by the Treasurer may frequently occur. The amounts should be kept by the Treasurer and a voucher drawn for them in his favor at the end of the period of audit and recorded under the department of Sundry Expenses.

Trustees handling the property of the lodge should keep a set of books of their own. All income collected by them should be turned over to the Secretary, who should make a proper record thereof and pay it over to the Treasurer in the usual way, taking his receipt therefor and deposited by him. When any funds are placed in the hands of the Trustees a regular voucher should be drawn in their favor in the name of the Chairman of the Board of Trustees. At the end of the financial year, or at such times as desired, the Trustees should make a full report to the lodge, showing the amount received for investment, the disposition made of it, the notes or bonds in their possession, the interest or profit accrued thereon, the present values of such securities, if any; interest or profit due and unpaid on such securities and the amounts paid to the Secretary. This report should be verified by the auditing committee. It should also be the duty of the Board of Trustees at the beginning of each term to make an inventory of the property of the lodge of whatsoever kind, hall, paraphernalia, stationery, furniture, library, investments in their hands, bank deposits, as shown by the books of the Treasurer, and on the liability side such amounts as the lodge may owe. This should be placed in the hands of the auditing committee and made a part of the minutes of the meeting at which presented.

The foregoing is to be taken as advice. There may be other methods of managing the financial affairs of a lodge, but where the brethren have had no experience this will be found useful reading.

LECTURE XXX

MASONIC JURISPRUDENCE

THE Code of the Missouri Grand Lodge, as recommended by the Committee on Masonic Jurisprudence, is contained in the Proceedings of the Grand Lodge Session 1920, beginning on page 132. This calls for a trial committee, whose session is not held in open lodge. In all former times it has been the rule that all trials for unMasonic conduct should take place in open lodge in the highest degree in which the accused has been initiated. All appeals from the findings of the lodge trial lie, first to the Grand Master, and secondly to the Grand Lodge in regular session. The sources of Masonic law are as follows:

1. The statutes of the Grand Lodge revised to date.
2. Decisions of Grand Masters, made between regular sessions of the Grand Lodge, which have been subsequently approved by the Grand Lodge.
3. Decisions of the Grand Lodge Committees on Appeals and Grievances approved by the Grand Lodge, so far as they apply to the case under consideration.
4. Decisions of other Grand Lodges, their Grand Masters and committees approved by them, so far as they apply in cases where our own law is silent.
5. Decisions of the Grand Lodge Committees on Jurisprudence, which have been approved and adopted by the Grand Lodge.
6. The Ancient Landmarks of Freemasonry.
7. The Ancient Charges.
8. The three ritualistic obligations.
9. The three ritualistic charges to candidates.
10. The ritualistic charges and regulations submitted to the Master on his installation.
11. The high standard of moral law as taught in the rituals of Freemasonry, practiced in its customs and generally admitted as respectable conduct in civilized society.

It may be thus seen that in order for a brother to be, in the sight of the Fraternity, guilty of a Masonic offense, it is not necessary that he shall have broken any written law. There are thousands of immoral and malign acts which a man may commit and never break any recognized law of the land, and that the law of the land can in no way punish. This is not true of Masonry, for the severest punishment known to the Order may reach him while the law is powerless. Masonry knows no civil law. Masonic wrongs against a brother Mason cannot be compounded for money damages. All offenses against Masonic law are, necessarily, criminal in their nature, and upon conviction are punished, either by reprimand, suspension from Masonic privileges for a definite time, or expulsion from the Order altogether. Should a brother have violated a statute of the Grand Lodge it is the duty of the lodge to which he belongs to prefer charges against him, and if he is found guilty assess a punishment of suitable severity. If the lodge fails in this duty it may be required to perform it by order of the Grand Master, and should it neglect to obey the Grand Master's order, have the charter arrested forthwith. And should any punishment assessed be, in the opinion of the Grand Master, insufficient for the offense, or should the offender be acquitted in face of clear evidence against him of guilt, the Grand Lodge may order a transcript of the evidence sent up to them and the brother be again tried before that body. The fact of having been acquitted in a particular lodge does not prevent further trials for the same offense, should additional evidence be forthcoming. No quibble of the law can here save an offender from a strict trial on the merits of the offense. On the other side it must not be forgotten that the several specifications of the charge must mention some real Masonic offense or moral delinquency, some overt act or some special neglect of duty which in good morals he was bound to perform. The accusation must also specify some approximate time and place at which the offense was committed and just the exact nature and manner of his offending.

It may not be generally known or realized, but a Mason is amenable for his Masonic conduct to the lodge in whose jurisdiction he may be sojourning, equally as to the lodge to which he belongs, and a charge of unMasonic conduct may be preferred against him in either lodge, though when such a charge is made against a brother in any other lodge than his own, and the proper indictment filed, it is right that the lodge in whose jurisdiction the offense was committed should notify the accused brother's lodge and transmit a copy of the charges and specifications, and ask a waiver of the right of trial or request that lodge to try him. Should the brother accused be found guilty and expelled from the Order, the lodge that tried and expelled him holds jurisdiction of his future career, and it alone can restore him to good Masonic standing, or in their stead the Grand Lodge on appeal.

A Mason also owes Masonic duty to the lodge in whose jurisdiction he happens to be sojourning, and is bound to obey its
summons in any matter, such as personal service in attending
upon the sick or distressed. This is why a Masonic traveler,
should he make a stop for any length of time within the jurisdiction of another lodge, ought to visit the lodge, make himself
known to its members and tender his services, in case they might
be needed, either for work in the lodge or in any other capacity
in which one of its own members might be expected to serve.
This is no more than right, because he himself may at any time
need such services in accident or distress. He would then feel
more at liberty to call for them.

It is the right and duty of any Mason hearing a complaint
against the conduct of a brother to ascertain if the complaint
be well founded and if, in his opinion, it is, to report the matter
to the Master of the lodge, together with all the facts known
to him and the names of such witnesses as may come to his
knowledge. It is then the procedure of the Master to request
the Junior Warden to formulate charges and prepare to take
testimony. With him the Master shall appoint a grievance
committee, who shall make such an investigation as a Grand
Jury might make in a criminal case in the regular courts of the
land, to ascertain if the charges be sufficiently well founded to
warrant a trial. The Junior Warden shall present before such
committee the evidence that may be in the possession of the
officers of the lodge and the committee should make a report,
generally within twenty days, of the findings. Should this report show sufficient evidence to warrant a trial, the Master
should appoint a day, not less than twenty days nor more than
twenty-five days, from the finding of the investigating committee
for the trial, and the accused should be summoned to appear.
A copy of the charge and finding of the grievance committee
should be furnished the accused. The officer serving the notice
should make a return as to the manner in which the summons
was served, whether by personal notice, by registered letter,
addressed to his last known place of residence and receiving
the post office receipt of delivery signed by the brother notified,
or by leaving a copy of the summons at the brother's residence.
It is of importance that the returns should show the time at
which the accused received the summons, as he is entitled to
twenty full days' notice, if he can be found. Where it is impossible to find him and he appears to be away from home, it

then is proper to grant a continuance for a reasonable time.

In making out the charge or indictment the Junior Warden, an office which corresponds to the position of prosecuting attorney, should arrange the specifications under the proper heading form taken from the Book of Constitutions. He should then in his mind locate the particular Masonic law violated in each specification. For the assistance of such as may have this duty devolve upon them we will analyze the points that may be found in the various sources of law, as follows:

1. Revealing the secrets of Freemasonry improperly to some person not a Mason or to some Mason of a lower degree, either by spoken word or by some kind of writing or sign, as by means of the deaf and dumb alphabet. The intent and result constitute the offense. The attempt that does not succeed would constitute an offense of another kind.

2. Neglect or unnecessary refusal to aid a Masonic brother in distress or his family. This would include refusing to take his turn with the other members in taking care of a sick brother.

3. Cheating, wronging or defrauding a Masonic brother or his widow or orphans.

4. Cheating, wronging or defrauding a Masonic lodge.

5. Neglect or refusal to obey the summons of a Masonic lodge or of a brother Mason when given or coming to him in a constitutional manner.

6. Revealing the secrets of a brother Mason when received in confidence.

7. Striking a brother Mason, other than in the necessary defense of person, family or property.

8. Assisting in conferring the Masonic degrees upon improper or unqualified persons.

9. Masonic communication with clandestine, suspended or expelled Masons, knowing them to be such. It is possible that under this head might be counted the visitation of lodges of Masons in countries and jurisdictions not recognized by this Grand Lodge.

10. Violating the chastity of a brother Mason's female relatives.

11. Proposing persons for initiation in a Masonic lodge unknown to the sponsor as being men of good character, or men of notoriously bad character.

12. Disobedience of some of the laws, rules and regulations of the lodge or Grand Lodge under which the lodge is held. Most of the statutes of the Grand Lodge are statutes regulating procedure which, if not followed, not only render the procedure void, but occasionally throw great expense upon the lodge. Knowingly violating these statutes should be punishable. Occasionally an act is

forbidden in the jurisdiction in which a brother may be sojourning that is not forbidden by the laws of the jurisdiction to which the brother belongs. In such a case it is not usual for the lodge in whose jurisdiction the accused may be merely sojourning to prosecute. If his conduct becomes a notorious scandal, the Grand Master may order his exclusion from communications of the Order.

The application of Masonic law and custom as derived from the Ancient Charges must be considered obsolete, so far as they relate to the Operative Craft, but so far as they relate to the conduct of one Mason toward another or to the profane world they must be considered good principles of law. From these regulations and usages is derived the authority to punish drunkenness and excesses of any sort, quarrelsomeness, slander, public profanity, sexual immorality, idleness, neglect to support the family and bad behavior in the lodge room and ante-rooms.

When improper and dishonest official conduct is to become the charge, it must be remembered that the lodge cannot try the Master. Therefore, when he is the person accused of misconduct or malfeasance in office, the charge should take the form of a complaint to the Grand Master, asking that the Master of the lodge be compelled to perform his duty. This complaint or indictment must recount the facts with time and place and names of witnesses, in precisely the same way as though the matter was to come before the lodge or grievance committee for trial, though the heading should take the form of a petition. The process resembles a mandamus suit in a court of equity. Any member may do this on his own account and probably the complaint of a profane to the Grand Master, if it involved scandalous conduct on the part of a Master of a lodge, would be sufficient to cause the Grand Master to institute a trial, when he was satisfied of the rightfulness of the complaint, even though the circumstances might be unknown to the lodge, or being known, neglected by them. Any other officer, save the Worshipful Master, may be tried by the lodge for the neglect of his official duty, just as well as for any other offense. The duties of any particular officer that he may be required to perform are to be found:

1. In the Book of Constitutions, under the heading of Duties of Officers.
2. In the Charges, given in the Installation Ceremony.
3. The special duties of the Master that are found in the rules and regulations submitted to him previous to his investiture.

Should any officer of the Grand Lodge fail or refuse to perform any duty devolving upon him under the list of duties appertaining to his office as laid down in the Book of Constitutions, a charge must be prepared in the form of a petition to the Grand Master, asking that said officer be compelled to perform his duty, and should the Grand Master fail to act the petition may be presented to the Grand Lodge in regular session. The lodge is not expected to interfere in any mere matter of debit and credit between brethren of the Order unless the question of fraud is involved.

The Book of Constitutions and the Trial Code give the forms which the various summonses must take, both to the accused to appear and make answer to a charge and the witnesses to appear and give evidence. Any Mason within the jurisdiction of the Grand Lodge may be summoned as a witness, and is bound to appear or show a good and sufficient reason for not appearing. The testimony of any person not a Mason may be taken, he making oath to the evidence given by him before competent legal authority, such as a notary public or justice of the peace authorized to administer an oath. If the trial took place in open lodge a profane could not be present at the trial, but his deposition might be taken, due notice being given to the accused of the time and place so that he might be present, either in person or by attorney, and ask such questions as he desired or cross-examine the witness. Under the new code this difficulty would not exist and the witnesses could appear before the trial committee as before a profane court. This is one of the main objects of the code, to enable the jury to judge of the credibility of the testimony. When on account of distance and expense of journey it may be necessary to take affidavits, notice of time and place must be sent to the accused for the same reasons as in taking any ordinary deposition.

At lodge trials the accused is permitted to have an attorney, though in all cases the attorney must be a member of the Order, and for many reasons this rule holds good, even though the trial may be held before a trial committee and not in open lodge. For one reason it is necessary that the attorney should become familiar with much of the internal workings of the lodge which could not properly come to the knowledge of a profane. The accused must make answer to the charges within a certain length of time or stand in contempt of summons. The answer may be in one of three forms:

1. Guilty as charged and asking the clemency of the lodge. Following such an answer no trial need be held or testimony taken. The lodge or trial committee will immediately proceed to determine the punishment to be assessed.
2. Not guilty. Following this the date of the preliminary hearing will be set and the accused and witnesses summoned to appear and the regular trial follow.
3. The acts charged may be admitted but the claim be made that the acts do not constitute a Masonic offense under the peculiar circumstances in which they took place. Such being the answer the date for hearing will be set and the various summonses sent out.

At the hearing, or at the subsequent trial, if the accused fails to appear or to file answer, as before stated, either in person or by attorney, the lodge should obtain from the Secretary evidence that the proper notices and summonses have been sent and the method by which they were served. If it appears that the accused has had all proper notices and no excuse has been presented, either in person or by attorney, the lodge may proceed against the accused for contempt of summons. If there is no evidence that the accused has actually received these notices, it is proper that a continuance be granted for a reasonable time in hope that personal service can be obtained, though if the offense is a grave one the lodge may proceed to trial and expel the accused for contempt. The Grand Lodge can remove the ban, upon appeal, and order a new trial on the merits of the charge.

When the day of trial is at last arrived and all things ready and all parties being present, the Master should appoint a stenographer to take down the proceedings. We would advise that the Master appoint the lodge Secretary or some other competent brother from the very first to keep what the French call a "dossier" of the case. That is, there should be a file or common binding in which a record of all the proceedings are kept, and this separate from the regular minutes of the lodge, so that all matters pertaining to the case can be found at any time desired. For instance:

1. The original complaint or accusation in writing and signed by the party or parties making the first report of the offense, giving the names and residence of witnesses. In short, the complainant's story in full.
2. The appointment of the grievance committee, under the leadership of the Junior Warden.
3. Notices sent to witnesses stating time and place of hearing, of which the complainant is the main witness, and

such as he brings with him or has knowledge of. These notices should show on the back the time and manner of service. Report of grievance committee or true bill against accused.

4. The complete regularly formulated charge with each specification in full, with time, place and circumstance and Masonic offense committed.

5. The summons to the accused to attend and make answer, with time and place. This should show on the back the manner of service, time of service, in such a manner as will show record that the law has been complied with as to number of days' notice the accused must be allowed to file answer.

6. Answer of the accused.

7. Notices sent of time and place of trial to accused and witnesses, with returns as to manner and time of service.

8. If under the Trial Code, jury notices, panel, challenges and final seating of same.

9. All depositions and affidavits, copies of notices to accused of the taking of such, whether or not such affidavits were admitted in the case.

10. Records of the trial from opening to closing, with all testimony and rulings.

It will be easy to see that should a transcript later be required to be sent up to the Grand Master, that all that would be necessary would be to copy the dossier and have it properly certified by the officers of the lodge under seal.

The stenographer, then, is a very important person. Of course, he must be a member of the Order and should be under oath. The first thing is the seating of the jury, a panel of twelve disinterested Master Masons of good standing in the lodge, who are not related in any manner or degree to the accused, or a witness either for or against the accused, and who have neither formed nor expressed any opinion as to his guilt or innocence, from which number a trial jury of six is selected. The twelve summoned must appear or be subject to a charge of contempt. If, on the date set, the twelve is not complete, the chairman may fill the vacancies out of those present. If this is not possible the trial may be postponed until such can be secured. When it is impossible to secure a proper panel of twelve in the accused brother's own lodge, a sufficient number may be selected from some neighboring lodge. These twelve shall answer, on their Masonic honor, all questions that may be asked them touching their qualifications to sit as jurors, either by the Junior Warden or the accused, or by the chairman of the trial committee. Any of the twelve may be challenged for good cause and each side has three preemptory challenges and the six remaining shall constitute the Trial Jury. When finally chosen the chairman shall charge the jury against discussing the case among themselves, or with any witness, or with the accused, and he shall forbid any other person from talking with them about the case, and should anyone attempt to talk with them they shall immediately refer the matter to the trial chairman, and they shall keep their minds free and open until the conclusion of the case, and this same charge or warning shall be given them at every recess or adjournment. Any disobedience of this warning shall constitute a Masonic offense. The trial may be adjourned from day to day until the trial is completed. While the trial is not held in open lodge it is customary to hold it at the ordinary place where the lodge meets. The Junior Warden may have any attorney to assist him, if he thinks advisable, providing said attorney be a member of the Order.

The first procedure, after the jury is finally seated, is to read the formal charge or indictment with its various specifications. After this is read the accused or his attorney may read the answer. Next the Junior Warden will present the testimony against the accused. When he has completed the direct examination the attorney of the accused may have opportunity to cross-examine the witnesses. The same rules regarding leading questions that apply in ordinary courts should be observed. The witness, on direct examination, should be allowed to tell his story in his own words, with only such questions as will tend to refresh his memory. On cross-examination he may be asked any question, calculated to test the truth of his testimony.

When all the witnesses for the prosecution have been examined, the accused may produce his testimony, the Junior Warden cross-questioning them, as he deems proper. The accused may go on the stand in his own behalf or not, as he thinks best, but if he does go on the stand he must subject himself to cross-examination like any other witness. He is not obliged to furnish any evidence against himself, and the prosecution should not withhold any evidence that would tend to the exculpation of the accused.

When all the testimony is heard the attorneys, or the Junior Warden and the accused, may argue the case and each present his own side as best he may. When the argument is closed the jury may retire and make up their verdict. They must choose a foreman, who shall take a vote as to whether the accused is guilty or not.

The vote must be by ballot and if a majority of the jury find him guilty they must then proceed to vote on the question of the punishment. Each specification should be voted on separately. If the entire jury vote for expulsion the accused will be declared expelled. If less than the whole number vote for expulsion, then the question must be put on suspension for a definite time. If a majority vote for suspension, they will proceed to vote on the longest time suggested, and so down until some time shall be determined on. If less than a majority vote for suspension, then a reprimand must be administered in open lodge by the Master or by some brother appointed by him.

Upon arriving at a verdict they must reduce the verdict to writing. This writing must be returned to the chairman of the trial, who, if he finds it in proper form, shall announce the same and shall cause the same to be filed with the Secretary of the lodge, who shall immediately endorse the verdict, as filed, with the date thereof.

At the next communication of the lodge after the trial the verdict must be read in open lodge. If the verdict be for expulsion, the Master shall declare the same in open lodge and the accused shall stand expelled from that date. If the verdict be for suspension, the Master shall declare the brother suspended for the time and period mentioned in the verdict. If the verdict be for reprimand the Master shall administer the same in open lodge. If the guilty brother is not present, the Master shall summon him to appear at the time stated and receive the reprimand. The testimony of all witnesses shall be given orally and reduced to writing, in short-hand where practicable.

All Masons giving testimony must give it on their Masonic honor; all profane witnesses, on oath administered by an officer authorized to administer oaths. The record and testimony, filed in a court of competent jurisdiction, duly certified, showing indictment or information, arraignment, conviction and sentence, or acquittal of the accused, according to the forms of law for the same offense for which he is being tried by the lodge, is legal and competent evidence, for or against the accused, but is not conclusive as to the guilt or innocence of the accused. Where pleadings in a civil suit to which a Freemason is a party, and in which he had or has the right and opportunity to appear, present the issue as to his guilt or innocence of a Masonic offense, the pleadings and judgment or decree therein are competent evidence in a Masonic trial for the same offense, but it is not conclusive as to the guilt or innocence of the accused.

In working under the code, whenever in the judgment of the Junior Warden or the accused depositions are expedient, the chairman of the trial committee may appoint three competent Master Masons not interested in the result of the trial or kin to the accused, to take the testimony of witnesses who are unable by reason of physical disability or other cause to attend the trial, or who reside outside the jurisdiction of the lodge, or by profanes who are unwilling to attend the trial. The testimony, when so taken, must be reduced to writing, subscribed and sworn to by the witnesses in the manner before mentioned, and certified to by the committee taking the same and filed with the secretary of the trial committee.

It is proper that the entire dossier of the trial be reduced to type-written form for permanent record. The chairman must make an itemized account of the expenses of the trial, which may include traveling expenses of members of the committee, the necessary mileage and per diem as allowed in civil cases, expenses in taking depositions, the services of stenographer and actual cost of serving the necessary notices required by the statute, which items shall be paid by the lodge. Any person desiring a complete transcript of the evidence ought to pay for it, but if the Worshipful Master is satisfied that the accused is unable to pay for a transcript, or for the attendance of his witnesses, the Worshipful Master may order the same paid by the lodge.

APPEALS—The accused and the accuser or any member of the lodge in which a case has been tried have the right of appeal and no others. The appeal must be taken within ten days after the verdict is read in open lodge and spread upon the records, provided, however, that the Grand Master may order the lodge to take an appeal at any time. When the notice of the appeal is filed, in due form, with the Secretary, he must note the date and immediately send a certified copy to the Grand Secretary of the Grand Lodge, together with a certified copy of the dossier, which need not include the testimony, though the complete record is likely to be required sooner or later. The appellant must, within sixty days after the filing of the notice of appeal, file with the Secretary a statement of such errors and objections as may constitute his reason for a new hearing.

It is a comparatively easy matter for the stenographer to make four copies of the records of a trial by means of carbon printing. More than this would be difficult, as it would require an entire fresh copy. So it is always better to have the stenographer make these carbon copies when writing up the original. When the Grand Lodge simply wishes an abstract of the most important points in the evidence, the Secretary or the Junior Warden may make this, and when completed it ought to be submitted to the opposite side. It is well to have the two sides of the case agree as to what the salient points of the case are when submitting an appeal. What one side might think very important the other side might consider trivial, so when the abstract is made and submitted to the opposite side it is proper for them to endorse their approval on the back of the abstract.

The Committee on Appeals and Grievances of the Grand Lodge, to which these matters are referred by the Grand Master, may, should it see fit, disregard the proceedings in the lower body altogether and try the case, de novo, on its merits. Generally, however, it is the custom for the committee to recommend that the judgment of the lower court be affirmed, or that the case be reversed and a new trial ordered before the lodge. The committee is not confined in any manner to the evidence contained in the abstract, or for that matter in the entire record, but may summon witnesses and hear and apply facts in its possession.

It is believed that trial under the new code will render appeals on behalf of the prosecution rather rare, though convictions will be more frequent and the punishments more adequate than they have been in times not long past. The trial is more likely to be conducted in a just and clean manner, without any prejudice or partiality, than when conducted in open lodge, subjected to the temporary passions of the members. When a case is reversed by the Grand Lodge and sent back to the particular lodge for a new trial, appeal may be taken a second time to some ruling of the lodge and again the case reversed.

In case the lodge expel the brother, the Grand Lodge may restore to good Masonic standing, but not to membership in his lodge. The lodge may acquit and the Grand Lodge set aside the acquittal and try the case itself. Whatever penalties the lodge may inflict it can at any time remove and restore the brother to good standing and lodge membership. When suspension is ordered for a definite time, as soon as that period has expired the brother is automatically restored to membership and good standing. Dues are not chargeable during suspension. In some jurisdictions fines as a means of punishment are assessed. That has never been the custom under this Grand Lodge. When the Grand Lodges assesses punishment, after a trial held before its own committee, the Grand Lodge alone can remove the ban. When the Grand Lodge is petitioned to call up a case where a brother has been expelled by his lodge and his lodge declines to restore him, it usually requires letters from Masons who live in his neighborhood that since his expulsion he has lived a respectable, moral life. This is also the custom, where a brother has stood suspended for several years for non-payment of dues and his lodge declines to reinstate him.

This comment may be made in regard to Masonic offenses: The lodge is apt to look upon them in far too lenient a manner, and as a rule the punishments assessed are far too light. It is found that witnesses are very hard and bitter in their estimate of an offender before he is brought to trial, but know very little of their own knowledge when called to give testimony concerning these offenses when questioned before a trial committee. Their evidence is usually of a hearsay character that cannot be used as fact. All the friends of the offender are present at the trial when it is held before the lodge, but find it convenient to remember nothing of the offense charged. They who were swift to scandalize his character outside either fear his enmity should they give evidence against him, or vote for any adequate punishment should he be found guilty, or knowing that they have been unfair in their previous condemnation develop a very sudden friendship for him. It is best to avoid trials whenever possible, as they not infrequently cause dissension in a lodge.

When a brother has exhibited conduct which appears reprehensible, let the Master or some venerable brother go to him and endeavor to show him the direction in which his conduct seems to be leading him. We are of the opinion that every lodge needs a censor mori, some venerable man, a minister of the gospel when possible, someone who is not only old enough to have had experience and has pretty well subdued his own passions, and also one who has sufficient mental ability to command the respect of the average brother. It ought to be his duty to keep his eye on the younger members, try to keep some track of their families, their goings out and their comings in, learn something of their daily walk and conversation, keeping books on them, setting down the good as well as the bad. Let him have personal knowledge so that when a brother seems to be starting on a downward path he may go to him and at least convince him that the lodge has taken enough interest in him to know what happens to him. In many of our lodges it is quite justifiable for any brother to get the idea into his head that the lodge brethren do not care whether he is prospering or in adversity, whether he is sick or well, whether he is setting a good example to others or ruining his own reputation and neglecting his family. It is a pretty undesirable thing that the first notice the lodge takes of one of its members is to condemn him for some unMasonic conduct. It looks as though it might be that he had not received much instruction as to what sort of conduct the lodge approved and what it condemned. It is not wise either to be constantly reprimanding a brother because his conduct is in your opinion rather light and frivolous, perhaps what might be expected of one of his age. We do not care particularly to see ivy clinging too closely to a young oak tree, nor mushrooms growing from its roots. Lightness, frivolity, occasionally looking upon the wine when it is red, perhaps being a trifle wild as to women, foolish in spending money, what is generally known as sowing wild oats, are the sins to which those of youthful years are especially addicted. The old, the sedate, the gray-headed, have no mind to these things and reckon them far more heinous than fraud, selfishness, coldness and hardness to those who ought to be held near and dear. The elders are more given to such sins, and considering the evil effect of these latter faults on a community they ought to be rated a great deal more severely than they are. It is pretty difficult to find any brother who is willing to go to such an one and admonish him, or inform him of the unhappiness he is causing, or threaten him with the disapproval of the lodge. He walks sedately, does not get drunk or use profanity. He probably goes to church and is very careful of spending his money foolishly, even when he has a plenty and might well be able to be generous with it. Such conduct is far more dangerous from a moral point of view than the former, and full as much in need of the attentions of the censor mori.

LECTURE XXXI
CONCLUSION

WE regret exceedingly that our book is not better, but we are conceited enough to say that if anyone had written a book as good we should not have written any book at all. Doubtless the subject-matter will be added to and improved for many generations. When Christopher Columbus had once made his egg to stand on end there was not a single man in the ship but could stand his up a thousand times more dexterously. We have for more than a quarter of a century cherished a great affection for Masonry, and our only grief is that she is not more worthy the love we bear her. We do not intend to miss any opportunity to try and make her so. We have always looked upon Freemasonry as a kind of religion, and regarding all matters of religion there have always been two classes of minds, the conservative and the radical, the dogmatic and the natural, the literalists and the symbolists. These minds will ever make themselves heard in Freemasonry. We have great sympathy for the literalist in religion, but our brains are not arranged in such a manner that we find it possible to believe things easily, especially those things which we think are untrue.

St. Paul says: "If Christ is not risen from the dead, then is our preaching vain, and why stand we in jeopardy every hour?" This is the attitude of the literalist. There is martyr stuff in them and we respect them, and when it is combined with kindness and pity and generosity of heart, these men are the very salt of the earth. But on the other hand, suppose the literalist to be narrow, superstitious, bigoted and without any sense of brotherly affection. He becomes as was Torquemada, a most dangerous man. To the symbolist revelation is only a delayed discovery of natural phenomena. Legend, tradition, history, if you please, can only be a partial view at the best. Their use is principally to save people from unpleasant experiences and to make men more kind. Make them cultivate that charity and tolerance that hopeth all things, believeth all things, beareth all things and endureth all things for a friend.

We believe that Speculative Masonry was born in an age when the literalist was making things mighty unpleasant. When religious intolerance was making Protestantism about as unhealthy as Roman Catholicism ever dared, when a man's life was never safe from the persecution of the dominant creed, when education, morality and even charity were considered but dangerous signs of a revolt against orthodoxy, then we believe was Speculative Masonry born, in the fervent hope that its secrecy and privacy might be a refuge for those who considered the humanitarian phase of religion of far more importance than any creed which Theologians had the nerve to manufacture. It has been such a refuge in spite of the literalists, who have from time to time been admitted within its fold, and from the earliest days have never neglected an opportunity to try and narrow the Institution down to the limits of the prevailing creed.

But despite, we say, all the efforts to pin the Institution down to some particular dogma Freemasonry has stuck to symbolism. She still allows every brother to interpret her symbols as may seem to him right, and requires only that he shall fulfil as near as a human being can the answer to the question asked by the Prophet Micah more than three thousand years ago: "What doth the Lord require of thee but to do justly, love mercy and walk humbly with thy God?" If men live thus wars and heart-burnings will cease.

We have so far as possible, considering our limited learning, endeavored to inform the reader as to what some of the symbols appearing in Freemasonry mean. We have done this entirely without prejudice, and if any brother honestly thinks they mean something different he has the long recognized privilege of interpreting them in another way. "The world is large enough for me and thee."

What matters it what faith or creed
My brother holds,
If to him through thought and deed
The truth unfolds?
What matters it what name he bears
If on Life's way of pain and cares
He bears the sign?
For his own soul must learn the right,
And his own eyes must see the Light,
Not mine or thine.

The same sun shines on all men's ways
And chooses none.
How should I think he spread his rays,
On mine alone?

The Life Eternal dwells in all,
Into his soul perchance may fall
The germ of power.
How shall I then pronounce his doom,
When in my brother's heart may bloom
The Holy Flower?

"May the blessing of Heaven rest upon us and all regular Masons. May brotherly love prevail and every moral and social virtue cement us."

FINIS.

INDEX

LODGE AND CRAFT